# Fritz Haber

# FRITZ HABER

## Chemist, Nobel Laureate, German, Jew

Dietrich Stoltzenberg

Chemical Heritage Press
Philadelphia, Pennsylvania

Printed in the United States of America.

For information about CHF publications write
Chemical Heritage Foundation
315 Chestnut Street
Philadelphia, PA 19106-2702, USA
Fax: (215) 925-1954
Web site: www.chemheritage.org

Library of Congress Cataloging-in-Publication Data
Stoltzenberg, Dietrich, 1926–
    [Fritz Haber. English]
    Fritz Haber : chemist, Nobel Laureate, German, Jew : a biography / by Dietrich Stoltzenberg.
        p. cm.
Includes bibliographical references and index.
    ISBN 0-941901-24-6 (acid-free paper)
    1. Haber, Fritz, 1868–1934. 2. Chemists—Germany—Biography. I. Title.
QD22.H15S7613  2004
540'.92—dc21
                                                                2003010808


Book interior designed by Patricia Wieland
Book jacket designed by Mark Willie, Willie•Fetchko Graphic Design
Printed by Thomson-Shore

*Von der Parteien Gunst und Hass verwirrt*
*Schwankt sein Charakterbild in der Geschichte.*

Blurred by the favor and the hate of parties,
His image wavers in our history.

(Translation by Charles E. Passage)


From the prologue of *Wallenstein* by Friedrich Schiller.
Spoken at the reopening of the theater know as the Schaubühne,
in Weimar in October 1798.

# Contents

# Illustrations

———◆◆◆———

All photos are courtesy of the Max Planck Society (Archiv zur Geschichte der Max-Planck-Gesellschaft, Berlin-Dahlem), except as otherwise noted. The Smith Collection is the Edgar Fahs Smith Collection, University of Pennsylvania Library.

# Foreword
# to the
# American Edition

WHOEVER SEEKS TO WRITE A BIOGRAPHY OF FRITZ HABER NEEDS TO have patience, persistence, and insight as well as a knowledge of physical chemistry. In addition the biographer must show understanding of Haber's character and empathize with his personality and his single-minded ambition and thinking.

My father, during his sixty-six years, witnessed Germany's history and fate—from the Second Empire to the Nazis. Whereas the new *Kaiserreich* with its Prussian jingoistic enthusiasms shaped his early life, in his middle years and old age he had to face sickness, a new and hostile regime, and ultimately exile. His personal life was emotionally troubled and rarely harmonious—and last but not least there was Judaism. He had many successes and received many honors, but there were also failures that he could not or would not explain. As professor and practical organizer Haber was closely involved with science policy and with the encouragement of research within Germany and beyond its boundaries. These time-consuming duties, which he took upon himself, were often vexatious and at times unsuccessful and even useless. And there were other setbacks, especially between 1914 and 1918, when he devoted himself to applied chemistry in the service of the fatherland. The responsibility for chemical warfare rested on his shoulders, and despite the passage of years it has never been lifted. The ingenious chemical weapons neither had the anticipated effect nor added to his reputation.

Dietrich Stoltzenberg has devoted several years to the study of Fritz Haber's complicated and involved life, using documents and letters that were either long neglected or inaccessible. His comprehensive biography of my father was first published in German in 1994. Stoltzenberg described Haber's many-sided activities. He also dealt with the ethical and personal problems of a chemist in war and peace to give a well-rounded and fair picture of the man and his work. There is a further and personal point to be made: for over ten years after his death my father's achievements were ignored in his native country because of his Jewish origins. Later, in a very different political climate, no one could find the time, energy, and patience to embark on the task of writing such a biography. With the publication of this biography, the gap was filled at last. And now, with the support of the Chemical Heritage Foundation, it has been translated into English in a shortened version that retains the essential features of the original work.

For me this book conveyed an impression of Fritz Haber as an imaginative personality, a chemical genius who deserves our admiration, but also as a stubborn man, sometimes hard to understand and inwardly perhaps lonely. The verse inscribed on a silver cigarette case given him by his friends on his sixtieth birthday may serve as a motto for Dietrich Stoltzenberg's book. Freely translated, it reads:

> Enjoy the gaieties of life
> And its serious sides as well.
> Nothing alive has a single cause,
> It is always many-sided.

> (Freut Euch des wahren Scheins
> Euch des ernsten Spieles
> Kein lebendiges ist Eins
> Immer ist's ein Vieles.)

Lutz Haber
Bath, March 1998

# Preface
# to the
# American Edition

I N 1996 THE CHEMICAL HERITAGE FOUNDATION REACTED POSITIVELY
to the idea of publishing a translation of the original Haber biography. Later
the books department of the American Chemical Society agreed to include
it in their joint enterprise with the Chemical Heritage Foundation, the
Modern Chemical Sciences Series. When the ACS closed its books department in 1998, soon after the manuscript was completed, it fell to CHF to
publish the volume. I am especially grateful to Theodor Benfey, one editor
of that series, who has encouraged and enabled this undertaking from the
beginning. I also thank Anthony Travis, Edelstein Center, Hebrew University of Jerusalem, the other editor of the series; Jenny Kien, Jerusalem, for
the basic translation of this abridged version; Arnold Thackray, president of
the Chemical Heritage Foundation; and Frances Coulborn Kohler and her
staff at CHF, without whose ambitious work this American edition would
not have been possible.

Since the publication of the original biography in 1994, several articles
and books about Fritz Haber have appeared. Among the most important
are Adolf-Henning Frucht and Joachim Zepelin, "Die Tragik der ver-
schmähten Liebe: Die Geschichte des deutsch-jüdischen Physikochemikers
und preussischen Patrioten Fritz Haber" (The tragedy of a disdained love:
The story of the German-Jewish physical chemist and Prussian patriot Fritz
Haber, *Mannheimer Forum* [1994/95], 63–112); Ralf Hahn, *Gold aus dem
Meer: Die Forschungen des Nobelpreisträgers Fritz Haber in den Jahren 1922–
1927* (Gold from the sea: The research of Nobel laureate Fritz Haber in the
years 1922–1927; Diepholz: GNT-Verlag, 1999); a short essay by Roald
Hoffmann in *The Same and Not the Same* (New York: Columbia University
Press, 1995); Vaclav Smil, *Enriching the Earth: Fritz Haber, Carl Bosch, and
the Transformation of World Food Production* (Cambridge, Mass.: MIT Press,

2001); Margit Szöllösi-Janze's biography, *Fritz Haber 1868–1934: Eine Biographie* (Munich: Beck, 1998); an article by Szöllösi-Janze, "Von der Mehlmotte zum Hollocaust: Fritz Haber und die chemische Schädlingsbekämpfung während und nach dem ersten Weltkrieg" (From the mealmoth to the Holocaust: Fritz Haber and chemical pest control during and after World War I; in *Von der Arbeiterbewegung zum modernen Sozialstaat: Festschrift für Gerhard A. Ritter zum 65. Geburtstag*, edited by Jürgen Kocka, 658–682 [Munich: Saur, 1994]); and an article by Joachim Zepelin, "Professor Fritz Haber: Forschungen im Dienst des Krieges" (Research in service for war, *Praxis Geschichte* 9 [1995], 55–57).

In closing, I thank my beloved wife once more, for her patience and assistance while I prepared this shortened version of the original biography of Fritz Haber.

Dietrich Stoltzenberg
Hamburg, December 2003

## Note on the Translation

This translation is based on a first version by Jenny Kien of Jerusalem. Theodor Benfey went over that version, especially the quotations from primary sources. The whole was then compared with the original German by Frances Kohler and retranslated as necessary during the editing. Help with the German was given by Arthur Daemmrich and with Polish place names by Richard Ulrych. The foreword was recast in English by Lutz Haber himself.

In the text, names of academic institutions and societies have been translated, with the German given in parentheses on the first mention. Names of companies based on personal names (Bayer, Hoechst) have been treated the same way. Companies not easily recognizable from a translated form (Metallgesellschaft) are left in German, with an English translation in parentheses on first mention. Companies known by an acronym (BASF) are so identified, with the full German name and English translation in parentheses on first mention. Names of government bodies have usually been given in English, with occasionally a German original in parentheses.

In the endnotes, names of depositories and journals are in the original German, and titles of published sources appear in the original language with a translation in parentheses. The index includes entries for the German form of the more frequently cited companies and societies.

# Preface
# to the
# German Edition

———◆◆◆———

Iɴ 1985 ᴀ ᴍᴇᴇᴛɪɴɢ I ᴀᴛᴛᴇɴᴅᴇᴅ ᴀᴛ ᴛʜᴇ Uɴɪᴠᴇʀsɪᴛʏ ᴏғ Hᴀᴍʙᴜʀɢ ᴅᴇᴀʟᴛ with the responsibility of the scientist. At this conference I was repeatedly confronted with the name of Fritz Haber. I knew his name from my earliest youth because my father, Hugo Stoltzenberg, my mother, Margarethe Stoltzenberg-Bergius, and my uncle, Fritz Bergius, had told me about their association with him.

Subsequently the Institute for the History of Science and Technology at the University of Hamburg held a seminar on a similar theme. The heated discussion that took place after my contribution on Fritz Haber led me to decide to write this biography. Apart from this volume, only Morris Goran's short biography, *The Story of Fritz Haber* (University of Oklahoma Press, 1967), tells Haber's story, and Goran's book is characterized by friends and relatives of Fritz Haber as "often not very true." There is also a novel about Haber's life, written by H. H. Wille and titled *Der Januskopf* (The Janus head; Berlin: Buch Klub 65, 1970).

Years of work in the archives and many conversations followed my decision to write this book, but I was exceptionally lucky. The archives of the Max Planck Society in Berlin-Dahlem had set up the Johannes Jaenicke Collection only a few years before I began. Jaenicke had been Fritz Haber's assistant in the Kaiser Wilhelm Institute for Physical Chemistry and Electrochemistry in the 1920s, and he later became the director of the laboratories of the Metallgesellschaft AG in Frankfurt am Main. At the beginning of the 1950s the Haber family and some of Haber's former colleagues asked him to write a biography of Haber. In order to support this undertaking, a call for information was published by the Max Planck Society, the German Bunsen Society for Physical Chemistry, the German Chemical Society, the

Society of German Natural Scientists and Physicians, and the Union of German Physical Societies (Deutsche Bunsengesellschaft für Physikalische Chemie, Gesellschaft Deutscher Chemiker, Gesellschaft Deutscher Naturforscher und Ärzte, and Verband Deutscher Physikalischer Gesellschaften). Jaenicke collected numerous documents in the course of the next twenty years and had many discussions with colleagues, friends, and relatives of Fritz Haber. Unfortunately, he was not able to write the biography, so my work constitutes a lasting memorial to him.

During the eight years of my research I received support from many people and organizations. First I would like to mention Lutz (Ludwig Fritz) Haber, Fritz Haber's younger son. Without his trust and his unfailing and active assistance I would not have been able to write this biography. The same holds for Eckart Henning, director of the Archive on the History of the Max Planck Society, and his assistants, who enabled me to examine the documents of the Jaenicke Collection and many other documents on the history of the Kaiser Wilhelm Society and the Max Planck Society, and who always helped and advised me.

It was possible for me to work in many other archives, institutes, and libraries, in particular the Breslau City Archives; the Federal Archive in Koblenz; the Military Archive and the Research Station of the Bundeswehr in Freiburg; the library of the Foundation of Prussian Cultural Property in Berlin; the Central Archives of the former Academy of Science in Berlin; the General State Archive in Karlsruhe; the Archive of the College of Technology in Karlsruhe; the former Central Archive of the German Democratic Republic in Merseburg and Potsdam (now the Geheimes Staatsarchiv Preussischer Kulturbesitz, Berlin-Dahlem); the Leo Baeck Institutes in London and Jerusalem; the archives of the Hebrew University of Jerusalem; the archives of the Weizmann Institute in Rehovot, Israel; the Bancroft Library of the University of California, Berkeley (where I was able to examine the literary estate of Emil Fischer); the Millikan Collection at the California Institute of Technology, Pasadena; and the library of the Institute for the History of Science and Technology at the University of Hamburg and the Hamburg State Library. I spoke with many people and received many suggestions, for example, from Fritz Stern, of New York; Ruth Sime, of Sacramento, California; Guenther Wendel, of Berlin; and Jost Weyer, of Hamburg. Also helping with the publication of this biography were Christoph Meinel, of the University of Regensburg; Ms. Remenyi-Schneider, of

Regensburg, who looked through the manuscript; and Peter Gölitz and Thomas Mager from the publishers, VCH.

I wish to thank especially my dear wife, Eva, who followed my work for many years with great patience as well as active support and criticism. Without the assistance of those mentioned—and those not mentioned, for the list would grow too long—I would never have been able to complete this book.

Dietrich Stoltzenberg
Hamburg, February 1994

# Prologue

———◆◆◆———

THE SUBTITLE OF THIS BIOGRAPHY, *Chemist, Nobel Laureate, German, Jew,* characterizes the unusual yet paradigmatic life of a German-Jewish scientist during the period of the German Second Reich and the Weimar Republic.

Fritz Haber is unusual not only because his scientific work had consequences that are still felt today in so many fields of the natural sciences—physics, physical chemistry, and biochemistry, as well as such applied fields as chemical technology and agricultural sciences—but also because he led the way on the political side of the scientific life. With Haber, the scientist and the German patriot went hand in hand.

Haber held many positions: as director of various scientific institutes; as a member of the senate of both the Kaiser Wilhelm Society and the Prussian Academy of Sciences; as a professor at the University of Berlin; as a founder and vice president of the Emergency Association (Notgemeinschaft) of the German Sciences (precursor of the German Forschungsgemeinschaft [Research Association]); and as president of the Union of German Chemical Societies and vice president of IUPAC (International Union of Pure and Applied Chemistry). These positions so enlarged his knowledge and experience that his advice was often sought and his opinions could not be ignored, even in the highest political circles.

He achieved his scientific success through hard work and constant all-out dedication. He worked his way into the fields of electrochemistry and thermodynamics, which were critically important for his research, in a most astounding and quite unusual fashion—without having an intellectual mentor in any of the scientific schools. With tenacious application—and the ability to motivate his leading assistants to extraordinary levels of achievement—he succeeded, despite the opposing opinions of leading physical chemists, in developing the synthesis of ammonia from its elements into a technically viable process.

Yet Fritz Haber was not spared his share of failure and false steps. Born a Jew and fully aware of being Jewish, he belonged to the large circle of Jews in Germany who wanted to demonstrate their "Germanness" through their accomplishments, particularly by serving the state. Haber thus participated actively in war research and inaugurated the employment of chemical weapons, whose development and use he supported until his death. He never denied this position and took full responsibility for this chapter in his life. His attitude was "for humanity in time of peace, for the fatherland in time of war."

Fritz Haber's activities during World War I later cast a long shadow on his life and works. It requires a considerable investment of empathy to penetrate the mindset and motivations of the participants in World War I, especially of those in leading positions who also fought the war with chemical weapons.

Like so many German Jews, Haber was moreover forced to realize that all his expressions of patriotic German sentiment counted as nothing before the anti-Semitic hatred of the National Socialists. He, too, had to recognize that he was a member of a people that, since its exile from Israel, had been unable to win the right of permanent abode in other countries. This realization came too late for Haber, if indeed he ever realized it to the fullest extent.

Fritz Haber's life was not only extraordinary; it was also paradigmatic. His forebears' ascent from simple wool dealers who traveled through the villages and small towns of Posen and Galicia to respected citizens and councillors of Breslau, the capital city of Silesia, is typical of the advancement of the Ashkenazim, the Jews who originated in Eastern Europe.

Haber's life as a member of the educated class of the nineteenth century is also archetypal. A career like his father's, as a merchant in dyes and chemicals for textile products, did not attract him. He wanted to study at the university, to take part in the intellectual currents of his time, among them the rise of the natural sciences.

Haber also experienced the obstacles that Jews in particular had to overcome; therefore he can be seen as an example of the "assimilated" Jew. But it was not his conversion from Judaism to Christianity (Haber was not a particularly religious person) that cleared his way. It was his tenacious will and the dedication of his intellectual and physical powers that enabled him to climb the heights. This concentrated effort ruined his health and caused him to neglect his private life—wife and family. He lost out in this sphere of life because he expected, even if subconsciously, that both his wives would adapt themselves to fit his needs and lifestyle.

Haber was obviously a man of his times, and just as he was molded by the intellectual currents of that era, so he later shaped the tasks that fell to his lot. He did indeed see the world changing. He had insights that were directed toward the future. Thus Haber saw the potential of getting enough nitrogen fertilizer through the synthesis of ammonia not as the end point of a process, but only as a temporary solution to the problem of feeding the ever-increasing world population. He saw for the future other, more natural—today we would say more environmentally friendly—ways.

And just as Haber exhibited vision in his own work, so he developed a style of work with his assistants and the guests in his institutes that was, and still is, a paradigm for any form of creative work. Today we would say that he motivated his assistants and gave them freedom for self-realization. This was the real reason that Fritz Haber was so honored by his assistants, even when the work did not lead to the desired goal, as in the project to reclaim gold from seawater.

For those of us living at the turn of the twentieth century, the life and achievements of Fritz Haber in his time constitute a paradigm worth considering, for its negative as well as its positive aspects, and a spur to us to reflect on our own achievements and aspirations.

# Abbreviations
# Used in the Notes

---

**Archives**

MPG

Archiv für die Geschichte der Max-Planck-Gesellschaft, Berlin (Archive for the History of the Max Planck Society)

**Journals**

| | |
|---|---|
| *Ber. Deutsch. Chem. Ges.* | *Berichte der Deutschen Chemischen Gesellschaft* |
| *Z. Angew. Chem.* | *Zeitschrift für Angewandte Chemie* |
| *Z. Anorgan. Chem.* | *Zeitschrift für Anorganische Chemie* |
| *Z. Elektrochemie* | *Zeitschrift für Elektrochemie* |
| *Z. Phys. Chem.* | *Zeitschrift für Physikalische Chemie* |

## Chapter 1

# Forebears

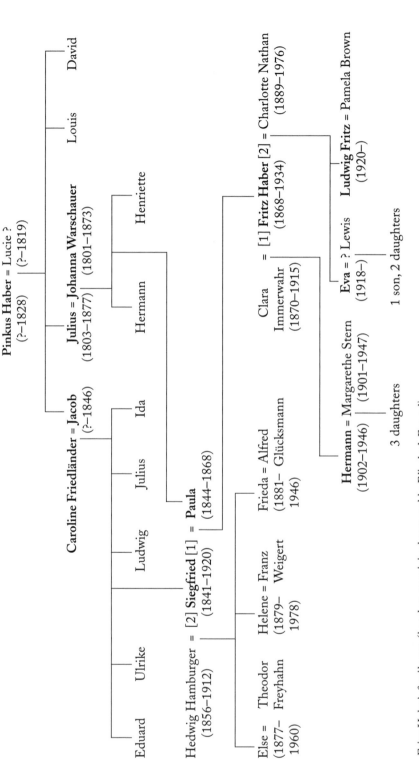

*Fritz Haber's family tree (based on an original prepared by Elisabeth Freund).*

*Previous page: Map of the area of the Austro–Hungarian Empire where Fritz Haber's family originated. Country borders shown are modern.*

THE ORIGIN OF THE NAME HABER REMAINS UNCLEAR. SOME SOURCES suggest that the Habers originated in Habern in Bohemia,[1] but it seems certain that this name was especially common among the eastern European Jews in the Polish region. There were, for example, the corrector (a person who has the ability to correct religious scriptures) Mordechai Jacob Haber (1846–1917) from Vilna (now Lithuania), who wrote the first secular Hebrew textbook, and Isaac Eisig Haber, a rabbi from Tykocin and Suvalkai in northeastern Poland, who published works on Jewish rites. It is from this Polish-Jewish region that Pinkus Selig Haber must certainly have come.[2] He is the first named forefather on Fritz Haber's family tree (see opposite page).

Fritz Haber's great-grandfather came from Kempen. This little town lies about sixty kilometers from Breslau in the former Prussian province of Posen, only twenty kilometers on the other side of the Silesian border. Pinkus Haber died in 1828. He was apparently married to a Lucie or Louise. Of their four sons—Julius, Jacob, Louis, and David—only Julius's year of birth, 1803, is known. From this birth date one can assume that Pinkus must have been born by 1780. It has been reported that he was a wool dealer.

Kempen was a market town with a large Jewish population. In Pinkus Haber's earlier years Jews did not have the same rights as the rest of the Prussian population, even though in the eighteenth century the demand for equal rights for Jews formed part of the middle-class demand for equality before the law. But it was still a long time before such demands were met. It took the emancipation of the Jews in France after the revolution in 1791 and Prussia's catastrophic defeat in 1806–1807 to bring a change. Society and state had to be modernized. Compulsory guild membership was abolished, and freedom to practice a trade was instituted between 1807 and 1811 by the Prussian reform legislation. An edict issued on 11 March 1812 "concerning the civil situation of the Jews" proclaimed: "Those Jews who now reside in our states and who have general privileges, naturalization papers, letters of safe conduct, and concessions, are with their families to be treated as local citizens and citizens of Prussia."

These reforms and this edict constituted an important stage in the process of the emancipation of Prussia's middle class and its Jews. The Jews reacted with hope. Young Jewish men volunteered for military service and participated in the War of Liberation of 1813–14. Here lie the origins of what was later termed German-Jewish patriotism, a sentiment so deeply rooted in Fritz Haber.

Pinkus Haber was apparently a participant in the War of Liberation. This ancestor of Fritz Haber's probably took advantage of the Jewish emancipation. He became an independent wool dealer, though he could not conduct this trade in Kempen since the emancipation laws were not yet valid in the province of Posen, where about 42 percent of Prussian Jews lived. Because of this restriction he most likely journeyed to Silesia, as did many other Jews at that time and in the following decades. In Breslau (Wrocław today) he founded the wool business that his sons, Julius and Jacob, eventually took over, but it is unclear whether he continued to reside in Breslau. It is mentioned in the family tree that Pinkus Haber died in 1828 and his wife in 1819, both in Kempen.

Pinkus Haber's two sons, Fritz Haber's grandfather Jacob and his great-uncle Julius, carried on their father's wool business. Jacob died early in 1846 while on a business trip to Brody, leaving his wife Caroline and their six children. His brother Julius then helped his sister-in-law by founding a branch of his business in Brieg and transferring ownership to her, which gave her an independent income. Her children attended the Brieg high school and, according to Fritz Haber's half sister, Else Freyhahn, often got together with their uncle Julius's family, the "Bernstadt Habers."

The wool business underwrote their prosperity. Whereas Pinkus had traveled from place to place as a dealer offering his wares for sale and buying wool from the shepherds, his sons developed what was to become a flourishing commercial company with buyers, agents in other towns (Brieg and Bernstadt), and a central office in Breslau.

Wool prices, however, high in the first decades of the nineteenth century, fell considerably in the 1880s, and then both production and turnover fell. It is not surprising that the next generation of Habers was not particularly inclined to enter the paternal business.

Fritz Haber's father, Siegfried Haber, was the third child of Jacob and Caroline. He was born on 6 February 1841. During Siegfried's early childhood Jacob Haber's young family lived in Brieg, a Silesian market town on the left bank of the Oder River. In 1850 the population was about ten thousand, which included two hundred Jews.

Siegfried's older brother Eduard, born in 1837, led a rather adventurous life. He lived for some time in Central America and then later in Hamburg. Fritz had little contact with him. Siegfried's older sister, Ulrike, was hardly mentioned at all by Fritz. One of Siegfried's younger brothers, Ludwig, became a merchant in a Dutch company and was a great success. He was sent to Africa and then later, as the company's leading representative, to England. At the beginning of 1874 he went to Hakodate, one of Japan's northern harbor cities. There, as consul, he also represented German interests, but he was murdered in August of that same year by an anti-European samurai. Fritz Haber visited his uncle Ludwig's grave in Hakodate during his stay in Japan in 1924.

Siegfried's third brother was Julius, born in 1844. Else Freyhahn characterized Julius as "without a doubt Caroline's most gifted son and also the most important." He studied law and became a district judge and later was appointed a judge in the Supreme Court in Leipzig. An advocate with an extremely high reputation, he also became president of the German Bar Association and Chief Justice. Julius and Siegfried died in the same year—1920.

Siegfried's youngest sibling was his sister Ida, born in 1864. According to Else Freyhahn, she was a woman of high spirits with a wonderful sense of humor. She married a merchant, Simon Spiro, whose home was in Ostrowo in the administrative area of Posen. The family later moved to Breslau. Ida was an ideal aunt and looked after Fritz during his earliest childhood, since his mother died at his birth.

Siegfried thus grew up surrounded by a large band of children. He was only five years old when his father died. But his uncle Julius took over care of the fatherless family, and his mother also showed amazing energy in raising the children by herself.

Siegfried befriended his cousin Hermann, who was only a year older. Siegfried Haber's memoirs contain stories about hikes that the two made, to and from Brieg and elsewhere. Hermann Haber was supposed to take up his father's wool business, but he ran into difficulties when the Silesian wool trade came increasingly under pressure from foreign wool imports. Besides his business Hermann was also interested in politics. He was city councillor and leader of the Liberal People's Party in Silesia. He also pursued an interest in literature and was managing director of the Breslau newspaper, *Die Breslauer Zeitung*, for which his nephew Fritz later wrote editorial pieces. Hermann Haber was a loving uncle to Fritz and once even took him into his house when he was having difficulties at home. Fritz Haber later told his niece Elisabeth Freund that he owed his whole upbringing to his uncle Hermann. He asserted that without his uncle's help he would never have convinced his father to let him study chemistry.

After finishing school, Siegfried learned the merchant's trade at S. E. Goldschmidt and Son in Breslau. His apprenticeship in this company was a decisive experience in his life. Shortly after completing it, he founded his own company and began dealing in dye pigments, paints, and pharmaceuticals.

In the early years of the business the dyes were primarily substances prepared from indigenous plants. Madder, cultivated in Silesia, contains one to two percent of the red colorant known as alizarin in its roots. This dye, when combined with various metal compounds, affords a variety of colors known as *madder lakes*. Another indigenous plant from which dyes were prepared was woad (*Isatis tinctoria*), which had been cultivated in Thuringia from ancient times. This plant provides a blue colorant similar to indigo.

Siegfried continued his business until the beginning of the twentieth century, when he was well into his seventies. The dye business had changed dramatically during the second half of the the nineteenth century. At first the import of such foreign dyes as Indian indigo made an ever-increasing part of the trade, and good connections were established with the import companies in Hamburg. Then the first synthetic alizarin came on the German market in 1871. The price of this synthetic product sank from 60 marks per kilogram in 1870 to one mark by the turn of the century. Synthetic indigo, first introduced in 1897, also replaced its natural analog. In that year synthetic indigo cost 16 marks per kilogram while the natural product cost 18 to 20 marks. By 1913 the price of the synthetic product had sunk to 8 marks, and Germany became a net exporter rather than importer of indigo. Thus Siegfried Haber experienced during his lifetime the same type of changes in the dye business that his uncle Julius had experienced thirty to forty years earlier in the local wool industry. His dye and pharmaceuticals business, however, grew into a lucrative venture from the 1860s through the 1890s.

Siegfried Haber intended, even as a youth, to marry his cousin Paula, the youngest daughter of his uncle Julius. She was about two years younger than Siegfried. As Elisabeth Freund states, "Paula was pretty and the darling of the Bernstadt Habers." Both Julius and his wife opposed a marriage between cousins. This caused a serious family fight, but the young people were victorious and married in 1867. Siegfried was just twenty-one years old. Their son Fritz was born on 9 December 1868. Paula died on 31 December from complications of childbirth, leaving Siegfried alone and in despair. There followed a gloomy period during which Siegfried's and Paula's sisters looked after Fritz. The father now lived only for his business and withdrew entirely from all other activities. Six years after Paula's death he met Hedwig Hamburger at the house of relatives. She was nineteen years old, extremely pretty, and an excellent piano player. Siegfried immediately fell in love with her, and they married soon after.

Siegfried and his second wife had three daughters. The eldest was Else, born 30 June 1877. She eventually married her cousin once removed, Theodor Freyhahn (son of Henriette Haber Freyhahn, the daughter of Siegfried's uncle Julius), who later became *Sanitätsrat* (a member of the board of health) in Berlin. After her husband's death Else kept house for her half brother, Fritz, until he died. She moved with him to England and died there in 1960.

Siegfried's second daughter was Helene. She married a medical practitioner, Franz Weigert of Stettin, who died in the Theresienstadt concentration camp in December 1942. Helene traveled from England to the United States and later lived in Chicago. She was almost a hundred years old when she died in 1978.

The youngest daughter was Frieda. She married Alfred Glücksmann, who later became mayor of Guben in the Niederlausitz. Both went to Palestine before World War II began, and Frieda died there in 1946. After his wife's death Alfred returned to Germany. For his entire life Fritz Haber had very good, often very close connections with his half sisters.

Siegfried Haber became a city councillor in 1905 and was reelected in 1911 and 1917. After a change in the legal prerequisites there was another election in 1919 in which he was not reelected, most likely because of his age and at his own request. In the same year he died at the age of eighty.

The most impressive documentation of Siegfried Haber's death comes from his son, Fritz. He had hurried to Breslau on receiving news of his father's serious illness. From there he wrote to his second wife, Charlotte, and his son Hermann:

> Dear Wife, dear Son,
>
> Next door, in the large corner room, my father is gradually sleeping his way into death. It is sometimes so quiet through the open door that, frightened, I creep to his bed because it seems to me that he is no longer alive. Yesterday when I came he still spoke with me, tired because of the morphine but with a clear spirit. He was serious and completely filled with the idea that he has lived out his life and all his wishes are concentrated on the one hope that he leave "on the express train." Now the infection that started overnight in both lungs will bring fulfillment of his wishes, a fulfillment that was not quite certain yesterday. I am thinking about how much joy he gained from activities that were not for personal gain. From 1895, when he became a member of the Town Assembly, up to 1919, when he left the council, it was a source of pride and joy—in good times satisfaction and in bad times an inner help—that he could use his strength and experience for the service of the city. Many have this idealism. But, in addition, he had a confident self-restraint, so that in his public life nothing appeared tempting or worth doing that he would be unable to do or that exceeded his strength. Therefore everything that he tried succeeded well. Not living just for oneself but for greater tasks and for solving problems not related to oneself because one's strength and powers are equal to the task! How strongly I feel his character now that he is leaving us.[3]

## Endnotes

[1] *Die Familiennamen der Juden in Deutschland* (The family names of the Jews in Germany) (Leipzig: Zentralstelle für deutsche Personen und Familien, 1935); and M. Freudenthal, *Leipziger Messgäste* (Frankfurt am Main: J. Kauffmann, 1978).

[2] Elisabeth Freund, "Zu dem Stammbaum der Familie Haber" (On the Haber family tree), 30 Sept. 1957, Max Planck Gesellschaft (MPG), Dept. Va, Rep. 5, 128.

[3] Fritz Haber to Charlotte and Hermann Haber, undated, MPG, Dept. Va, Rep.5, unnumbered.

*Chapter 2*

# Childhood
# and
# Youth

*Paula Haber, Fritz Haber's mother.*

*Previous page: The Elisabeth High School in Breslau, as it was until around 1903.*

ＡFTER THEIR MARRIAGE SIEGFRIED AND PAULA HABER TOOK AN apartment on the Schweidnitzer Graben, where the old fortifications of Breslau had previously stood and where there was now a green belt around the city. They were happy to be together after all the disagreements with Siegfried's mother, Caroline, and Paula's father, Julius. Hermann, Paula's brother and Siegfried's friend and cousin, had given them great support and now visited them frequently. With Hermann's young wife, Rudolfine, they made small excursions into the city's surroundings. It was a wonderful, happy year.

Siegfried had yet to establish properly his recently founded dye business and thus spent much time in his office in the Antonienstrasse in the heart of the city. Paula was a delicate, pretty, and cheerful woman, but her pregnancy in the year after their marriage was difficult. Siegfried was worried but eagerly awaited the birth of his first child. Fritz was born on 9 December 1868. The birth was difficult, and it considerably weakened Paula. All the doctors' skills were of no avail, and she died three weeks later on New Year's Eve. This was a terrible shock for Siegfried. For weeks it was impossible to talk to him, and the aunts and older cousins looked after the newborn child and the household.

It must have seemed that the father blamed the child for the mother's death. This is probably the major reason that in later years the relationship between father and son never became close and that tensions often arose. Siegfried became completely engaged in his work; he was hardly ever in the apartment and had little to do with his son. Fritz was looked after by Siegfried's sister Ida and the cousins. A housekeeper, a Mrs. Wohlgemut, was hired, but she spent most of her time keeping the household in order. Fritz's uncle Hermann also took care of him, and even as a small boy Fritz was often in his uncle's house. Little Fritz was a bright child; his thirst for knowledge showed even in his early years, and he amazed his aunts with many questions.

In Breslau, primary schools were attached to the old, well-esteemed high schools. Fritz Haber was enrolled in the Johanneum School, a liberal institution open to children of all religions. It was first established in 1872 as a "simultaneous school"; that is, the Catholic and Protestant religions as well as the Jewish religion were regarded as having equal rights.[1] These schools were distinguished by their progressive spirit and sensitive treatment of the children. There was no Prussian drilling, as was often the case elsewhere, a situation that certainly made Fritz very happy.

In the meantime his father married again. The family moved to a new apartment at Königsplatz, which was even closer to Siegfried's office. Life at home changed considerably. After some early difficulties Fritz established a trusting relationship with his stepmother.

Fritz developed more and more into a gifted student who loved to read stories and who learned poems by heart. He recited these at home to his stepmother, but his father showed little appreciation for his skills. Uncle Hermann, however, was very interested, for he also had a literary bent. Fritz even began to write little verses himself, a habit he retained throughout his life. Self-expression in poetry, composing letters in verse, or writing short poems in a poetry notebook were features of Fritz's childhood years.

At school Fritz noticed a tension between Christian and Jewish pupils in spite of the tolerance espoused in the education. Needling, taunting, and gibing were constant. From his father Fritz learned that he had to act carefully and considerately to avoid provoking jealousy or anger among the Christian merchants. But as the young boy had contact with only his closer relatives outside school, these strictures did not make much of an impression. He must, however, have thought about the problem at times, and he probably spoke to his uncle Hermann about it, because Hermann was very interested in politics and was about to take on a leading position with the progressive Liberals in Breslau.

Fritz Haber changed schools when he was eleven years old. He went to the Elisabeth High School, which was oriented strictly toward the humanities. This school was connected to the main old Protestant church, St. Elisabeth's, and had originally been a convent school. It was still housed in a dark, old building with poorly lit and badly ventilated classrooms. The

*Fritz Haber as a child in a play uniform, with a weapon.*

whole style of the school was much stricter and more in the Prussian humanistic tradition than that at the Johanneum. It is not known why Fritz Haber attended this particular school, but it is possible that its location nearer the Königsplatz may have been a principal factor. Various sons of acquaintances and relatives also attended this school: the son of a good acquaintance of Fritz's father, Eduard Koebner; the cousin of his stepmother, Ernst Hamburger; Ernst's brother Max, a friend of Fritz's for many years; and Emanuel Ehrlich, the son of the well-known architect Paul Ehrlich. Even though the school had strong connections to the Protestant Church, there were many Jewish (or as they were also called then, Mosaic) pupils. Half the members of Fritz's class were Jewish. Thus here too, in spite of the quite conservative and reactionary teaching, anti-Semitism hardly played a role. Occasional anti-Jewish digs or remarks by teachers made little impression on the pupils.

The school was above all a humanistic institution. The German language and classical literature, along with an introduction to the Prussian philosophy of Immanuel Kant or Johann Fichte, made up much of the lessons. In addition, teaching of the classical languages, Latin and Greek, began in the lower classes. Verses were recited from the original text of the *Iliad* and the *Odyssey,* Sophocles was read, and the Greek world of gods and myths was explored. Apart from the standard texts, Caesar's *De bellum gallicum*, Cicero's *De officiis,* and Sallust were also read. Plutarch's comparisons of Roman and Greek statesmen and military leaders made the weaknesses and cruelties of the great heroes clearer to the pupils. Perhaps here lies the origin of the refined and slightly exaggerated style of speaking that became so characteristic of Fritz Haber.

In his later school years Fritz's horizons expanded beyond his immediate school circle. He often went to the theater. The then very famous Meininger Hoftheater came almost every year to give a guest performance in Breslau, and the pupils were particularly attracted to their performances. A wider circle of students, including those from such other schools as St. Magdalen's School, the Johanneum, and the so-called Royal High School, formed an "anti-classic circle," as it was called by Eduard Koebner.[2] This group was also later visited by university students. A connection to the Academic Literary Club (Akademisch Literarischer Verein) developed; this was a sort of university fraternity, and both Jewish and Christian students as well as high school pupils in their later years could become members.

In the club literary and aesthetic matters were discussed. There were also "serious conversations between men," as Koebner describes it. These conversations included discussion of social and political questions, all the more because many of the boys' parents were actively engaged in local politics and in some cases occupied leading positions in the liberal or conservative parties. From his Uncle Hermann and his father, Fritz Haber knew about those barriers that, although not obvious, repeatedly confronted Jewish citizens who aspired to higher positions in the public sector, at the university, or in the judiciary. Fritz's uncle Julius certainly discussed some of his observations of signs of anti-Semitism with his brother Siegfried. Fritz was now old enough to listen in and to understand the conversations. His father kept up the Jewish religious traditions, as did most of the relatives, without necessarily having any close contact to the synagogue. They supported the Jewish community and would sometimes attend communal functions if they had a social or educational purpose. Later Fritz Haber would have to confront the conflict between his Jewish background and his striving toward full integration into the German Christian society, but that conflict now played a small role. In these years his pride in being a German was paramount. From this point of view the political differences and friction between the religions were minor.

Besides the humanities, mathematics and science were taught in the high school. Mathematics was considered a major subject because of its logical construction and the mental discipline it required. The mathematics teachers at Elisabeth High School gave stimulating lessons and made high demands on the pupils. As the same teachers were also responsible for giving science lessons, mathematics was emphasized in the science subjects as well, especially physics. This education was of great value to Fritz Haber when he later entered the field of physical chemistry. The chemistry lessons were very modest: chemistry was covered only in a short appendix in the comprehensive physics textbook, and no chemical experiments were carried out at school. Pupils interested in this subject had to learn it on their own.

We do not know what first aroused Fritz Haber's interest in chemistry. Of course, his father had some knowledge of the subject, and his trade in dyes and medicaments had numerous points of contact with chemistry. But a dealer in dyes does not need a great knowledge in this area, and Fritz's father did not seem to be greatly interested in the "chemical games" that his son was pursuing.

According to the accounts of his sisters and fellow pupils, Fritz began to carry out his first chemical experiments in his parents' apartment during his early high school years. At first he experimented secretly in his room. Naturally, this activity did not remain hidden long, because strange smells escaped and small explosions were sometimes heard. His experiments were therefore forbidden. Uncle Hermann finally helped Fritz, probably by providing a larger space in his apartment or in one of the larger storerooms that belonged to his wool business. Here Fritz could follow his interest in chemistry with fewer restrictions.

Fritz Haber completed his *Abitur* (school-leaving examination) on Michaelmas (29 September) in 1886, when he was seventeen. In the tabular listing of the graduates of the St. Elisabeth High School, the entry for Haber states that he attended the school for seven-and-a-half years, two years in the lower sixth form and one year in the upper sixth form.[3] In the section "Report on the maturity of the graduate and judgment regarding behavior and effort in the School Leaving Certificate" are the words, "Sufficiently gifted, hard-working, advanced regularly, he has a sufficient knowledge—good—good." In his *Abitur* he received the following grades:

| | |
|---|---|
| German composition | Good |
| Latin oral (and extempore) | Satisfactory |
| Latin composition | Unsatisfactory |
| Greek translation | Good |
| Extempore exercises | Satisfactory |
| French extempore exercises | Satisfactory |
| Work in mathematics | Very good |
| History | Very good |

Fritz left the school with such a high level of knowledge that he was later in the habit of commenting that the end of his school years marked a decline in his general knowledge. His life, however, proved that this remark was certainly not valid.

He remained for some time in Breslau after graduating from high school, describing this period as "very carefree . . . but were this to be the best period of my life, then I would send myself as quickly as possible to the hereafter . . . I long to be away from here . . . Now I am definitely not going to study at the Polytechnic School in the immediate future but at the University in Berlin, and afterward, in the summer, I will go to Freiburg or Heidelberg."[4]

While at school Fritz Haber gave his intended profession as chemist. But his father, who was now forty-two years old and whose business was encountering difficulties because of the introduction of synthetic dyes, wanted his son to receive an education that would allow him to take an active part in his company. As far as Siegfried was concerned, Fritz should first complete a commercial apprenticeship or work for a period as an unpaid assistant.

But Fritz was still drawn to the study of chemistry. He made a final attempt to obtain his father's agreement. In a combined action with his uncle, and possibly his stepmother, who was very attached to him, he succeeded in changing his father's mind. Now he could realize his long-cherished dream of being admitted to the university.

But which university should he attend? Remaining in Breslau meant he would have to continue living in his parents' apartment. But he wanted to become independent of his rather authoritarian father, so he decided on the Friedrich Wilhelm University in Berlin. The capital, with its many cultural possibilities, such as theater, opera, and concerts, must have attracted him. The Habers also had friends and relatives living in Berlin. Thus, at the beginning of the winter semester of 1886–87, he traveled to the city that would become his stamping ground for many decades.

Fritz Haber also wished to study in Berlin because of the reputations of both the director of the Institute for Chemistry, August Wilhelm von Hofmann, and the great physicist Hermann von Helmholtz. However, both were already elderly by Haber's first semester, when he attended their lectures: Hofmann was sixty-eight and Helmholtz sixty-four years old. Furthermore, the two were no longer very interested in their lectures or in teaching. At this time young students found it extremely difficult to follow Hofmann's lectures, which were presented in a soft voice, and to understand the complicated mathematical equations that he wrote on the board. Hofmann's older students had studied with him during his periods in London and Bonn. His towering personality had nonetheless attracted many young people during his first years in Berlin, and he had succeeded in building there an institute that met in full the demands of the time.

This institute, constructed between 1865 and 1869, was situated between Dorotheenstrasse and Georgenstrasse opposite the university library. It had laboratory space for seventy students, a large lecture theater seating three hundred, numerous additional rooms and private niches for special projects, private laboratories, the usual storerooms, and apartments for research assistants and servants.[5] By the time Haber arrived, the institute was twenty years old. When Emil Fischer became Hofmann's successor in 1892, he described it thus: "Everywhere there was a lack of light and air, and much of the space as designed consisted of dark and unused corridors. . . . The ventilation was also quite inadequate. . . . Even the heating was in a sorry state; the peat ovens intended for the purpose functioned so badly that some of the students bought their own gas heaters."[6]

Apart from courses in his specialty with Hofmann and Helmholtz, Haber studied philosophy under Wilhelm Dilthey, who had taught in Berlin since 1882. Haber had already become acquainted with Kant's philosophical system at school and at the meetings of the Academic Literary Club in Breslau. The members of the club had discussed their ideas on thinking, wanting, and feeling, on knowledge, morals, and the effect of emotions. They had read *Critique of Pure Reason, Critique of Practical Reason,* and *Fundamental Principles of the Metaphysics of Morals* and had discussed with youthful enthusiasm the contrast between natural drives and moral tasks. The club members also read Schelling's *Lectures on the Philosophy of Art,* whose basic principle was that art is the highest and most complete of all forms. And at school Haber was taught, as the basis of the Prussian constitution, Johann Gottlob Fichte's dialectics—which state in part that every problem creates a new one—his teachings on duty, and his theory of the state.

Now, toward the end of his studies in Berlin, Haber became interested in Dilthey's ideas and attended his lectures. Dilthey was a master of historical analysis and wanted to clarify what form of expression a given society developed in a given period and how the society's growth and decline were mirrored in it. In his *Introduction to the Humanities and Social Sciences* (1883) he attempted to form a basis for the study of society and history.

During this period Haber wrote from Berlin to his friend Max Warburg, "I am the most respectable person under the sun." And he mentions meetings with fellow club members at which there were debates on "God and the world, soul and consciousness, idealism and realism. . . . I am swimming in an ocean of formal dialectic and logic."[7]

But on the whole Haber was disappointed by his first semester at the Institute for Chemistry in Berlin. Then the famous name of Robert Bunsen attracted him to Heidelberg, and for the summer semester of 1887 he went to that beautiful old university city.

The chemist Theodor Curtius has described the method Bunsen used when demonstrating gas analysis to his trainees as one that shriveled their pride in knowing everything. Curtius believed that Bunsen used exercises of this type to sharpen his students' observational skills, and this thread ran through his entire approach to teaching. Such arduous work encouraged the students to develop self-discipline and the ability to observe accurately, and the great confidence the method gave them allowed many to make significant discoveries later in quite different fields.

Reading Curtius makes one wonder whether Haber, who later described his period with Bunsen somewhat critically, did not after all gain critical knowledge and skills in Bunsen's laboratory. Later, as a professor at Karlsruhe, Haber carried out several experiments on the Bunsen flame, including some on light emission, or gave similar problems to others. His studies in Heidelberg also influenced the work on the analysis of gases he carried out while still part of Bunte's institute at Karlsruhe. The exact and patient study and precise execution of experiments that proved essential to Haber's later success in Karlsruhe probably originated in these first years of study in Bunsen's laboratory.

Haber received a further foundation for his later work from lectures he heard in differential and integral calculus given by the mathematician Leo Königsberger. At this time Königsberger was writing his textbook on differential equations. For Haber, Königsberger's clearly presented mathematical deductions formed a basis on which he could later build and expand his mathematical knowledge. Student and teacher formed a close relationship that was to last for many years.

Haber participated fully in the student life at Heidelberg. Fritz Milch, his fellow student, thought that Haber was going through a *Sturm und Drang* period. There were clashes in the fraternity, and Haber was even challenged on a "matter of honor" that led to a duel in which he received a sword slash in the face, as befitted a student of the times.[8] But many valued young Haber's company. Among the older men in the fraternity were many industrial chemists who came to Heidelberg from Mannheim and Ludwigshafen and participated in the functions and excursions. These functions, lectures, discussions, and social events were always stimulating and wide ranging. Haber was very open to this variety and enlivened the literary, philosophical, and scientific discussions.

From Heidelberg, Haber then went back to Berlin, this time to the Charlottenburg Institute of Technology (Technische Hochschule). His correspondence with Max Warburg during this period shows that he dragged himself through his studies with difficulty. His experience, like that of so many chemistry students who were driven between theory and practice and numbed by the monotony of student life, left him at times overwhelmed by the material to be learned.

Haber left Berlin in the summer of 1889 to undertake one year of voluntary service, as required by law, with the Sixth Field Artillery Regiment.[9] Volunteers were also allowed to attend lectures at the university in order to complete their education. Haber enjoyed being a soldier and from then on affected a military manner. He also got to know the boredom of a soldier's life. He wrote Max Warburg "from the noisy loneliness" of the Falkenberg artillery practice range, "this desolate vacation spot. . . . Here life is deadly boring, even though there are hours when you imagine that you have been transported to the comfortable leisure of a spa."[10] When Warburg later was slated to serve in the same regiment, Haber wrote to him about his experiences: "You will be miserably peeved, but if you quickly think yourself into the depths of the word *Wurschtigkeit* [indifference], you will find it bearable. Endless *Wurschtigkeit*, that is the main thing. I privately gave myself the motto 'It doesn't matter'—then come what may."[11]

After basic training was over, volunteer Haber was able to attend philosophy lectures at the University of Breslau, as his garrison was in its vicinity. He had been promoted to noncommissioned officer after a short period of service, a minor honor. During this period he again began to attend the Academic Literary Club in the evenings. Here the debates over current events and cultural matters that he was accustomed to from his school days were continued. On the weekends he frequently visited his uncle Hermann and his cousin, Carl Haber, who had begun to build up a lumber business in Breslau. He also went dancing and there met Clara Immerwahr, who was later to become his wife. The Immerwahrs were a respected Jewish family, the father a chemist and owner of a sugar factory and an estate in Polkendorf. Clara's grandfather, David, owned a novelty shop in Breslau, and the family owned a commercial building on the Ringstrasse around the Rathaus (town hall). Clara was about two years younger than Fritz. She had studied to be a teacher after leaving school but had never entered the profession. She later studied chemistry at the University of Breslau. How close the friendship they struck up at the dances became is hard to say, but Fritz never forgot this delicate young woman. The connection was still there twelve years later when they met again at a congress in Freiburg. Moreover, Clara's thesis director, Richard Abegg, was a friend of Haber's whom he had known since his first semester in Berlin.

Haber returned to Berlin in the autumn of 1890, where he became a student of Carl Liebermann's. Liebermann had succeeded Baeyer at the Royal Technical Academy (Königliche Gewerbeakademie), the predecessor of the Charlottenburg Institute of Technology, in 1872. He and Carl Gräbe had together determined the constitution of alizarin, the dye in the madder root, in 1868. Liebermann was also a professor at Berlin University. He was a fervent fighter for recognition of the Charlottenburg Institute of Technology as an educational institution with rights and standing equivalent to those of the university, and he remained in Berlin despite several other offers. After working out the alizarin synthesis, Liebermann continued to study alizarin homologues and the stages in the reduction of anthraquinone.

Perhaps this research motivated Fritz Haber to choose Liebermann as his new teacher and later as his doctoral supervisor. The economic consequences of the alizarin synthesis, which caused the collapse of madder cultivation in Silesia, had affected Fritz's father's dye business profoundly. This choice of study led Haber further into the field of organic chemistry, which had hardly counted in the curriculum at Bunsen's institute in Heidelberg. For three semesters Haber attended Liebermann's highly polished lectures. He found the lectures of Otto Witt on the chemical technology of dyes also stimulating. Among other work, Witt had in the 1870s formulated a theory of organic dyes, and he was one of the first to distinguish between chromogens and auxochromes.[12] Haber also attended a course by F. R. Weber on general chemical technology, which he later described as worthless.

At this time the Charlottenburg Institute was undergoing great change. Laboratories and machine rooms, modern in comparison with the standards of the day, were being set up, and imposing and impressive buildings in the late empire style were being erected on the Kurfürstenallee. The Kurfürstenallee led to the train stop at the Zoological Gardens, and at this time the whole area was just one large building site. On Hardenbergstrasse stood the Art Academy and the Conservatory of Music—so that even then, as today, students dominated the scene in this section of the city.

The capital of the German state was fast becoming the center for the sciences and the arts for the whole nation. Besides the new educational institutions, new theaters were also being built, such as the Metropol and the theater located on the Schiffbauer Damm. The Theater des Westens (Theater of the West) and the Neue Schauspielhaus (New Playhouse) were soon to follow. The students were extremely interested in this theater life, and Haber was especially attracted to the splendid performances in the Deutsches Theater.

He had thoroughly familiarized himself with the Liebermann institute by the semester of 1889–90 and had acquired a broader understanding of the field of organic synthesis. Liebermann's work and that of his assistants and students during this period dealt not only with anthracene and anthraquinones but also with other fields in the synthesis of natural products and dyes.

Liebermann assigned Haber the task of examining a particular reaction with piperonal, a fragrant substance with a heliotrope-like odor. The reaction to be examined corresponded to the first stage of Baeyer and Viggo Drewsen's synthesis of indigo. For this work Haber received his doctorate from Friedrich Wilhelm University in May 1891.[13] It was clear to him that his doctoral dissertation was not exactly a masterpiece. He stated in a letter to Max Warburg: "The thesis is miserable. One and a half years of new substances prepared like a baker's bread rolls . . . and in addition, lots of negative results just where I was looking for significant results, and further, results that I cannot even publish because I fear that a competent chemist will find them and prove to me that the camel is missing its humps. One learns to be modest."[14]

Since the Charlottenburg Institute of Technology did not grant doctorates until 1899, Haber had to present his thesis at the University of Berlin. There the examiners were Hofmann for organic chemistry; Karl Friedrich Rammelsberger, who had occupied the chair for inorganic chemistry at the Institute of Technology since 1874, for inorganic chemistry; and for physics August Kundt, the physicist who had taught at the university since 1888 and who became well-known for his powder patterns for measuring the speed of sound. Haber's inability to answer Kundt's question on how to measure the resistance of electrolytic solutions spoiled his grade. Given that Haber later carried out significant scientific experiments in the field of electrochemistry, his bad grade shows only that the ability a pupil displays during an examination gives no indication of which area the pupil will later master.

At this time a graduate student who took his doctorate under the philosophical faculty was also examined for his knowledge in philosophy. Haber's examiner for this field was Wilhelm Dilthey, a teacher he respected highly. It is no wonder that Haber received the grade of "very good" from Dilthey, which improved his overall grading, so that his final grade was *cum laude*. This score was not especially good, but Haber was pleased that he had passed this hurdle. His friend Richard Abegg received his doctorate from Friedrich Wilhelm University at the same time, so they, together with other fellow students, celebrated their new Dr. phil. degrees to the hilt.

## Endnotes

[1] R. F. Schaefer to Johannes Jaenicke, 22 Sept. 1957, MPG, Dept. Va, Rep. 5, 337.

[2] Eduard Koebner to Margarethe Haber, Coates Papers, MPG, Dept. Va, Rep. 5, 1429.

[3] Archivum Ponstwowa, Wroclaw, files of the Breslau magistrate, no. 32203.

[4] Fritz Haber to Max Warburg, 3 Oct. 1886, Haber-Warburg correspondence, MPG, Dept. Va, Rep. 5.

[5] Karl Heinig, "Das chemische Institut der Berliner Universität unter der Leitung von August Wilhelm von Hofmann and Emil Fischer" (The Chemical Institute of the University of Berlin under the direction of August Wilhelm von Hofmann and Emil Fischer), in *Forschen und Wirken: Festschrift zur 150. Jahr–Feier der Humboldt Universität zu Berlin, 1810–1960*, ed. Willi Göber and Friedrich Herneck (Berlin: Deutscher Verlag der Wissenschaften, 1960).

[6] Emil Fischer, *Aus meinem Leben* (From my life) (Berlin: Julius Springer, 1922), 146.

[7] Haber to Warburg, 23 Jan. 1887, Haber-Warburg correspondence, MPG, Dept. Va, Rep. 5.

[8] Fritz Milch to Johannes Jaenicke, 24 April 1950, MPG, Dept. Va, Rep. 5, 1485.

[9] Prussia introduced one year's voluntary service in the army in 1867, a practice taken over by the German state. A law on military service dated 9 November 1867 states: "Young educated people who pay for their own clothes, equipment, and lodging during their period of service, and who have demonstrated the skills they have learned to the extent required by the regulations, will be given leave to enter the reserves after one year of service in the army. Depending on their abilities and achievements, they may be nominated to officer's posts in the reserves or the militia."

[10] Haber to Warburg, 28 June 1890, Haber-Warburg correspondence, MPG, Dept. Va, Rep. 5.

[11] Haber to Warburg, 25 Nov. 1891, from Szczakowa, in Galicia, ibid.

[12] Jean d'Ans, "Zum Geburtstag von Otto Nikolaus Witt," *Chemiker Zeitung* 77 (1953), 279; Otto Noelding, "Otto Nikolaus Witt," *Ber. Deutsch. Chem. Ges.* 49 (1916), 1753–1830.

[13] Fritz Haber, "Über einige Derivate des Piperonal," *Ber. Deutsch. Chem. Ges.* 24 (1891), 617.

[14] Haber to Warburg, 13 Feb. 1890, Haber-Warburg correspondence, MPG, Dept. Va, Rep. 5.

Chapter 3

---

# Years
# of
# Study and Travel

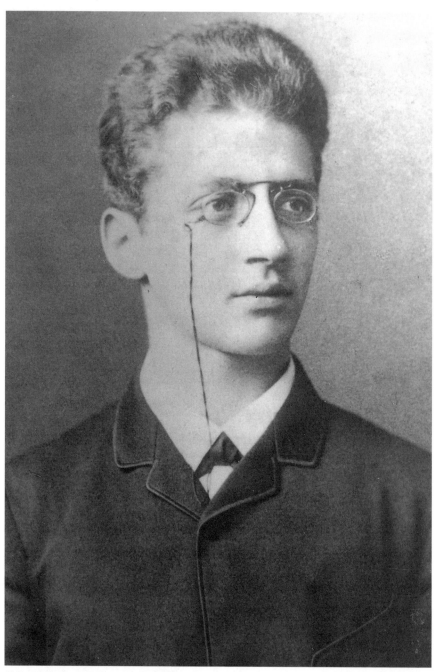

*Fritz Haber in 1891, as a recent Ph.D.*

*Previous page: The title page of* Chemisch-technische Untersuchungsmethoden, *by Haber's professor Georg Lunge.*

Fritz Haber was now twenty-two years old. He had led a relatively free and independent life during his years of study and had only occasionally thought about what he would do when he finished. He probably would have preferred to remain at a university. Richard Willstätter believed that Haber would have liked to work with Wilhelm Ostwald in Leipzig at this time.[1] Ostwald's Institute for Physical Chemistry in Leipzig was on the upswing and was attracting many young students and graduates. However, Carl Liebermann apparently advised Haber against this move. A further indication that Haber wanted to go there comes from a letter from his friend Richard Abegg to Ostwald, written in July 1891.[2] In the letter Abegg applies for a position in Ostwald's institute but also requests a position "for Dr. Haber, who has already approached you in the same matter." Haber must also have expressed this intention directly to Ostwald.

After graduation Haber returned to Breslau, where his father still held the opinion that his son should enter the family business. The confrontations that arose between father and son over the next few months made the differences in their characters increasingly evident. Siegfried Haber was a prudent businessman who weighed his actions carefully. His attitudes toward work, fulfillment of duty, order, and discipline determined the course of his activities not only in his business life but also in the domestic arena, the everyday life of the family—at least when he was at home in the evening. Fritz, who had proved during his studies that he too could succeed through disciplined work, did not want to submit to his father's domination. He felt that some of his father's actions and decisions were narrow-minded, his harsh treatment of him uncalled for, and the work in the business dull and boring.[3] But he was forced to submit to his father's will.

Siegfried decided that his educated son should now do a practical apprenticeship after spending so much time on theory. Fritz was to work in various chemical companies to learn their modes of operation and financial methods and to gain the experience required for a position in the family firm. Siegfried Haber had far-reaching business and family connections and was thus able to arrange various apprenticeships; these positions did not, however, bring much financial remuneration. But they were not unattractive to the son. He knew that he had no experience in chemical technology and perceived this as a deficit. And the apprenticeships would allow him to escape somewhat from his father's influence.

The first post was at an alcohol distillery in which the residual liquors from molasses after distillation were thickened down to extract potash. The distillery, Grunwaldt and Company, was in Budapest, where several such factories operated. Fritz started working there in the spring of 1891. Budapest was then a city with a population of nearly half a million people and a varied cultural life. Fritz reported from Budapest to Max Warburg: "It is wonderful here, and I am very satisfied with my work."[4]

The second position was in the first Austrian ammonia-soda factory to operate by the Solvay process. Willstätter stated that the factory was located in the province of Galicia, in Szczakowa. It is known that the Aussiger Verein made soda at this time using the Leblanc process, which was increasingly being replaced by the process developed by Ernest Solvay.[5] In 1882 Solvay built a small plant close to the salt mines of Wieliczka in Galicia, not far from Krakow. This plant and others that later came into operation supplied local markets, for high costs of transport did not permit distant parts of Austria-Hungary to be supplied centrally.[6] It was almost certainly in this small Solvay factory that Haber became acquainted with the ammonia-soda process.

Szczakowa itself must have been an extremely boring place. Haber describes it in a letter to Max Warburg:

> Life here is quite monotonous. I am learning some things about production and am gaining an eye for technical realities and questions. . . . Social life is nonexistent, the people and their circumstances are very limited, with the possible exception of the director. . . . The district is a wasteland of sand, swamp, and fever that offers nothing, absolutely nothing. The village—perhaps ten houses, apart from the factory buildings, in which I include the workers' houses that the factory built.

But he also saw the positive side of his stay there.

> As to the soda factory—a splendid and energetic intelligence, sustained by large amounts of money, dominates here. Since probably almost no ammonia-soda factory elsewhere on the continent would allow a study of its operation, I have reason to be very happy about the opportunity that came my way to work here.[7]

Haber appears to have worked for only a short period in this factory, for in the beginning of 1892 he was to be found at a cellulose factory, the Feldmühle Paper and Cellulose Works (Papier- und Zellstoffwerke). There he became familiar with a completely different area of chemical industry. The manufacture of cellulose had undergone a great upsurge during this period, after Benjamin Chew-Tilghman had discovered the sulfite process in 1866 and Eilhard Mitscherlich had improved on it and introduced the process to Germany. In the 1880s the Feldmühle erected one of the first large cellulose plants and became one of the leading cellulose manufacturers.

Haber now learned how defective his technological education had been. He lacked an overview of technical processes, which interested him far more than plant economics and financial operations. He must have expressed his feelings convincingly to his father, because Siegfried agreed that he should advance his technical knowledge by studying at an institute for chemical technology. He decided on the Polytechnic College in Zurich, where Georg Lunge, a distant relative of the Habers, was head of the chemical technology department.

This college, later the Swiss Federal Institute of Technology (Eidgenössische Technische Hochschule), was founded between 1848 and 1854 and had achieved an outstanding reputation. The school had excellent teachers, especially in the departments of chemistry and industrial chemistry: Georg Frobenius, Hans Landolt, Johannes Wislicenius, and later Arthur Hantzsch and Viktor Meyer. Among them was Georg Lunge (1839–1923), originally from Upper Silesia, who had obtained his doctorate in Breslau and studied with Robert Bunsen and Gustav Kirchhoff.[8] Here, along with other projects, Lunge examined the composition of gases in the nonluminous zone of the Bunsen flame. (Haber too was later to investigate the water-gas equilibrium in the Bunsen flame.) Lunge went to work in industry in 1860. He then went to England, where he occupied various leading posts in the English chemical industry and worked on the manufacture of sulfuric acid by the Glover tower process, on the chemistry of coal tar, and on the manufacture of sodium carbonate (soda). He acquired a reputation from his many excellent publications, and in 1876 he took up the chair of chemistry at the Polytechnic School.

Under his leadership the Polytechnic became one of the leading schools of chemical technology in the world. Lunge's main interests while in Zurich lay in the field of inorganic chemistry. He published a handbook on the soda industry in 1879, and he carried out research on the technical manufacture of sulfuric acid (lead chamber and contact processes). But he also remained active in the field of coal-tar chemistry and pioneered new methods in analytical chemistry: he brought methyl orange into use as an acid-base indicator, he was one of the first to begin working with standard solutions and standardized volumetric substances, and he introduced the nitrometer for use in gas analysis. Especially familiar to all older chemists is the collective work *Chemisch-technische Untersuchungsmethoden* (Research methods in chemical technology), edited first by Lunge and later by Lunge together with Ernst Berl.[9]

Haber came to know Lunge as an active teacher in the laboratory. Lunge loved intensive discussions with his assistants and students about their research problems. He was quick to recognize their abilities and supported them as much as he could. Lunge had one of his typical "controversies" with Alfred Werner, one of the assistants whom Haber met at this time. As Berl described it, Lunge let fly at Werner with the following words: "You're fired! You are no use to me here because you are far too good for this position. I know that your father has a little money. With his and my help you could spend a year studying in Paris."[10]

Haber stayed in Zurich for one semester. He learned about applied inorganic and new analytical methods and benefited from meeting such outstanding chemists as Arthur Hantzsch and F. P. Treadwell. He also maintained his connection with Zurich later, when Richard Willstätter and Hermann Staudinger, among others, were teaching there.

After this semester, in the autumn of 1892, Siegfried Haber urged his son to enter the family business and support him in his work. Fritz's father was now more than fifty years old and was understandably concerned about a successor for his company. Times had not become easier for his business. Synthetic alizarin had mainly replaced the natural madder, and the same was expected to happen soon with indigo. The import business via Hamburg was still flourishing, and trade in other chemicals necessary for dyeing was still favorable. But turnover and profits were not what they had been a decade before. Fritz probably saw these difficulties and realized their implications. He had certainly gained an insight into dye chemistry with Liebermann, and in Zurich he had become acquainted with modern improvements in process technology. He was thus much more skeptical than his father about the company's long-term prospects.

Fritz Haber could not have found it easy to work in his father's business, where his duties included purchasing raw materials and products for resale. He soon clashed with his father, who watched his expenditures very closely. For example, Siegfried refused to take any form of credit from the banks during times when the company's funds were reduced, even though this might have increased his sales. Father and son had a confrontation during the cholera epidemic in Hamburg in 1892, when large amounts of chloride of lime were needed for disinfection. Fritz thought he could make a profitable business transaction under the circumstances. But the epidemic had already subsided by the time he closed the deal on the purchase of lime, which led to a substantial loss. His father was extremely angry and accused him of lacking business acumen. This assessment was certainly exaggerated, but he was not completely wrong: in later life Fritz was not always lucky with money in financial transactions. In any case, father and son saw that cooperation in the business was impossible. This period ended with Fritz's decision to opt for an academic career, which even Siegfried now realized was more suitable.

Fritz Haber had maintained close contact with his old friends, acquaintances, and relatives during the summer months in Breslau. At home his half sisters were in that "in-between" age, from eleven to fifteen years old, and they enjoyed the company of their big brother, whom they had always adored and admired—as probably his stepmother did, too. Fritz also met often with his favorite uncle, Hermann, who died a few years later; the old wool business came to an end with his death. In addition Fritz visited his friends from the Academic Literary Club. Although the circle had changed a great deal, the social milieu was good, and Fritz was happy to participate. He liked to drink a glass of wine, and he shone there by declaiming verses and stories that he composed to fit the occasion. This short period was certainly a pleasant one.

He met an old friend in the Academic Literary Club, Siegfried Czapski, who was later to become a director of the Carl Zeiss Works (Carl Zeisswerke) in Jena. Czapski had connections to the University of Jena, and it was probably he who now persuaded Haber to enter that university.

In 1892, when Fritz Haber went to Jena, it was the central university of the Thuringian states. The university had been founded in 1548 by the Saxon Elector Johann Friedrich as a center for maintaining Lutheran beliefs. It was confirmed as a university in 1558 by Emperor Ferdinand. Goethe and Schiller were active here in Jena at the beginning of the nineteenth century. Later the Zeiss Works in Jena developed into an imposing enterprise. Ernst Abbe, the director of the company, and Zeiss himself actively promoted the university, no doubt for the good of their company. Abbe founded the Carl Zeiss Foundation, whose most notable function was to support the university.

The Institute for Chemistry (also generously supported by Abbe) had been under the directorship of Ludwig Knorr since 1889.[11] Knorr had studied in Munich, Heidelberg, and Erlangen; in 1882 he took his doctorate in Erlangen, where he remained for three more years as a privatdocent. In 1888 he went to Würzburg for an associate professorship. By 1883 he had already synthesized antipyrine (1,5-dimethyl-2-phenyl-3-pyrazolone) in collaboration with the Hoechst Dyeworks (Farbwerke Hoechst) and had a reputation as an excellent organic chemist.

The documents in the archives of the University of Jena indicate that Haber must have worked with Knorr as an independent assistant.[12] In the university's list of staff from the winter semester of 1892 he was registered among those who had the right to attend lectures without being matriculated. He matriculated in the winter semester of 1893–94. The documents do not reveal, however, whether Haber occupied the post of *Assistent* (research assistant).

A variety of investigations were under way in Knorr's laboratory when Haber began to work there. These were all designed to clarify the new theory of tautomerism; Haber's work also helped establish this theory.[13]

Haber found it more and more urgent to move into the field of physical chemistry during this period, as he wanted to apply for an assistantship with Wilhelm Ostwald. In Jena he attended lectures on this subject for the first time. They were given by a later director of the Zeiss Works, Rudolf Straube, a theoretical physicist who had received his habilitation (qualification to be a teacher in a German university) in 1893.

Once again Haber tried to join Wilhelm Ostwald's group of assistants.

He wrote to him in November 1893, asking him to expound his ideas on the reciprocal relationship between emitted and chemical energy and requesting a meeting to discuss the matter.[14] Ostwald agreed. Just two days later Haber went to Ostwald's institute in Leipzig, but he had to wait patiently for another day until Ostwald received him. Nothing is known about the results of the conversation; in any case, it did not gain Haber access to Ostwald's institute. Later, when Haber was already in Karlsruhe, he tried once more to gain Ostwald's ear. Much later, when answering congratulations from Ostwald on the occasion of his sixtieth birthday, Haber wrote: "Twice I seemed a hair's breadth from acceptance into your group of assistants."[15]

Before we turn to the events that led to Haber's decision to go to Karlsruhe, another decision he made in Jena needs to be discussed: his conversion to Christianity. It has never been clear why he decided on this step. Johannes Jaenicke believes that Haber was "now quite determined to try for a career within the university. First of all, he cleared away the obstacle that made access to this goal incalculably harder," namely belonging to the Jewish religion.[16] We can certainly understand Haber's position at that time, although his choice must have been difficult. Haber's friend Richard Willstätter remained true to his Jewish faith, but he had to pay for it even before 1933.

Another possible motive might stem from Haber's participation in the reserves. While in Jena he served with a Thuringian artillery regiment, and after his change of religion he could have applied for an officer's position. Yet he did not, probably because he did not believe his application would be accepted. He remained at the rank of a noncommissioned officer.

Now came the decisive point in Haber's academic career. If he was to succeed in the academic world, he needed to obtain the post of *Assistent* at either a traditional university or an institute of technology. A friend asked him how long he wanted to remain "in this bleak hole" of Jena, especially after Ostwald had not accepted him.

Why Haber decided on Karlsruhe is not clear. It may have been because Karlsruhe was situated in one of the most liberal German states. Once Haber had decided, Ludwig Knorr gave him a letter of recommendation to Carl Engler, the full professor of chemistry in Karlsruhe. Haber left Jena in the spring of 1894 and traveled to Karlsruhe without being certain of what awaited him. It is impossible to establish whether this trip was "an awkward coincidence," as Richard Willstätter believed.[17] However, this "coincidence" changed Haber's life. Karlsruhe was to hold this versatile wanderer for seventeen years. There he would finally find his way into physical chemistry and physics, almost completely without a teacher and without any help. He developed into a self-taught man who divested himself of all prior influences and created his own field of work.

## Endnotes

[1] Richard Willstätter, *Aus meinem Leben* (From my life), 2nd ed., ed. A. von Stoll (Weinheim: Verlag Chemie, 1958), 242.

[2] Richard Abegg to Wilhelm Ostwald, 20 July 1891, Ostwald Nachlass, Archiv der Berlin-Brandenburgischen Akademie der Wissenschaften.

[3] Rudolf Stern, *Fritz Haber: Personal Recollections*, Leo Baeck Institute Yearbook 8 (New York, 1969), 73.

[4] Fritz Haber to Max Warburg, 29 July 1891, Haber-Warburg correspondence, MPG, Dept. Va, Rep. 5.

[5] Ernest Solvay, "Coup d'oeil retrospectif sur le procédé de fabrication de la soude de l'ammoniaque" (A retrospective glance at the ammonia-soda process), *Proceedings of the 5th International Congress of Pure and Applied Chemistry* 1 (1903), 408–417; W. H. Nicholls, "Ernest Solvay—an Appreciation," *Journal of Industrial and Engineering Chemistry* 14 (1922), 1156. The Österreichische Verein (Austrian Union) für Chemische und Metallurgische Produktion was located in Aussig in Bohemia and is commonly called the Aussiger Verein, or simply the Verein.

[6] Julius Glaser, *Die chemische Industrie Österreichs und ihre Entwicklung* (Austria's chemical industry and its development) (Berlin: Verlag Bornträger, 1918), 37.

[7] Haber to Warburg, 5 Nov. 1891, Haber-Warburg correspondence, MPG, Dept. Va, Rep. 5.

[8] Ernst Berl, "Georg Lunge," *Journal of Chemical Education* 16 (1939), 453.

[9] Georg Lunge and Ernst Berl, eds., *Chemisch-technische Untersuchungsmethoden* (Research methods in chemical technology), 8th ed. (Berlin: Springer Verlag, 1931–40).

[10] Berl, "Lunge" (cit. note 8), 459.

[11] Fritz Chemnitius, *Die Chemie in Jena von Rolfinck bis Knorr, 1629–1921* (Chemistry in Jena from Rolfinck to Knorr, 1629–1921) (Jena: Fromman, 1929).

[12] H. Schrader to Johannes Jaenicke, 21 Mar. 1958, MPG, Dept. Va, Rep. 5, 426.

[13] Ludwig Knorr and Fritz Haber, "Über die Konstitution des Diacetbernsteinsäureesters" (On the structure of diacetosuccinic acid esters), *Ber. Deutsch. Chem. Ges.* 27 (1894), 1151–1167.

[14] Fritz Haber to Wilhelm Ostwald, 21 Nov. 1893, Ostwald Nachlass, Archiv der Berlin-Brandenburgischen Akademie der Wissenschaften.

[15] Haber to Ostwald, 1928 (date unknown), ibid.

[16] Johannes Jaenicke, "Fritz Haber: Beiträge zu seiner Biographie" (Fritz Haber: Contributions to his biography), *Fridericiana: Zeitschrift der Universität Karlsruhe* 35 (1984), 3.

[17] Richard Willstätter, *From My Life: The Memoirs of Richard Willstätter*, trans. Lilli S. Hornig (New York: W. A. Benjamin, 1965), 258. Orig. *Aus meinem Leben* (cit. note 1).

*Chapter 4*

# The Glorious Years
# in
# Karlsruhe

*Fritz Haber in a drawing by Backhaus (1903).*

*Previous page: Fritz Haber with his assistants in Karlsruhe in 1909 (see also p. 60).*

A T THE CLOSE OF THE NINETEENTH CENTURY KARLSRUHE WAS THE capital city of the Grand Duchy of Baden, which had developed into a focus of liberalism in Germany. Such institutions as the School of Art (Kunstschule) and the Trade School (Gewerbeschule) had helped turn Karlsruhe into a city whose high educational level was generally acknowledged. Of central importance was the Institute of Technology, founded in 1825 by Grand Duke Ludwig.[1] It arose from the merging of the School of Architectural Drawing (Architektonische Zeichenschule)—founded in 1768, reorganized by Friedrich Weinbrenner in 1798, and extended by a school of architecture—and the School of Engineering (Ingenieurschule)—founded by Johann Gottfried Tulla in 1807. The institute that resulted from the merger was first called a Polytechnic College (Polytechnische Hochschule). After further organizational changes and expansions in the next decades Friedrich Redtenbacher saw to it that science was introduced into the technical workshops and that closer ties were formed between theoretical and technical mechanics.

Redtenbacher's successor, Franz Grashof, demanded in 1864 that the polytechnic colleges gain university status. In 1865, consequently, the Karlsruhe school received a full university constitution with the right to appoint professors and to have autonomous administration; it was thus made equal to the universities. The name Institute of Technology (Technische Hochschule) was bestowed at this time.

Chemical research at the college was carried out at the laboratory that Carl Weltzien founded in 1851, which was one of the best regarded chemical research laboratories of the time. Of special significance for the college was the founding in 1860 of BASF, the Badische Anilin- und Sodafabrik (Baden Aniline and Soda Factory) in Ludwigshafen-Mannheim. Close contacts arose between BASF and the college that have endured until today. In the same year the International Chemical Congress, which played an essential role in the history of chemistry, took place in Karlsruhe.[2] In 1868 Weltzien's successor, Lothar Meyer, made an essential contribution to the setting up of the periodic table of the elements.

## Teaching and Research in Chemistry at Karlsruhe in Haber's Time

At the end of the nineteenth century, research and teaching in the field of chemistry at the Karlsruhe Institute of Technology were greatly influenced by two people: Carl Engler and Hans Bunte.

Carl Engler (1842–1925) received his doctorate from the University of Freiburg in 1864, on the basis of work he carried out in Weltzien's laboratory in Karlsruhe.[3] He then went to Halle, where he received his habilitation and the title of privatdocent in 1867. In 1876 Engler was appointed full professor of chemical technology at the Polytechnic College in Karlsruhe and director of its laboratory of chemical technology, which had been set up by his predecessor, Karl Birnbaum, who also established the Institute for Chemical Technology in 1872.

Once he began his professorship, Engler devoted himself to the problems of dyes and of the dye industry. The application of colorants in dyeing and textile printing, as well as the study of synthetic materials for textiles, received special attention at the Karlsruhe Institute of Technology. A dye laboratory was set up in the Institute for Chemical Technology in 1881. Paul Friedländer, an associate professor and a student of Adolf von Baeyer's, directed this laboratory from 1887 on. After Fritz Haber received his habilitation, Engler delegated the teaching in the fields of dyeing and fiber technology to him.

Engler followed advances in the dye industry with great attention. The lecture he gave on 1 September 1884 at the general meeting of the German Engineers' Society (Verein Deutscher Ingenieure) in Mannheim, "Über den heutigen Stand der Teerfarbenindustrie" (The current status of the dye industry) demonstrates that interest. Engler began his research in the field of petroleum in the same year, and over the decades he benefited from the growing interest in this area. His journeys to the oil fields of eastern Galicia, the Caucasus, and, later, North America show how systematically he proceeded, gaining wide-ranging knowledge of where oil occurred and on how to make it accessible for development.

In 1887, on Lothar Meyer's departure for Tübingen, Engler took over

Meyer's professorship in chemistry and at the same time became director of the Institute for Chemistry, which he enlarged considerably. Here he continued his oil research.

In his tribute to Engler on his eightieth birthday, Fritz Haber expressed great gratitude and veneration.[4] Willstätter called the text a "splendid, warm, loving portrait," and he mentions that Haber always spoke of Carl Engler and also of Hans Bunte "with great modesty, true to his original relationship to these much older men, his superiors, with a fine perception of the special character, of the wonderful humanity of these scholars, and with a deep feeling of gratitude."[5]

Bunte was the other person who directed teaching and research in chemistry at the Karlsruhe Institute of Technology. He also supported Fritz Haber in his early years, and Haber revered him for the rest of his life.[6]

Born in 1848 in Wunsiedel, Bunte attended high school in Erlangen. His university studies were in Stuttgart, in Heidelberg with Robert Bunsen, and in Erlangen, where he received his doctorate. He then worked in Munich, where his activities were increasingly concentrated in the field of gas illumination and fuel technology. He became the General Secretary of the German Society of Gas and Water Professionals (Deutscher Verein für Gas- und Wasserfachmänner). Here he became acquainted with Carl Engler, and in 1887 he was appointed his successor as professor for chemical technology in Karlsruhe. He kept up the fields introduced by Engler and greatly expanded studies in gas and fuel technology. Through him Karlsruhe became the center of scientific and technical research in this area. Bunte also founded the so-called Gas Institute on the grounds of the Karlsruhe Gas Works, which his son, Karl, subsequently directed.

Fritz Haber's first papers in Karlsruhe were molded by Bunte's fields of research: his investigations of the pyrogenic reactions of aliphatic compounds, the determination of ethylene in the presence of benzene vapors, the combustion of gas for illumination, and the process of combustion in gas-powered machines. Haber's habilitation thesis also dealt with a theme from this area.[7]

Thus was the stage set when Haber entered Karlsruhe. Both Engler's and Bunte's institutes maintained a close connection with technology and the industrial application of scientific results. This type of scientific investigation, which focuses on technical application and therefore requires organized collaboration between industrial technology and academic research, was of decisive significance for Haber's future.

## Haber's Career in Bunte's Institute

The first months in Karlsruhe were not an easy time for Haber. His reception by Engler was less than enthusiastic, since his scientific achievements at this time were still limited. Engler referred him to Bunte, who finally agreed to appoint him *Assistent* in his institute in the summer semester of 1894.

The subject areas under study in this institute were new ground for Haber. He now had to familiarize himself quickly with them and get qualified as rapidly as possible. On Bunte's advice he began with an investigation into the thermal decomposition of hydrocarbons. He made quantitative assays of all the products formed by this decomposition, which other researchers had failed to do. He examined critically the analytical methods to be used and made many improvements. The result of this investigation can be summarized in what was then known as Haber's rule: the thermal stability of the carbon-carbon bond is greater than that of the carbon-hydrogen bond in aromatic compounds and smaller in aliphatic compounds.

Haber's first independent investigations, which formed his habilitation thesis, are still viewed today as classic works in the then largely unknown field of pyrolysis. They bear the hallmarks of his later work: thoroughness and rejection of an imprecision based even partially on belief rather than firm knowledge. During this period, which included many studies of the decomposition of gases important to technology, Haber made his first connections with the combustible fuel industry. He found contact with the users of his research a stimulating experience, and it influenced the further development of his interests. Until the end of his life he repeatedly worked on the problem of combustion processes in gases.

Haber sent his habilitation thesis to Wilhelm Ostwald, to "renew our lapsed acquaintanceship," as he put it in the accompanying letter. He had certainly not given up hope of a closer relationship with Ostwald.[8] Ostwald reviewed the thesis positively but did not respond. Haber kept working at Karlsruhe, now as privatdocent.

Haber's responsibilities as docent in Bunte's institute over the next few years are laid out in a letter from Bunte to the Grand Duchy's Ministry of Education, dated 12 March 1897.

> Instruction in dye technology, accompanied by practical exercises, was carried out by Professor [Paul] Friedlander up until 1895. When he left, no official replacement was available. In the winter semester of 1896 the second

*Wilhelm Ostwald.*

assistant at the Laboratory for Chemical Technology, Dr. Haber, received his habilitation and his *Privatdozentur*. The intention was for him to take over the teaching of dye technology, an area of chemical technology with which he was familiar because of his earlier research.[9]

Bunte here refers to Haber's position in his father's company and his stay in Lunge's laboratory in Zurich. He goes on to explain that Haber "taught in the summer semester of 1896 without receiving any payment other than the students' fees." The same document further mentions that "the department of chemistry has authorized financial support for the above-mentioned for a fact-finding trip to obtain information on the latest advances in practical aspects of dyeing."[10] Haber made this trip to Silesia, Saxony, and Austria in the autumn of 1896. A second trip followed in the summer of 1897, during which he also explored electrochemistry. These opportunities to expand his knowledge show how much trust was placed in his abilities.

In the same letter Bunte mentions "an important branch of the chemical sciences": electrochemistry.[11] Over the eighty years since the days of Humphry Davy, Michael Faraday, Friedrich Kohlrausch, and Johann Wilhelm Hittorf, this subject had developed into a field that was attracting many young scientists. Svante Arrhenius's ionic theory, Wilhelm Ostwald's work in Leipzig, and Walther Nernst's work in Göttingen formed a foundation on which the structure of modern electrochemistry was to rest.

Haber had followed developments in this field since his time in Jena. After he applied three times without success for an *Assistent*'s position with Ostwald, he must have realized that he would have to work his way into this field by himself, without being a member of one of the large established schools. His friend Hans Luggin helped him in this endeavor. Luggin came from Klagenfurt in Austria and had studied physics in Graz, where he became acquainted with the work of Nernst and Ostwald. He had also met Arrhenius there and followed him to Stockholm in 1894. In 1896 he came to Karlsruhe, where he received his habilitation in November 1897. Hans Luggin had the heart-warming charm typical of many Austrians, which attracted Haber, particularly as Luggin had received a thorough education in the area that Haber wished to enter. They soon developed a close relationship, and Luggin guided his friend in endless discussions. Luggin taught Haber well and stimulated him on many fronts.

The young privatdocents taught a practical course for which Luggin gave the theoretical lectures. Luggin was also authorized to teach physical chemistry. He was probably a prospective candidate for the planned chair in physical chemistry, but he died on 5 December 1899. Haber tended him on his deathbed with great devotion. He grieved deeply after the death of his friend and always praised him as someone who had eased his path. Lasting proof of this friendship is to be found in Haber's *Grundriss der technischen Elektrochemie auf theoretischer Grundlage* (Outline of technical electrochemistry based on theoretical foundations), published in spring 1898; Haber acknowledges his indebtedness to Luggin in the foreword.[12]

This book also gives an introduction to the research in electrochemistry that Haber had published from 1896 to 1898. The most important of these papers, which gained him widespread recognition, dealt with the reduction of nitrobenzene.[13] His thorough knowledge of organic chemistry allowed him to tackle this topic.

These papers received a lot of attention from both electrochemists and organic chemists and stimulated further investigation in the area of electrochemical reduction and oxidation. Haber presented his results in 1898 at the congress of the German Electrochemical Society (Deutsche Elektrochemische Gesellschaft, subsequently the Bunsen Gesellschaft für Angewandte Chemie) in Leipzig. Wilhelm Ostwald writes about this in his autobiography *Lebenslinien*:

> Still a third new beginning is to be reported from this meeting. A young researcher described electrochemical investigations of organic compounds, presenting a large number of findings at breathtaking speed. He was strongly and unjustly attacked by a somewhat older colleague, so that I felt that as chairman I had to intervene on his behalf. His name was hardly known then but later became very well known. It was Fritz Haber.[14]

In December 1898, however, Ostwald wrote an unidentified colleague: "I quite agree with you that Mr. Haber first needs to be 'seasoned' somewhat. His knowledge is good, and he sets his tasks rationally, but he has only been in electrochemistry for two years and therefore does not yet have sure judgment."[15]

Haber was not accepted readily into "illustrious" circles. However, he maintained a tremendous output and worked to the limits of his capacities without considering his health, a work ethic he retained for the rest of his life.

Along with his assistants, Haber carried out further investigations in the most varied areas of electrochemistry. Collaborative projects with his friend Georg Bredig, who at this time was working under Wilhelm Ostwald in Leipzig, brought new discoveries on the phenomenon of the dispersion of various metals during electrolysis at high voltages.[16] Haber's results obtained during the further course of this work contributed greatly to the formulation of the theory of conduction potentials.

With incredible energy and great tenacity Haber worked his way into a variety of areas during his first four years in Karlsruhe. His work was followed with interest by the students of Ostwald, Nernst, and Arrhenius, and of course by his friends Abegg and Bredig. Bunte was surprised by his new coworker's abilities and supported him insofar as his funds permitted. Engler began to discuss with Haber his own areas of petroleum and problems of autoxidation, and Haber soon included these subjects in his own work.

Haber's duties at Bunte's institute included teaching as well as research. He taught chemistry of gases to a growing circle of students, gave lectures and practical courses on dyeing and spun materials, and taught technical electrochemistry to an increasing degree, first with his friend Luggin, then later by himself. Once he was awakened to a specific area, there were no bounds to his scientific interest.

True, there were also those who were jealous of him; some regarded Haber as an intruder who had pushed his way into their own fields—and not only those in Bunte's institute. There Bunte protected him. The circles around Nernst in particular expressed their dissatisfaction, which is not at all surprising. Nernst himself was prone to expressing strong opinions on various colleagues and young aspiring scientists. But Haber did not let such direct or concealed attacks touch him. He developed a pronounced self-confidence that various colleagues and students remarked on, especially later. But when he won a friend or awakened the interest of a student, he showed a genuine sympathy for all their problems and difficulties, whether at work or in private matters.

Bunte applied to Engler for further authorization allowing Haber to teach in the area of chemical technology of spun fibers and dyeing, at the same salary. Engler then passed this application on to the ministry.[17] After the ministry forwarded it to the chief of the cabinet of the grand duke, Haber was invested with an associate professorship—made *Extraordinarius*—by the Grand Duke Friedrich von Baden on 6 December 1898.

## Marriage and Friends

Haber had now achieved a tenured position at Karlsruhe. His income was still quite modest, but he probably continued to receive subsidies from his father. His financial situation also improved because the number of his students and of those attending his lectures increased. In addition he had begun paid consultancies for various companies in Karlsruhe, on flatbed printing of textiles (to produce a colored ground), for example. Thus he could afford to think of marrying.

His first love was Clara Immerwahr, whom he had met in Breslau during his military service, as discussed earlier in Chapter 2. Clara had completed her teacher training in Breslau in 1892–93 but did not enter the profession. She had moved instead to the farm of her father, Phillip Immerwahr, at Oschwitz.

Clara's father had studied chemistry with Bunsen in Heidelberg and later became a factory director and commercial judge. He then retired to the Oschwitz farm as leaseholder. He seems to have been a kind and friendly person, but he must have been quite dependent on the company of his wife

*Clara Immerwahr (1870–1915), Fritz Haber's first wife.*

and daughters. He became very lonely after his wife died and his daughters were no longer living with him, and he died a few years after Clara left home. Her mother was described as a kind-hearted, conciliatory woman. Her date of death is not known. She was probably dead before Clara returned to the farm, since their friends who often came on visits to the farm at this time do not mention her.

Clara's father apparently did not forget his education after he retired. He corresponded with his fraternity and did a lot for younger and older members of this circle. He surely conducted technical discussions on chemistry at home. This background, combined with Clara's continuing feelings for her old flame, Fritz Haber, may have led her to take up the study of chemistry in 1896 at Breslau, a difficult undertaking for a woman at this time. She was the first woman to receive a doctorate from Breslau. Her iron will and work during the long hours of the night strained her health, but she succeeded. Her fellow students and friends described her as a sensitive, delicate person who was driven toward clear understanding and resolving disagreements, not only in her personal life but also in intellectual discussions.

Toward the end of 1897 Clara converted to Christianity and was baptized, to the great surprise of friends and relatives. At lunch one day she stated: "Father, I have been baptized." He accepted this revelation without a word. Later he said, "I will remain faithful to my flag."[18] This baptism was a further step toward an engagement with Fritz Haber. Near the end of her studies Clara took classes from Richard Abegg, who had come to Breslau in 1899. She established a close relationship with Abegg, as later correspondence with him shows. As he was also Haber's good friend, the connection with Fritz became that much stronger.

On 18 April 1901, Haber wrote to Clara's uncle, Georg Immerwahr:

> Fate has been kind to me. Your niece, Dr. Clara Immerwahr, of whom I was fond as a student and then for ten years tried very hard but unsuccessfully to forget, has said "yes" to me. We saw each other at the congress in Freiburg, spoke to each other, and finally Clara allowed herself to be persuaded to try a life with me.[19]

Soon afterward Haber and Clara traveled to her father "like a prince and princess in a fairy tale wrapped up in a dream," as Haber writes further in this letter. Soon preparations for the marriage began. Haber rented a large, comfortable apartment in the Moltkestrasse in the western part of Karlsruhe. The two were married on 3 August 1901.

Marriage naturally altered Fritz's social life. Now he and his wife could receive guests in their more spacious apartment in the Moltkestrasse and present them with the results of their culinary artistry. Haber's friend Hans Luggin spent much time at the home of the Habers. Other areas of Haber's life developed gradually. A circle of students gathered together with him in the evenings for a glass of beer and for excursions into the beautiful and varied countryside around Karlsruhe. Such undertakings were later organized by the small section of the new Chemical Society of the Karlsruhe Institute of Technology, a tradition that has continued to the present day.

In his bachelor days Haber had joined a group of young people of various professions who occasionally met for lunch or for drinks in a pub in the evening. This group, which later turned into a regular dinner circle, included the historian Karl Dauber, the German philologist August Marx, a forestry expert named Hausrath, and the painter Count Leopold von Kalckreuth. A horn with an emblem on which was written "Lying is permitted here" hung above the pub table where they regularly met. Later, when most of the members of this dinner circle had already married, they met on certain evenings for *Würstelessen*, or "muddle meals" in the Austrian dialect, in the homes of various participants. Lore Marx, Marx's daughter, reports that pasta dishes were often eaten in their Swabian household. Haber scorned pasta, calling it "mush." For Haber's fortieth birthday the Marxes presented him with a giant wisdom tooth, as he had now reached the age of maturity for a Swabian, and a bowl of *Spätzle* (small dumplings run through a colander) with the rhyme, "Dear Fritz, don't make a face [*Frätzle*], go eat the bowl of *Spätzle*."

Haber was also invited to Hans Bunte's. Once, while he was there for tea, Mrs. Bunte told him that they were planning a large party, and they had heard that he had a talent for writing and producing little sketches on such occasions. Haber produced a witty and charming caricature of Bunte's work on the technology of gases, and Bunte found it so amusing that he had it published by Verlag Oldenbourg. The piece ended with this grand finale:

> I still remember how on a leisurely day—
> Long ago, of course (it seems ages),
> In the forest with my Goethe I lay
> Leafing through the familiar pages.
>
> "Die Wahlverwandtschaften" (how much I like
> To read it again and again!)—
> Now I flew through it and thought how unlike
> People of today are from those of then.
>
> What I had achieved each day and year,
> Faithfully I counted it out;
> How little it was! I thought with drear
> And considered myself a lout.
>
> And yet Goethe's characters, the three,
> The captain, Charlotte, and the Baron
> They did damn little and were yet carefree;
> So one reads and so I dare own.
>
> Then suddenly it hit me, like a friendly glow
> More lovely than spring and sun—
> Those three still had what we lack so,
> Diogenes' barrel, now long gone.

Happy not only with ceaseless activity,
But happy too in quiet ease,
They were centered on a serenity,
Which we fools try to chase and seize.

And had we caught the sun, stars, and moon,
To light up our rooms at will,
The radiant shimmer that on Goethe's three shone,
Would be for us missing still.[20]

This poem expressed something that was already causing Haber difficulties during his years in Karlsruhe. His ceaseless activity, probably caused by his tremendous ambition, often made him nervous and tense.

After the Habers moved to a more spacious apartment, they often hosted large gatherings. Clara, however, was annoyed when her husband brought guests home without any warning. The guests were frequently from the Karlsruhe Institute, Lothar Wöhler, for instance, who with his wife was often at the Habers (later he went to Darmstadt). Or Paul Eitner, director of the Institute for Experimental Chemical Technology, and later Reginald O. Herzog, Aladar Skita, and Paul Askenasy visited. Guests, relatives, friends, and acquaintances from out of town also came and stayed with the Habers for longer periods, particularly Clara's father.

The institute excursions to the outskirts of Karlsruhe were a special form of social gathering, and later they were carefully planned. The then wife of Friedrich Bergius (who in 1931 received the Nobel Prize for his work on high-pressure coal-to-oil conversion) tells how Fritz Haber was able to relate wonderfully to other people, even outside the laboratory. These descriptions actually come from a slightly later period. They depict Haber's surroundings in Karlsruhe in the following years, during which his professional ascent continued—the time in his life regarded as his most brilliant scientific period.

As early as 1898 Engler and the institute senate both considered a separate chair for physical chemistry essential. Engler sent a letter to the senate in May 1899 concerning "the establishment of a full professorship of physical chemistry and electrochemistry."[21] The letter did not mention that negotiations had been under way with Max Le Blanc since mid-1898. Le Blanc had worked with Wilhelm Ostwald in Leipzig and later took up an industrial position at the Hoechst Dyeworks. When negotiations concluded in 1901, the chair was established, and Le Blanc was named professor and director of the Institute for Physical Chemistry.[22] Bunte tried to prevent his

protégé Haber from being pushed aside during these maneuverings. He succeeded at least in keeping the field of electrochemistry as part of his institute by declaring that it was "technical" electrochemistry and because of this
should be maintained in an institute of chemical "technology." Haber, caught
between the interests of the senate members and those of the leaders of the
chemistry department, felt cheated. He immersed himself in his work during this miserable period, which did not help his newly contracted marriage.
An assignment for the German electrochemical society, the Bunsen Society,
made at a meeting in Würzburg in 1902, helped him out of this predica-
ment by sending him to the United States on a fact-finding trip on electrochemical developments.

## The Trip to America

By the turn of the century the technical applications of electrochemistry
began to expand. Industrial electrochemistry did not become viable until
after 1867, when Werner Siemens developed a system for generating electricity on an industrial scale, using the principle of the electric dynamo. This
allowed the generation of large amounts of electrical energy from mechanical energy. The first power stations, which mainly served city lighting and
still used direct current, were built in 1882 in New York City and in 1883 in
Milan by Thomas Edison. The first plant in Berlin was built in 1884 and
provided current for only 2,500 lamps. The first power station using alternating current was built in Buffalo, New York. The largest power station
before the turn of the century was built at Niagara Falls and had three 5,000-
horsepower generators that produced alternating current.

The use of electrical current for electrochemical processes soon gained in
significance, especially in the extraction and purification of metals and in
the production of various chemicals, such as aluminum and alkali.

The last years of the nineteenth century saw the contacts between the
German and the American electrochemical societies intensify, through both
personal connections and the exchange of scientific publications. The American Electrochemical Society then held a conference at Niagara Falls from
14 to 21 September 1902, and the German society was also invited. J. H.
van't Hoff, president of the German Bunsen Society, had just been awarded
the Nobel Prize. His experiences on a journey to the United States had
given him the idea of sending a member of the society to America to
study electrochemical plants in this forward-moving country. He declared

himself ready to give 2,000 marks to help support the costs, and various bodies donated further funds. Fritz Haber was chosen to make the journey.

This assignment demonstrated his colleagues' trust in his expert knowledge and ability. He was expected to study the level of development of the electrochemical industry and the methods of teaching chemistry in America and to make suggestions from his findings for improvements in German electrochemical research and teaching as well as in the electrochemical industry.

Before Haber departed for the United States, however, he and Clara celebrated a happy occasion. On 1 June 1902 Fritz's son Hermann was born. The father was happy, and the mother was relieved, because the pregnancy had not been easy. Both loved their son tenderly and showed him every affection. Clara cared for him and fussed around him, trying to make him feel better whenever he was a little ill. Fritz's fondness for Hermann made it difficult for him to leave wife and child alone in Karlsruhe only a few months later while he traveled to America. His letters to Clara show his love and concern for both when, in tender words, he asks Clara to take care of herself and to watch her health.

Like many visitors before him and after, Haber was enthusiastic about New York. After the trip he gave a lecture at the Hofman House in Berlin on 18 January 1903, on chemistry teaching at the universities and on electrochemical technology in the United States. He expressed his reaction to the city:

> On entering the port of New York on a clear day for the first time, you receive a wonderful impression. There are more charming landscapes elsewhere, but I have never seen a comparable picture of economic bustle. This impression intensifies in the inner harbor and takes on almost oppressive proportions on entering downtown, where the means of transportation and traffic arrangements outstrip everything that we know on the old continent. At first glance all our knowledge from our own country appears tiny, as we subconsciously draw conclusions from what we see, using our own yardstick from home, and we imagine that the development of intellectual life here must bear the same relation that it would in Germany to the visible achievements of civil engineering, mechanical engineering, and electrotechnology revealed in this colossal transportation system.[23]

Haber soon traveled to the conference of the American Electrochemical Society at Niagara Falls. Here he was met by R. S. Hutton (later of Cambridge, England), who subsequently described his vivid memories of Haber.

Hutton reports that Haber had little knowledge of English: he apparently first began to learn it on the ship crossing the Atlantic. Hutton describes amusingly a talk that Haber must have delivered at a banquet in connection with the conference. Haber himself later described (to Hutton's wife in Cambridge in 1933) how he went to Hutton with the "English" outline of his speech and how Hutton, after looking through it, told him that he could not understand what he had drafted. Hutton then suggested that Haber give him the German version, and he would try to translate it into English. Haber finally gave part of the talk in English but then switched to German.

Hutton mentions that the group was exceptionally well treated during their visits to the plants and that no American visitors received such treatment. They were able to meet with many well-known leaders of the financial and industrial world, such as Charles Martin Hall, the inventor of the electrolytic process for extracting aluminum; Edward G. Acheson, later known for his work on carborundum and artificial graphite; Leo Baekeland, later famous for the manufacture of phenol-formaldehyde resins (Bakelite and Novolak); Frederick M. Becket, who subsequently became president of Union Carbide and Carbon Research Laboratories and vice president of Union Carbide; Charles E. Acker, who showed them his process for making alkali with a molten lead cathode; and Charles S. Bradley, who together with Robert D. Lovejoy developed the electric-arc process for fixing atmospheric nitrogen as nitrogen dioxide. Hutton was inspired and noted that it had been an amazing gathering of enthusiastic inventors and discoverers of new electrochemical ventures.

Haber's information-gathering mission was certainly not easy—and it required tact and empathy. Hutton wrote in his memoirs that

> Haber was perhaps a little too anxious to gather details of all we were shown, even when in some cases it was made clear to us that we were being treated exceptionally and that some of the information was given in confidence. Perhaps he [Haber] did not quite understand this . . . and I believe some of the Americans were a little unhappy when they saw his full report in the *Zeitschrift für Elektrochemie.*[24]

After the conference at Niagara Falls, Haber undertook a three-month trip through the United States. He reported his experiences on this trip and the information he had gathered on it and at the conference in the January 1903 lecture cited above. As president of the Bunsen Society, van't Hoff had suggested that he give the lecture, which was published in the *Zeitschrift für Elektrochemie.*

Today Haber's report is an important scientific historical document. It describes in detail various electrochemical processes used around the turn of the century in the United States. Haber also describes the American character:

> The spirit of enterprise is the natural legacy of their forefathers, who, regardless of what it was that loosened their bonds to their old homes, possessed the courage to found a new home in a distant land under strange and uncertain circumstances. Self-confidence is perhaps the most fundamental characteristic of the American spirit, both in individuals and in the people as a whole. This reveals itself in the greatest variety of forms: in the early independence demanded by the young generation; in the national sensitivity of the broad masses (as reflected in daily journalism); and in the rejection by the individual of every form of official domination, which we so often register with surprise.

He commented further on the economic situation in the United States:

> Here the founding of companies means overcoming greater distances and moving more materials than in the confined countries of Europe, and these tasks have to be solved in such a way that the human hand has to do as little as possible in the factory and the machine takes over as much human work as possible.[25]

Haber recognized clearly that this striving toward efficiency, which still holds in today's computer age, was even then especially developed in the United States. He was amazed at the high salaries in industry and compared them with the then-current salaries in Germany. He said that "the period of self-sufficiency has also started for chemistry, and in my opinion this will be the last generation in which the dependence of chemical industry on German influences is a general one." Haber could not have foreseen that this development would take place even faster, once World War I began.

At the beginning of his examination of the American university system Haber wrote:

> We are accustomed in Germany to viewing the universities as places that encourage theoretical knowledge. The technical branches have been removed to special educational institutions, the institutes of technology. The framework of the university in America is broader. It literally corresponds to the word *university* in that it includes branches of all possible subjects that can be taught at a university. That is, it includes the technical subjects and also those

institutions that are most similar to our technical colleges and are called institutes of technology or schools of applied sciences. . . . German universities . . . are public educational institutions. . . . American universities are private creations in the East and part public, part private in the Midwest and the West. . . . The fitting out of the schools and their institutes is splendid, and anyone judging by the outer decoration of the buildings, their facades and stairwells, will find German university buildings shabby at times. . . . It is an understandably human weakness that a person making a major donation for such a purpose should wish to create a memorial for himself at the same time.

As to the status of the teaching faculty, Haber found it "generally less favorable than in Germany." He mentions low regular salaries, little social status, and a lack of pension rights. Haber then described the differences in admissions requirements and in the actual teaching. "We demand a high school matriculation [the *Abitur*] . . . in principle the American university is satisfied with the one-year voluntary level [a Prussian school-leaving certificate]." He criticizes the learning by rote common in American schools. Here he was probably reminded of his time at school in Breslau and of the last classes in the upper forms, for German schools, too, used mainly this form of teaching. But Haber emphasizes the advantages in America, above all the "development of the technical outlook in the pupils . . . not present to the same extent in our schools."

As for the American bachelor of science and bachelor of arts degrees, Haber considered that the universities "discharge the student with an abundance of carefully learned factual knowledge . . . but with only a very limited scientific maturity." "It is ready-made science that is taught, as in schools, not science in the making, as at the university." Haber also said that "those universities at which plausible postgraduate work is carried out" are small in number.

Haber's descriptions of the type of chemistry taught are just as relevant today. He discussed what he considered to be "an exemplary characteristic" of American teaching.

The first chemistry lectures are accompanied by exercises in inorganic preparation . . . This corresponds to the natural tendency of the student. . . . In Germany we begin . . . practical courses with qualitative analysis, and thus we disappoint the expectations . . . of the young student. . . . Should not the practical courses use pertinent experiments that the student himself carries out in order to strengthen and deepen what is taught in the lectures? Were we to place preparative exercises at the beginning of courses . . . designed to offer every opportunity to learn a little of the art of experimentation that is so inseparable from our subject, then we would shift the drudgery from a place where it is experienced as oppressive and would move it where it can be borne much more easily.

During his trip through the United States, Haber met Alexander Smith, who taught at the University of Chicago. Smith had studied in Munich and strongly advocated teaching chemistry at the beginning of a university education. Haber was very impressed by his textbook, *A Laboratory Outline of General Chemistry,* for it described how chemistry courses were taught in America, much as Haber describes them above. On his return Haber used all his influence to have the book translated and distributed in Germany. After Ernst Riesenfeld declined, Haber, together with one of his coworkers, M. Stoecker, took over the translation into German.[26] On publication of the translation Haber tried to make the American system attractive to his colleagues, but he failed to effect any change in teaching methods at the universities.

Haber returned to Karlsruhe in mid-December 1902 to celebrate Christmas with his young family. In April 1903 he gave another lecture about his visit to America, to the local section of the German Engineers' Society. Here he limited himself mainly to the broad outlines of developments in America. One section from this lecture could have been given today rather than in 1902:

> We are familiar with the distorted view of the American as someone who chases after dollars without a break, and who, because of his wish to become rich, loses his feeling for law and order as well as any interest in the world of culture. But is this any more accurate than the distorted view of the German that we are confronted with over there? . . . We are seen as a people who are good at parades and who write bad lyric poetry, who fawn on those above them and treat harshly those below them, . . . who feel comfortable with a voluntary lack of independence in politics, who gladly accept the pressures imposed by the authorities and pass them on to their wives and daughters, whom they rob of freedom and the right to education both in marriage and in their lives generally.

And later: "The 'American Danger' has become a slogan, and it seems that Prince Bismarck's statement that the Germans fear only God is, in financial circles, gradually and seriously being amended by adding and 'the United States—a little.' "[27]

## Back at Karlsruhe: Research Problems and a Professorship

Haber again took up his teaching duties at Bunte's institute on his return from America and busied himself with work he had begun. The years that followed were extraordinarily fruitful for him.

Within the framework of his teaching on the technology of textile fibers he also dealt with dyeing and printing. Through his studies in this area he came into contact with Adolf Holz, who owned a silk and wool printing works in Rorschach. Holz had succeeded after many years of experimentation in using the process of lithography for printing on textiles. With his assistant Friedrich Bran, Haber now investigated this process and was able to provide explanations for the various steps used in the process; he then published the results.[28]

Haber's other research in this period dealt with autoxidation, a problem that played an important role in his scientific work. Carl Engler, who had gained considerable inspiration from his discussions with Haber, had drawn his attention to this field. According to Haber's investigations, autoxidation could be seen in electrochemical terms. Haber examined the various sorts of autoxidation by oxygen radicals formed in flames and explosions, and he established the difference between dry and wet autoxidation.[29] (Thirty years later he would return to these researches and contribute new ideas to the theory of radicals.)

During these years Haber completed his earlier work on electrochemical reduction, focusing on its physical aspects. In a series of brilliant investigations regarded as classics of electrochemistry, he developed the first general theory both for irreversible reduction (for example, the reduction of nitrobenzene) and for reversible reduction (for example, as shown in the quinone-hydroquinone system).[30]

Another largely uninvestigated field that Haber worked in was that of crystalline salts. Seeking to enlarge knowledge in this area, he focused on the special thermodynamics of the reactions of solids. He was the first to confirm that Faraday's laws also held for the electrolysis of crystalline salts.[31] Further work led to the theory of the glass electrode and its practical application, which is still important today for the measurement of electrolytic potentials.[32]

Turning to the electrochemistry of iron,[33] Haber dealt with passivity, a condition that arises temporarily in the non-rare metals (e.g., chromium, iron, nickel, aluminum, and zinc), causing them to show the chemical resistance of the precious metals. While engaged in this work, Haber came up against the corrosion of underground gas and water pipes caused by stray currents from streetcars, which then generally worked with direct current. This problem disappeared with the introduction of alternating current.[34]

This overview of the fields that occupied Fritz Haber and his assistants from 1902 to 1906 demonstrates the multiplicity of problems that attracted his interest. He spent most of his time in this period on electrochemistry, however. In his continual drive to form a close connection between research and industrial application, he viewed it as a great shortcoming that industrial practitioners of electrochemistry of the time took little notice of new theoretical results, probably because they had little training in physical chemistry.

To provide additional income, Haber also consulted in various areas of chemistry. This sideline brought him into contact with a range of industries, first with middle-sized companies, but later with such chemical giants as BASF, which then awarded him contracts for consulting. Such activities were quite normal then (as today) for leading chemists: Engler, Bunte, Nernst, and Ostwald as well as many other well-known scientists of the day were consultants.

Many of Haber's papers on the reactions of gases and on electrochemical processes led him to the field of chemical thermodynamics. Even during his first years in Karlsruhe, while his friend Hans Luggin was still alive, Haber was fascinated by the question of how the laws of thermodynamics influenced the course of chemical reactions and what practical consequences followed. In his lectures and in seminars carried out with his closest colleagues, he always tried to work out the thermodynamic relationships and to present them in clearly understandable terms.

As the chemical industry expanded, the predictability of chemical reactions, that is, the ability to measure chemical affinity, acquired decisive importance. In 1867 Marcelin Berthelot had succeeded to a certain extent in posing the right question, and he found nearly the right answer. He had asked why certain reactions continue spontaneously, whereas others do not. It was the old problem of affinity, but formulated somewhat more precisely. Berthelot believed that he had found the answer in the release or absorption of energy, and he concluded that those reactions take place spontaneously in which heat is released.

Berthelot's principle is correct in most cases, but from the beginning it was obvious that it had exceptions. Still, most chemists readily accepted the principle, because few understood the full significance of the second law of thermodynamics. The second law illustrates both the best and the weakest aspects of thermodynamics. Its clarity and strength lie in its general validity (for it can be applied not only to the metabolism of living organisms but also to the production of nuclear energy in the sun's interior); its disadvantage is its generalized formalism, which makes it so difficult to visualize the physical parameters it deals with. It was exactly this visualization that always interested Haber.

Berthelot's principle could not claim general validity and was therefore not acceptable for thermodynamics. Van't Hoff's great achievement was to have recognized the thermodynamic significance of affinity. Here the two relevant parameters are those also used in the second law: the conversion of the total energy that arises in a chemical reaction, and the part of the energy that can be changed into mechanical work. In 1880 Hermann von Helmholtz had formulated the exact mathematical relationship between total energy and the energy that can be converted to work, which he called "free" energy; van't Hoff showed that chemical affinity could be measured through this free energy. (Josiah Willard Gibbs had independently reached the same conclusions in 1876.)

Once van't Hoff had determined how to measure the energy contained in a substance, it seemed feasible to assume that every chemical equilibrium could be calculated. However, it soon became clear that it was impossible to calculate the absolute affinity—and thereby the equilibrium constant—because the integration constant of the second law for the difference in entropy at absolute zero was not known. In *Thermodynamics of Technical Gas Reactions: Seven Lectures,* Haber discussed at great length the problem of this "thermodynamically indeterminate integration constant"—as he termed it.[35] When Haber started working on the problem for the first time in 1903, he showed that the free energy of reactions between solids was almost equivalent to their heats of reaction.[36] The measurements were not sufficiently accurate, however, to allow calculations of the temperature coefficient.

When Nernst published his heat theorem in the following year, Haber quickly recognized its immense significance for his own research. Nernst was certainly better qualified than other scientists to tackle this problem. His earlier analysis of electrochemical reactions, which had led to the theory of the galvanic cell, had in previous publications already shown his solid knowledge of the field of thermodynamics.

After Haber's book was translated into English in 1908—this edition included Haber's thoughts on Nernst's heat theorem—it was regarded internationally as a classic treatise of high significance. Thus Gilbert N. Lewis and Merle Randall in the 1923 edition of their *Thermodynamics* called it "a model of accuracy and critical insight." There are three reasons why this book is especially valuable for the history of thermodynamics: its influence on the teaching of chemistry, the way in which it takes up a problem that Nernst solved in 1906, and Haber's systematic and critical overview of all thermodynamic data necessary for calculating the change in free energy in gas reactions. This overview appeared at just the right moment.

Gas equilibria had already been discussed earlier, and although Henri Le Chatelier in 1888 had pointed out the significance of specific heats in the calculation of equilibria over a wide temperature range, chemists generally did not recognize its importance and its practical value. Haber, however, spoke to chemists as a chemist, informing them clearly on reactions that were important to industry. He succeeded admirably at presenting this aspect of physical chemical theory and research: he wrote in an informal and straightforward style and developed his theme clearly and precisely, and his incorporation of entropy as a practicable and usable function caused chemists generally to embrace this concept. He was the first to use mole fractions in equations (for example, 0.5 $O_2$), and it was he who invented the term *equilibrium box* for the "reaction space" where equilibrium prevails in van't Hoff's thought experiment on the maximum work of gas reactions.[37]

The greatest part of Haber's book was devoted to a detailed thermodynamic treatment of important gas reactions from the point of view of existing thermal and equilibria data—and to the formulation of equations for calculating free energy. It was the first time that anything like this had been attempted. His masterful treatment of this difficult task and his discussion of the experimental determination of gas equilibria greatly advanced development and research.

The study of the thermodynamics of gas reactions was to form a firm foundation for the further development of Haber's work and that of his assistants. Without this knowledge they would not have managed the thorough, fruitful investigations of the reaction $N_2 + 3H_2 \leftrightarrows 2\,NH_3$ that in the end allowed them to succeed in fixing nitrogen from the air.

The quality of Haber's research in that area is better grasped in the context of the progress of his career: its difficulties, the hard work with which he overcame them, and the able assistants on whom he relied to translate his many fruitful ideas to reality. In 1901, when the chair for physical chemistry was created for Max Le Blanc, teaching and research in this subject were no longer the province of Bunte's institute. Bunte, however, knowing that Haber would find it hard to accept this exclusion, made repeated efforts to define the major direction of the institute's work—the chemistry of gases— so as to include the physicochemical aspects of gas reactions. Long before the new chair was established, Haber and his friend Luggin had successfully integrated the field of electrochemistry into the group of subjects covered by the institute, and therefore teaching and research in this area could easily continue there. The university prospectus for the department of chemistry of the Karlsruhe Institute of Technology in the winter semester of 1905 shows that Le Blanc held lectures on physical chemistry and on theoretical and technical electrochemistry and conducted the practical courses in physical chemistry and electrochemistry. The themes of Haber's lectures were the chemistry of gases and specialized technical electrochemistry. In addition, Bunte directed practical exercises in gas chemistry with Haber. Overlap was unavoidable. Haber was always frustrated by the need to accede to the wishes of his superiors, the full professors.

The Institute for Chemical Technology was considerably enlarged around the turn of the century. A new wing was built, an electrochemistry labora- tory was set up, and a large lecture theater was built on the upper floor. In January 1906 Bunte applied to the rector, asking that the institute be allowed to give additional lectures on applied physical chemistry.[38] After some deliberation the ministry finally approved Haber as teacher for this course.

Meanwhile, in 1904 Wilhelm Ostwald had applied for retirement from the University of Leipzig. He had just asked to be relieved for one semester of the burden of a major lecture course on the grounds of ill health. This request led to a sharp confrontation. At one faculty meeting he was re- proached for his arrogance and accused of forgetting his duty. His request was rejected, whereupon he submitted his resignation. Ostwald had previ- ously received an invitation to visit the United States; after his return from America on 11 May, his request to retire as from 1 October 1906 was accepted.

Le Blanc was proposed as Ostwald's successor, and he accepted the chair at the University of Leipzig in July 1906. The candidates considered as his successors in Karlsruhe were Richard Abegg, associate professor at the Uni- versity of Breslau and a friend of Haber's; Friedrich Förster, full professor at

*Fritz Haber with his assistants in Karlsruhe in 1909. Front, on the ground: Friedrich Kirchenbauer. Seated row, from the left: unidentified, Robert Le Rossignol, Unkowskaja, Paul Askenasy, Fritz Haber, Gerhardt Just, Alfred Leiser, Adolf Koenig, Oettinger. Long standing row, from the left: Friedrich Bergius, Reinhard Beutner, unidentified, Arkady Volotkin, J. E. Coates, unidentified, Setsuro Tamaru, unidentified, Paul Krassa, unidentified, Wilhelm Hirschkind, unidentified, H. J. Hodsman. Long standing row, fourth from the right: Zsygmund Klemensiewicz. On the lower steps, third from the left: Fusajiro Kotera. On the top steps, second from the right: Gordon F. Fonda.*

the institute of technology in Dresden; Haber himself; and Robert Luther, associate professor at the University of Leipzig. The committee for the appointment of the successor concluded at one of their meetings that "E. Förster and F. Haber are to be the first considered for the appointment, and they are to be considered equally, after them R. Abegg."[39] On receiving this recommendation from the senate of the Karlsruhe Institute, the Ministry of Education in Baden offered the full professorship for physical chemistry to Haber. In accepting the offer, Haber had thus reached the object of his ambitions.

## Haber's Group and His Colleagues

Haber, as director, together with his assistants produced many often-extraordinary publications that built an excellent reputation for the Institute for Physical Chemistry and Electrochemistry. The group investigated the most varied problems in widely different areas, such as flame reactions and the processes of combustion. With his coworker Gerhardt Just, Haber examined the emission of electrons in chemical reactions, and they debated the connections between heat changes and the observed electron emission.[40] He and his group also worked on mercury reactions in which amalgams are formed, and they carried out investigations on topics of practical significance, as on the quality of the glass used in the manufacture of wine bottles.[41] Haber collaborated with the physicist Fritz Löwe, an employee of the Zeiss Works in Jena, on developing an interferometer for gas analysis. Their work led to several improved measuring instruments, later used in many areas of science, technology, public health, and industrial safety.[42]

These many-faceted investigations would not have been possible had Haber not attracted an excellent staff. Many appear in a photograph taken in 1909, of him and his assistants gathered in front of the institute (see opposite). Haber is in the middle of the front row. In front of him sits his universally admired "servant," the technician Friedrich Kirchenbauer. Haber inherited him from Le Blanc, who said to Haber on the transfer of the institute: "In every institute the decisive factor is the director and his helper; the others are secondary." Haber did not quite agree with this opinion, but it was nevertheless clear to him how valuable to the institute this man, "so talented in mechanics," was. In a letter to Engler in which he proposed promoting Kirchenbauer to the grade of technician, Haber described him as an "unusual employee, of special value."[43] It was thanks to Kirchenbauer

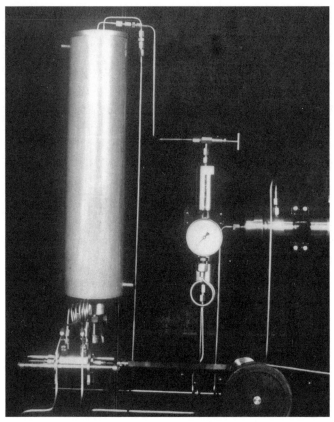

*The Haber–Le Rossignol apparatus for the synthesis of ammonia.*

that the high-pressure equipment for the synthesis of ammonia functioned as intended.

Paul Askenasy is sitting on Haber's left. He, too, came from Silesia, and Haber had known him for almost twenty years. He had been *Assistent* under Viktor Meyer in Heidelberg, then had gone into the electrochemical industry. He worked with Le Blanc for a short period in 1902 and then became the director of the Consortium for Electrochemical Industry (Konsortium für Elektrochemische Industrie) in Nuremberg. Haber had to use considerable persuasion to bring him to his institute in Karlsruhe. Askenasy received his habilitation in 1908 in the field of electrochemistry and became an associate professor in 1909.

The only woman in the circle sits next to Askenasy. Nothing is known about her except her last name, Unkowskaja. She appears to have been

Russian. Next to her, sitting very erect, as if fully aware of his own value, is Robert Le Rossignol. He was English, from the Channel Islands. He had already worked on ammonia with William Ramsay before coming to Karlsruhe. It was he who perfected the laboratory synthesis of ammonia to the point that BASF finally adopted it. Many of Haber's patents were registered in Le Rossignol's name also. (Unfortunately, in the 1920s, they had a mild disagreement over money.) Le Rossignol came to Karlsruhe in 1907 and worked on the dissociation of carbonic acid as well as on the ammonia equilibrium. Haber was enthusiastic about his ability to plan and build apparatus and once said to him: "You are a true engineer." Le Rossignol later worked at Leopold Koppel's Auer Company (see Chapter 6), even (after a short internment) during World War I. After the war he returned to England and worked for many years in the scientific laboratory of the General Electric Company in Wembley. In 1959 he wrote to Johannes Jaenicke, referring to Haber as "my dear old professor and friend. I last saw him in 1933, and I very much regret that I did not see him during his stay in Cambridge."[44]

The man with the beard to the right of Haber is Gerhardt Just, Haber's first *Assistent* in Karlsruhe. He received his habilitation in 1906 in the fields of physical chemistry and electrochemistry and during this period worked mainly on the emission of electrons from metals and on photochemistry. He lectured on photochemistry and also on liquefied and compressed gases. He later went to Berlin with Haber. Alfred Leiser sits next to Just. He taught methods of measurement in physical chemistry and lectured on the phase rule in metals. He, too, later worked with Haber at his institute in Berlin-Dahlem. At the very right of the photograph are two gas specialists: Adolf Koenig, who first went to BASF, then lectured as a professor in this area at the Karlsruhe Institute, and a Professor Oettinger, who ran the gas chemistry laboratory, as he had under Bunte.

Other assistants and colleagues among the forty shown in this photograph also deserve mention. Friedrich Bergius stands at the far left in the second row; during this time he worked on high-pressure synthesis under Haber in his personal laboratory. This research led to his publications on the hydration of carbon—the original coal-to-oil conversion—work carried out four to five years later at the Hannover Institute of Technology. For these and other publications and for practical work in this field he was awarded the Nobel Prize in 1931 jointly with Carl Bosch, who was also cited for his work on Haber's high-pressure ammonia synthesis. Standing in the second row, behind and between Unkowskaja and Askenasy, is Setsuro Tamaru, a Japanese colleague. Tamaru, who later became a professor at the Tokyo Institute of Technology, was always loyal to Haber. He was full of concern when Haber experienced difficulties in 1933 and tried to bring him and his assistants to Japan. Another Japanese colleague, Fusajiro Kotera, who later became director of Tokyo Industrial Research Laboratory (Tokyo Kogyo Shikenjo), is in this group, in the next to last row.

The multinational nature of Haber's circle of assistants should also be emphasized (not all of them are in the picture). Two Americans, H. J. Hodsman and Gilbert Walworth Morden, as well as at least four researchers from eastern Europe—Arkady Volotkin and those with the last names Mavetzky, Vladimirsky, and Isgarischev—worked in the institute. Two professors from Poland, Stephan Tollocsky and Ludwik Bruner, had worked with Haber previously in the Institute for Chemical Technology. Their field was the reduction of solid carbonic acid to carbon and the role of carbon in an oxygen-hydrogen combustion chain.

Another Pole, Zsygmund Klemensiewisz, appears near the right end of the second row, above Leiser and Koenig. He and Haber invented the glass electrode in 1909. Born in 1886, he studied in Lemberg (Lwów), and received his doctorate there in 1908. After Karlsruhe he received his habilitation in Lemberg, then went to Paris in 1933 and worked with Marie Sklodowska-Curie. In 1939 he was deported to the Soviet Union, succeeded in reaching London after many detours, returned to Poland in 1956, and became professor at the Institute of Technology in Gleiwitz (Gliwice). He died in 1963.[45]

The man standing between Le Rossignol and Unkowskaja is J. E. Coates, who later (in 1937) gave the Haber Memorial Lecture to the Royal Chemical Society in London. He worked under Haber on the formation of nitric oxide during the combustion of carbon dioxide; later he taught at the University of Wales in Swansea.

Standing between Haber and Askenasy is Paul Krassa, a distant relative of Haber's wife, Clara. He first met Haber in 1906 in Vienna, where Krassa was studying chemistry at the university of technology, when Haber was negotiating there for a professorship. In his short recollections of Haber, Krassa describes how this encounter was the deciding factor for his going to Karlsruhe, where he worked for three years in the institute.[46] He later went to the Güstrow Chemical Factory as the works director. Afterward he went to the Auer Company in Berlin, where he again maintained close contact with Haber and his wife. He was even married in Haber's house in Dahlem. After a short sojourn in Vienna, Krassa was appointed professor of physical chemistry and industrial chemistry at the university in Santiago, Chile. He continued to work there at the Instituto de Investigación de Materia Primas even after retirement, right up to the 1950s.

Reinhard Beutner, Haber's lecture assistant, can be seen just behind and to the right of Bergius. He went to the United States in 1924 and in 1936 became professor of pharmacology at Hahnemann Medical Center in Philadelphia.

Some of Haber's earlier assistants who were no longer working with him at the time the photograph was taken should also be mentioned. Samuel Grinberg worked with Haber as early as 1898 on the electrolysis of hydrochloric acid and the electrolytic formation of hydrogen peroxide. Franz Richardt had previously worked as Bunte's *Assistent* and finished his doctorate under Haber on the water-gas equilibrium in the Bunsen flame in 1904. He later worked for the Karlsruhe gas works. Franz Goldschmidt and Kurt Liese contributed to the work on stray earth currents. Fritz Fleischmann carried out experiments on the action of oxygen on magnesium chloride. G. van Oordt began working on beryllium only in 1904 and then became Haber's first assistant in the investigations on the ammonia equilibrium.

Max Mayer, from a Jewish family in Ulm, arrived at Karlsruhe in 1903. He had studied in Heidelberg and became Bunte's personal assistant when he first came to Karlsruhe. He received his habilitation in 1906 in the area of chemical technology. He later became one of Haber's closest friends and often advised him on professional questions and on problems of patent law. He became a director of the Auer Company and then went to Czechoslovakia in 1922 as managing director of the Aussiger Verein. After the Germans invaded Czechoslovakia, he fled to the United States.

Reginald O. Herzog, who became well known in the field of macromolecular chemistry, prepared his habilitation thesis under Haber in Karlsruhe. He later became involved in a considerable controversy with Staudinger over the structure of cellulose: Herzog championed the micelle construction of macromolecular compounds in 1925 and stuck to this opinion for a long time. He later worked in Berlin and had close contact with Haber in the 1920s.

Many other members of Haber's group of assistants could be mentioned.

The documents of the Karlsruhe Institute of Technology show that in 1910 Haber's institute included about sixty-five professors, docents (with habilitation), unpaid assistants, and doctoral students, not including those who completed practical courses or attended lectures.

No picture of Haber's life at Karlsruhe at this time can ignore his colleagues, whose views of him add another dimension to the portrait. In 1907 Hermann Staudinger, later a pioneer of macromolecular chemistry and a Nobel laureate in 1953, was appointed associate professor under Engler. In 1912 he succeeded Richard Willstätter at the Swiss Federal Institute of Technology in Zurich. Of this occasion he wrote:

> I was congratulated by many colleagues on being appointed to this prestigious professorship. Only Fritz Haber, whose . . . laboratory was in the same building as the organic department, came to me and said he must commiserate with me, for a wonderful period of undisturbed work was now over for me. He was totally correct.[47]

In a conversation with Johannes Jaenicke in the 1950s, Staudinger recalled incidents from the period he worked in the same building as Haber. One passage reads:

> Haber often came into the laboratory because, having once been an organic chemist, he was still interested. He would ask, "What are you doing there? All this is really not very sensible—these syntheses and ketenes." [Even in Strasbourg, Staudinger had been extensively occupied with the production and the properties of ketenes and diketenes, and he kept up this work in Karlsruhe.] "Do something intelligent in organic chemistry. Find out what cellulose is. You should incorporate physics into organic chemistry rather than carrying on with the same old organic chemistry."

Staudinger remarked that Christopher Ingold, for example, later took exactly this tack, and after that he himself did look a little more closely at cellulose. On Haber, Staudinger continued:

> We had a very intimate connection because I always poured water on his head. The organic chemistry laboratory was above the physical chemistry laboratory. If something blocked the drains and the water pumps were running, there was an enormous flood and the water ran down into Physical Chemistry.[48]

A cartoon in a student magazine confirms this image: it depicts Haber's laboratory as an aquarium and Haber as an enormous aquatic animal swimming around in it with his assistants. I had a similar experience fifty years later while cooking up preparations in the same organic laboratory under the direction of Rudolph Criegee and completing a physical chemistry practical course with Paul Günther. (There was, however, never enough water to swim in.) Staudinger described Haber at that time as "very impulsive and temperamental," and noted that

> he could talk about everything interesting, about art, literature, and about whatever was happening in the world.... Haber's lectures were always excellent. He was an unbelievably fast thinker. He was always interested and always hit the nail on the head.... He analyzed my lectures nicely and drew my attention to several points. He always found the right point.

Staudinger later found Haber "pompous and pontifical." He took it badly when Haber headed gas warfare during World War I, and they entered into a vehement controversy.[49]

Several other reports originating from the circle gathered around Haber evoke this period with enthusiasm, recreating the atmosphere in a lively way: they describe Fritz Haber as teacher, adviser, and person and note some of his idiosyncrasies.[50]

Karl Holdermann reports on the time when Haber was still working in Bunte's institute. Holdermann later worked at BASF and became known especially for his biography of Carl Bosch.

> With the more senior students Haber could walk up and down the corridor for a half or a whole hour, lecturing tirelessly on physicochemical themes. As a person Haber was deeply devoted to his students and was always happy to help with advice or by doing something for them. He gained great respect and admiration.[51]

Franz Richardt, who later worked in gas chemistry, gave an account of the same period:

> A seminar with Haber and two to five other people was wonderful and extremely enjoyable. Temperamental, which he was while an associate professor, he simply bubbled over; he had nothing of the dignity and the measured demeanor of a professor. The conversation flowed to and fro, from thesis to counterthesis. He always listened attentively to his students, armed with a cigar that he chewed more than he smoked; he countered quickly and often and loved to spice the conversation with a joke that fitted the situation or derived from it.[52]

Haber's cigar also stands out in M. Stoecker's memoir. (Stoecker translated Alexander Smith's book with Haber.) He describes how he came in contact with Haber when he attended his course on problems of gas chemistry:

> These courses were held on the upper floor of the Chemical Technology Institute in the gas analysis laboratory used for work involving mercury. At that time no one knew how enormously toxic mercury is. The only safety precaution was that the large workbench had a raised strip around it. Because mercury is not held back by such obstacles and because equipment was constantly failing, the room, including the floor, was saturated with mercury. Haber had invented the equipment for exact gas analysis over mercury. . . . Haber was an untiring Virginia cigar smoker who also was in the habit of chewing his cigar. He laid it with the chewed end on the bench, an excellent way to get mercury poisoning. Once Haber sat at a workbench, time ceased to exist for him. He was a stranger to the feeling of hunger that came over all the rest of us at one time or another. . . . We usually stayed pretty late in the evening.[53]

Rudolf Wizek also worked in Bunte's institute and later became the director of the Berlin Gaswerke. He thought that Haber, an intruder in this field, was far superior to his colleagues at the institute. He also remarked that, as a Jew, Haber was a controversial figure. In Karlsruhe he was the typical "odd man out" who

> quickly rid the people assigned to him of their slow, deliberate work pace. . . . Haber's supervision overflowed with suggestions. All those he supervised, after their astonishment about Haber's unbelievable versatility and knowledge of the literature of the field, gradually came to the valuable realization of the gaping holes in their own knowledge.[54]

Gordon F. Fonda recalls that Haber taught his assistants how to present their research.

> He taught me the proper way to write a paper or lecture. I had written my thesis in a logical order. First the experiments arranged in a sequence so that the step-by-step advance to the final conclusion seems obvious; and then the theory that is validated by the results. "Oh, no," said Haber, "that is completely wrong. You have to make it simple for the reader. You must turn it around completely. First comes the theory, and then it is validated by the things that you found." He expounded the same idea in a seminar. A student had reported on his findings in great detail. I found everything very interesting. But when he finished, Haber stood up and began his critique, which was

framed, to be sure, in a very amusing fashion, as was characteristic of his friendly manner. "You have presented us with a splendid arrangement of facts," he said, "but you do not seem to tell us what they mean. It is like a man who climbs a mountain and later tells a friend about it. He describes every detail of the excursion and omits none of his observations. But nothing describes the view that meets his eyes when he reaches the summit nor does he tell how it impressed him."[55]

Paul Krassa writes in his memoirs about the seminars that were held regularly: the seminars, in which work planned or carried out in the institute or other current topics were discussed, were the most interesting hours of the week. The discussions almost always continued at the pub, where a small circle met with Haber in the evening. Here he also told about his experiences, mixing serious and happy ones. On the way Haber directed work in the laboratory, Krassa writes:

> Haber left most of the general practical course in physical chemistry to his assistants, especially Dr. Just. But when he did come in and began talking with a student, then immediately a general discussion ensued, which was carried out at the blackboard and involved everyone. Such occasions made clear his pedagogical talent of connecting apparently unrelated areas, an ability that made his lectures especially interesting.[56]

Three anecdotes by Adolf Koenig from a letter he wrote his former colleague J. E. Coates complete the picture of Haber's laboratory life:

> If one of his students said something stupid or did something wrong in an experiment, Haber immediately let fly: "You robber and criminal, I will stab you in the belly with a rusty dagger." Then afterward he could walk to and fro for hours with the robber and criminal, giving him a private lecture.

> It happened once in a lecture that someone in the first row fell asleep and snored audibly. Haber stopped in front of him and said reprovingly, "Sir, when I was a student I too slept in some lectures, but I was considerate enough not to sit in the front row to do it."

> Once when they were talking about good and bad teachers of physical chemistry, Haber said, "I cannot make any judgment about that; I have never attended a lecture on physical chemistry."[57]

It would be presumptuous to add a summary to these impressive descriptions and memories. They speak for themselves. When Willstätter writes in his memoirs that Haber's period in Karlsruhe was his most brilliant, then he certainly was also speaking of the excellent and exemplary atmosphere in the institute. It is not surprising that such important scientific publications were produced there. The most outstanding work carried out during this period, however, was the successful treatment of the problem of the fixation of nitrogen.

## Endnotes

[1] *Das Grossherzogtum Baden in geographischer, naturwissenschaftlicher, geschichtlicher, wirtschaftlicher und staatlicher Hinsicht* (The Grand Duchy of Baden from a geographical, scientific, historical, economic, and national point of view) (Karlsruhe: Verlag Bielefeld, 1885).

[2] Richard Anschütz, *August Kekulé,* vol. 1, *Leben und Werken* (Berlin: Verlag Chemie, 1929), 163–209; Alfred Stock, ed., *Der internationale Chemiekongress in Karlsruhe, 3–5 September vor und hinter den Kulissen* (The International Chemical Congress in Karlsruhe, 3–5 September, onstage and backstage) (Berlin: Verlag Chemie, 1933).

[3] L. Ubbelohde, "Carl Engler," *Öl und Kohle* 13 (1937), 1189; Karl Pfeiffer, "Carl Engler," *Die Technische Hochschule Fridericiana Karlsruhe: Festschrift zur 125 Jahresfeier* (Publication on the occasion of the 125th anniversary) (Karlsruhe, 1950), p. 40; C. Schuster, "Carl Engler und die BASF," *Wissenschaft- und Technik-Schriftenreihe des Archivs der BASF* 14 (1976).

[4] Fritz Haber, "The Eightieth Birthday of Carl Engler," *Chemiker Zeitung* 46 (1922), 2.

[5] Richard Willstätter, *Aus meinem Leben* (From my life), 2nd ed., ed. A. von Stoll (Weinheim: Verlag Chemie, 1958), 245.

[6] Johannes Körting, *Geschichte der deutschen Gasindustrie* (History of the German gas industry) (Essen: Vulkan-Verlag, 1963).

[7] Fritz Haber, *Experimentaluntersuchungen über die Zersetzung und Verbrennung von Kohlenwasserstoffen* (Experimental investigation of the decomposition and combustion of hydrocarbons) (Munich: R. Oldenbourg, 1896).

[8] Fritz Haber to Wilhelm Ostwald, 22 April 1896, MPG, Dept. Va, Rep. 5, 838.

[9] Hans Bunte to the Ministry for Justice, Public Worship, and Education (Ministerium der Justiz, des Kultus, und des Unterrichts) in Baden, 12 Mar. 1897, MPG, Dept. Va, Rep. 5, 1523 (also in the Generallandesarchiv, Karlsruhe).

[10] Ibid.

[11] Ibid.

[12] Fritz Haber, *Grundriss der technischen Elektrochemie auf theoretischer Grundlage* (Outline of technical electrochemistry based on theoretical foundations) (Munich: R. Oldenbourg, 1898).

[13] Fritz Haber, "Über die stufenweise Reduktion des Nitrobenzols mit begrenztem Kathodenpotential" (On the stepwise reduction of nitrobenzene with limited cathode potential), *Z. Elektrochemie* 4 (1897/84), 506; Haber, "Über die elektrische Reduktion der Nitrokörper" (On the electrolytic reduction of nitrobodies), *Z. Angew. Chem.* 13 (1900), 433; Haber and C. Schmidt, "Über den Reduktionsvorgang bei der elektrischen Reduktion des Nitrobenzols" (On the process of reduction in the electrical reduction of nitrobenzene). *Z. Phys. Chem.* 32 (1900), 271.

[14] Wilhelm Ostwald, *Lebenslinien: Eine Selbstbiographie* (Lifelines: An autobiography), Vol. 2 (Berlin: Klasing & Co., 1926), 253.

[15] Wilhelm Ostwald, 21 Dec. 1898, Ostwald Nachlass, Archiv der Berlin-Brandenburgischen Akademie der Wissenschaften.

[16] Georg Bredig and Fritz Haber, "Über Zerstäubung von Metallkathoden bei der Electrolyse mit Gleichstrom" (Pulverization of metal cathodes during electrolysis with a constant current), *Ber. Deutsch. Chem. Ges.* 31 (1898), 2741–2752.

[17] Hans Bunte to the Rector and the Senate of the Technische Hochschule Karlsruhe, 8 Nov. 1898, MPG, Dept. Va, Rep. 5, 1527, and Generallandesarchiv, Karlsruhe.

[18] Haber to Georg Immerwahr, 18 April 1901, MPG, Dept. Va, Rep. 5, Nachtrag Lutz Haber.

[19] Ibid.

[20] Fritz Haber, satirical sketch of Bunte's work on gases (Munich: R. Oldenbourg, 1892).

[21] The Department of Chemistry to the Senate of the Technische Hochschule Karlsruhe, 31 Mar. 1899, Generallandesarchiv, Karlsruhe.

[22] Letter of appointment, 9 Oct. 1900, No. 974, Ministry for Justice, Public Worship, and Education in Baden, 13 Oct. 1900, file no. 32786, MPG, Dept. Va, Rep. 5, 1537 (also in the Generallandesarchiv, Karlsruhe).

[23] Fritz Haber, "Über Hochschulunterricht und elektrochemische Technik in den Vereinigte Staaten" (On university education and electrochemical technology in the United States), *Z. Elektrochemie* 9 (1903), 291–303, 347–370, 379–406, 514.

[24] R. S. Hutton, Notes and Recollections of Professor Fritz Haber, MPG, Dept. Va, Rep. 5.

[25] This and following quotations on pages 52–54 are from Haber, "Über Hochschulunterricht und elektrochemische Technik" (cit. note 23), 291.

[26] Correspondence between Fritz Haber and Ernst Riesenfeld, MPG, Dept. Va, Rep. 5; and Alexander Smith, *A Laboratory Outline of General Chemistry*, trans. into German by F. Haber and M. Stoecker (*Praktische Übungen zur ein Führung in die Chemie*) (Karlsruhe: G. Braun, 1904).

[27] Fritz Haber, "Technische Bilder aus den Vereinigten Staaten und Deutschlands Stand auf der Weltausstellung in St. Louis" (Technical descriptions of the United States and Germany's display at the World's Fair in St. Louis), *Z. Elektrochemie* 9 (1903), 893.

[28] Fritz Haber, "Über ein neues Zeugdruckverfahren: Der textile Flachdruck" (On a new process of calico printing: Lithography printing on textiles), *Zeitschrift für die Farb- und Textilindustrie* 1 (1902), 1.

[29] Fritz Haber, "Über Wasserstoffperoxyd, Autoxydation und die Gaskette" (On hydrogen peroxide, autoxidation and the gas chain), *Physikalische Zeitschrift* 1 (1900), 419; "Nachtrag" (Addendum), *Physikalische Zeitschrift* 2 (1900), 130; Haber and F. Bran, "Über die Autoxydation: Teil I" (On autoxidation: Part I), *Z. Phys. Chem.* 34 (1900), 513, and Teil II (Part II), *Z. Phys. Chem.* 35 (1900), 81, 603; Haber, "Über die Autoxydation und ihren Zusammenhang mit der Theorie der Ionen und der galvanischen Elemente" (On autoxidation and its relation to the theory of ions and galvanic elements), *Z. Elektrochemie* 7 (1901), 441.

[30] Fritz Haber, "Über die elektrische Reduktion von Nichtelektrolyten" (On the electrical reduction of nonelectrolytes), *Z. Elektrochemie* 7 (1900), 269; Haber, "Zur Theorie der Indigoreduktion" (On the theory of the reduction of indigo), *Z. Elektrochemie* 7 (1900), 607; see also A. Binz, *Z. Elektrochemie* 9 (1903), 599; Haber and R. Russ, "Über die elektrolytische Reduktion" (On electrolytic reduction), *Z. Phys. Chem.* 47 (1904), 257.

[31] Fritz Haber, "Bestätigung des Faraday'schen Gesetzes beim Stromdurchgang durch heisses Porzellan" (Confirmation of Faraday's laws on current through hot porcelain), *Z. Anorgan. Chem.* 57 (1908), 154.

³² Fritz Haber and Zsygmund Klemensiewicz, "Über elektrische Phasengrenzkräfte" (On the electrical forces at phase borders), Z. Phys. Chem. 67 (1909), 385.

³³ Fritz Haber, "Über galvanisch gefälltes Eisen" (On iron precipitated galvanically), Z. Elektrochemie 4 (1897/8), 410; Haber, "Über die löslichen Alkalisalze des Eisenoxydes und der Eisensäure" (On the soluble alkali salts of iron oxide and ferric acid), Z. Elektrochemie 7 (1900/1), 215; Haber, "Über die Ferritlösungen" (On ferrite solution), Z. Elektrochemie 7 (1900/1), 724; Haber, "Nachweis und Fällung der Ferroionen in der wässerigen Lösung des Ferrocyankaliums" (Detection and precipitation of the ferrous ion in an aqueous solution of potassium ferrocyanide), Z. Elektrochemie 11 (1905), 842.

³⁴ Fritz Haber and Franz Goldschmidt, "Der anodische Angriff des Eisens durch vaga-bundierende Ströme im Erdbereich und die Passivität des Eisens" (Anodic attack on iron by stray currents in the earth and the passivity of iron), Z. Elektrochemie 12 (1906), 49; Haber and K. Liese, "Über die Messung der Dichtigkeit vagabundierender Ströme im Erdbereich" (On the measurement of the density of stray currents in the earth), Z. Elektrochemie 12 (1906), 829; Haber and Paul Krassa, "Weitere Beiträge zur Kenntnis des Eisen-angriffs in der Erde" (Further contributions to understanding the attack on iron in the earth by stray direct currents from streetcar lines), Z. Elektrochemie 15 (1909), 705.

³⁵ Fritz Haber, Thermodynamik technischer Gasreaktionen: Sieben Vorträge (Munich: R. Oldenbourg, 1905); trans. A. B. Lamb as Thermodynamics of Technical Gas Reactions: Seven Lectures (London: Macmillan, 1908), chapter 2.

³⁶ Fritz Haber, "On the Fundamentals of Chemical and Electrical Energy," Electrochemi-cal and Metallurgical Industry 3 (1905), 292.

³⁷ Haber, Thermodynamics, trans. Lamb (cit. note 35), 55.

³⁸ Hans Bunte to the Rector and the Senate of the Technische Hochschule Karlsruhe, 20 Jan. 1906, Generallandesarchiv, Karlsruhe.

³⁹ Handwritten report, "On the new appointment of the Chair for Physical and Electro-chemistry at the Technische Hochschule," 31 July 1906, signed by Carl Engler and Hans Bunte, Generallandesarchiv, Karlsruhe; and extract from the meeting of the committee for appointment of the successor, MPG, Dept. Va, Rep. 5, 1555 (also in the Generallandesarchiv, Karlsruhe).

⁴⁰ Fritz Haber and Gerhardt Just, "Austritt negativer Elektronen aus reagierenden Metallen" (The emission of negative electrons from reacting metals), Annalen der Physik 30 (1909), 411. See also Haber, "Elektronenemission bei chemischen Reaktionen" (Electron emission in chemical reactions), Verhandlungen der Gesellschaft Deutscher Naturforscher und Ärzte 83 (1911), 215.

⁴¹ Fritz Haber, "Eine Bemerkung über die Amalgampotentiale und über Einatomigkeit in Quecksilber gelöster Metalle" (Some remarks on the amalgam potential and on the monovalence in metals dissolved in mercury), Z. Phys. Chem. 41 (1902), 399; and Haber and H. Schwenke, "Über die elektrochemische Bestimmung der Angreifbarkeit des Glases" (On the electrochemical determination of the susceptibility of glass), Z. Elektrochemie 9 (1904), 143.

⁴² Fritz Haber and Fritz Löwe, "Ein Interferometer für Chemiker nach Rayleigh'schem Prinzip, etc." (An interferometer for chemists based on the Rayleigh principle), Z. Angew. Chem. 23 (1910), 1393.

⁴³ Fritz Haber to Carl Engler, 22 Sept. 1908, Archives of the University of Karlsruhe, Haber Collection.

⁴⁴ Robert Le Rossignol to Johannes Jaenicke, 30 Aug. 1959, MPG, Dept. Va, Rep. 5.

⁴⁵ M. Konopacki and J. Szpilecki, "Prof. Dr. Zsygmund Aleksander Klemensiewisz (1868–1963)," Wiadomoisi Schemiczne 17:3 (1964), 137; and R. Piosik, "Die Glaselektrode und ihr

Miterfinder Zsygmund Klemensiewisz (The glass electrode and its co-inventor Zsygmund Klemensiewisz), *Mitteilungen der Gesellschaft Deutscher Chemiker, Fachgruppe Geschichte der Chemie* 8 (1993), 50.

[46] Paul Krassa, "Meine Erinnerungen an Haber" (My recollections of Haber), MPG, Dept. Va, Rep. 5, 1470.

[47] Hermann Staudinger, *Arbeitserinnerungen* (Recollections of work) (Heidelberg: Dr. A. Huethig Verlag, 1961), 3–4.

[48] Johannes Jaenicke, notes on a conversation with Hermann Staudinger, MPG, Dept. Va, Rep. 5, 1505.

[49] Ibid.

[50] C. Krüll, "Die Kontroverse Haber-Staudinger um den Einsatz chemischer Kampfstoff im 1 Weltkrieg (The controversy between Haber and Staudinger over the introduction of chemical warfare in World War I), *Nachrichtenblatt der Deutschen Gesellschaft für Geschichte der Medizin, Naturwissenschaft und Technik* 27 (1977), 32; and Krüll, "Fritz Haber und Hermann Staudinger: Eine Auseinandersetzung um die gesellschaftliche Verantwortung des Naturwissenschaftlers" (Fritz Haber and Hermann Staudinger: A controversy on the social responsibility of the scientist), unpublished manuscript in the Institute for the History of Science and Technology, University of Hamburg.

[51] Karl Holdermann, "Erinnerungen an F. Haber" (Recollections of F. Haber), 17 June 1954; and Holdermann to Johannes Jaenicke, 1 Feb. 1958, MPG, Dept. Va, Rep. 5, 1299.

[52] Franz Richardt, "Notizen über meine Arbeiten unter Haber im Frieden und im Krieg" (Notes on my work under Haber in peacetime and during the war), MPG, Dept. Va, Rep. 5.

[53] M. Stoecker, "Erinnerungen an Fritz Haber aus den Jahren 1901–1904" (Recollections of Fritz Haber during the years 1901–1904), 2 April 1955, MPG, Dept. Va, Rep. 5, 371.

[54] Rudolf Wizek to Jaenicke, 15 Sept. 1960, and R. Wizek to Prof. F. Kaempf, MPG, Dept. Va, Rep. 5, 421.

[55] Gordon F. Fonda to Jaenicke, 30 Oct. 1957 and 12 Feb. 1958, MPG, Dept. Va, Rep. 5, 123.

[56] Krassa, "Erinnerungen an Haber" (cit. note 46).

[57] Adolf Koenig to J. E. Coates, 7 Oct. 1934, MPG, Dept. Va, Rep. 5, 1390.

*Chapter 5*

# Nitrogen Fixation

*Carl Bosch in 1913.*

*Previous page: The Leuna Works at Merseburg, 1916–17. From a painting by Otto Bolhagen.*

THE TERM "FIXATION OF NITROGEN" WAS INTRODUCED INTO TECHNICAL language during the last decades of the nineteenth century. Today it is generally used by chemists to signify the bonding of atmospheric nitrogen in organic and inorganic compounds. But it was first used to describe the biological process by which plants take up nitrogen from the atmosphere. Such plants were then called "nitrogen collectors," in contrast to those plants that need nitrogen-containing nourishment, or "nitrogen eaters."

## The State of the Art at the Turn of the Century

A growing population requires raising the yield of foodstuffs from the soil. Between 1800 and 1900 the German population rose from 25 to 55 million. The only way to produce the additional food these people needed was to add artificial fertilizers containing nitrogen, potassium, and phosphorus to the soil. It gradually became clear that for nitrogen, biological and animal sources alone would not suffice, that a mineral fertilizer like saltpeter would be needed. While phosphate and potassium fertilizers were freely available in western Europe, especially in Germany, it was difficult to expand the production of nitrogen fertilizers to the degree needed. For a long time a major source of nitrogen was ammonia liquor, a by-product of gas works. Other sources were guano and the saltpeter deposits to be found in the Andean countries of South America—Peru, Chile, and Bolivia. From 1879 to 1883, in the so-called saltpeter war, these countries fought viciously over the precious deposits in the Atacama Desert. Around 1900 experts predicted that the saltpeter deposits would be exhausted in about thirty years. Solving the problem of obtaining nitrogen from the air to manufacture soluble nitrogen compounds had therefore become one of the most urgent needs for humanity.

Haber encountered the problem of fixation of nitrogen during his tour of America in 1902, when he visited the Atmospheric Products factories at Niagara Falls, where nitrogen was oxidized in electric-arc furnaces.[1] How to use oxidation to bind nitrogen from the air occupied him and his assistants for several years.

It had long been known that nitric oxide is formed by electrical discharges in the atmosphere during thunderstorms. (Haber once calculated that rain deposits an average of several tenths of a gram of bound nitrogen per square meter of the earth's surface; this concentration, however, was too low for economical exploitation.[2]) In the 1890s several researchers recognized that using an electric arc, which concentrates a great amount of energy in a small space, yielded higher concentrations of nitric oxide. The arrangement of the arc played an essential role, so various patents were registered for suitable configurations and also for the flow rate of the gases in and out of the apparatus. The most important were those of A. A. Naville and P. A. Guye in 1895, McDougall and Howell in 1899, and Robert Lovejoy and Charles Bradley in 1901. The plant in Niagara Falls was based on this last process. The patents that proved crucial, however, were those of Kristian Birkeland and Samuel Eyde in 1903. They based their process on a principle developed by the Pauling brothers of Austria, who had built a plant in 1905 at the Salpetersäure Industrie Gesellschaft (Nitric Acid Industrial Company). H. Pauling later reported on this process in a monograph.[3]

Plants using the Birkeland and Eyde process were built in Norway, where electricity was especially cheap because hydroelectric power was easily available. After the first plant in Norway was successful, an international consortium invested in further expansion of the Norwegian plants. BASF participated in this consortium and built a test plant in Ludwigshafen. They had employed Otto Schönherr to study the reaction in 1897. In 1907 he patented a method of production with a steadier arc than had been attained by Birkeland and Eyde.[4]

Academic scientific research too had increasingly focused on oxidation of atmospheric nitrogen using an electric arc. A major question was the effect of temperature on how much nitric oxide is formed. Various researchers, among them Wilhelm Muthmann and H. Hofer[5] and Max Le Blanc, held the view that more oxide is formed as the temperature rises. Nernst had also occupied himself with this question. He and others found that although nitric oxide is stable at very high temperatures, as the temperature falls the equilibrium $N_2 + O_2 \leftrightarrows 2\ NO$ shifts more and more to the left. This shift can also be deduced from the negative heat of formation of nitric oxide. To obtain nitric oxide in sufficient concentrations requires very high temperatures. To avoid decomposition on cooling, the substances have to be "quenched," that is, the temperature has to be brought down from nearly 3,000°C to below 1,000°C as rapidly as possible. Birkeland and Eyde's procedure—in which the temperatures achieved in the flame of the electric arc were reduced suddenly by using a strong electromagnet to pull the arc flame into a disc through which air is blown—addressed this problem in a relatively effective way.

Thus, at the beginning of the twentieth century, the fixation of nitrogen by oxidation in an electric arc was carried out on a commercially feasible scale for the first time. This feat was achieved in countries with access to cheap electricity. Even so, the cost of the nitric acid and the nitrate made that way could compete with the natural sodium nitrate from Chile only if energy costs remained very low. And the great amount of energy needed made it impossible to produce enough saltpeter to break dependence on Chilean saltpeter.

Other procedures for fixing nitrogen were based on ammonia production. One method (already mentioned) extracted it from the water gas that was a by-product of the destructive distillation of coal in gas and coke works, a process that became increasingly significant in the last third of the nineteenth century. The amount of bound nitrogen produced by gas and coke works varied considerably since it depended on the level of iron production, which consumed the fuel that was the primary product of the distillation. According to Walter Eucken, 110,000 metric tons of bound nitrogen were produced in this way in Germany before World War I, but the estimated amount fluctuated between 65,000 and 120,000 metric tons.[6] This amount covered only about half of what Germany needed at that time, and demand rose sharply during the war. This method, however, produced more nitrogen compounds than the other methods available.

Ammonia was also produced by the cyanamide process. Here finely ground calcium carbide is brought to react with nitrogen at high temperatures:

$$CaC_2 + N_2 \rightarrow CaCN_2 + C + 72 \text{ kcal}$$

This reaction was discovered in 1898 by Fritz Rothe and was tested for industrial use by Adolf Frank and Nikodem Caro. The bistable equilibrium moves to the left with increasing temperature. Heating to about 1,000°C is needed only once: as the reaction is strongly exothermic, it then continues spontaneously. Residual amounts of carbide can be removed with water. The desired product, calcium cyanamide (or lime-nitrogen), is the calcium salt of cyanamide (NC-NH$_2$). On being heated with steam, it decomposes and ammonia is formed:

$$CaCN_2 + 3\ H_2O \rightarrow CaCO_3 + 2NH_3$$

The action of soil bacteria in water effects the same decomposition gradually at relatively normal temperatures, producing intermediates in the process.

Calcium cyanamide produced by the Rothe-Frank-Caro process became a significant nitrogen fertilizer in the early 1900s, particularly after 1914, and ammonia production using the same process was also commercialized at this time. The first plants were built in Trostberg, Bavaria, and in Knapsack, near Cologne. Some 5,000 metric tons of bound nitrogen were produced in this way before World War I.

Various other processes were also investigated, such as the reaction of barium oxide with carbon and nitrogen, which leads to barium cyanide. This compound decomposes in the presence of steam to ammonia and barium hydroxide. BASF tested this method between 1902 and 1908. Finally there were attempts in France to produce ammonia from aluminum nitride. Carl Bosch at BASF also looked into this process.

The possibility of synthesizing ammonia directly from elemental nitrogen and hydrogen continued to attract researchers. One was Wilhelm Ostwald, who on 12 March 1900 wrote to the management of BASF that he had

> discovered a method for combining free nitrogen (e.g., from the air) with hydrogen gas to make ammonia. The material and energy costs are so low that the price of synthetic ammonia would be a small fraction of the present price of bound nitrogen.
>
> The method has been tested in the laboratory. . . . I do not need to expand upon the significance of this synthesis for agriculture. . . . Furthermore, it is easy to get nitric acid from ammonia using atmospheric oxygen. In case you wish to contact us about the technical set-up and the financial estimates for the discovery, I would be pleased to receive any appropriate suggestions.[7]

That year Ostwald applied for a patent on a process for manufacturing ammonia and ammonium compounds from atmospheric nitrogen and hydrogen. The patent contained the essential characteristics of the scaled-up synthesis carried out later: elevated temperature, high pressure, a catalyst (here iron or copper), and recirculation of the gases. Ostwald stated his view of the patent's worth in his autobiography at the beginning of the 1920s:

> As the expert immediately recognizes, the basic ideas on the synthesis of ammonia, which has become so important, were clearly and unambiguously stated then [March 1900]. Thus I am justified in calling myself the intellectual father of this industry. I have certainly not become its real father, for all the difficult and varied work needed to create a technically and economically viable industry from the right ideas was carried out by those who took on the abandoned infant.[8]

Why, however, had Ostwald abandoned the "infant"? Various people have reported on the dramatic happenings that led to Ostwald's decision: Ostwald himself; his daughter, Grete Ostwald; and Karl Holdermann in his biography of Bosch.[9] After registering the patent, Ostwald negotiated with BASF, Bayer, and Hoechst. BASF repeated Ostwald's experiments. They found that the small amounts of nitrogen formed actually came from the nitrogen present in all commercially available iron. A repeat of this experiment in Ostwald's laboratory confirmed this result. Ostwald withdrew from the contracts already made with companies and dropped his patent application. Thus, this attempt to produce ammonia from its elements on an industrially feasible scale failed, and Ostwald's intellectual "infant" had to be developed by others.

## Haber's Contribution to the Fixation of Nitrogen

### Early Investigations

Haber's earliest work on nitrogen fixation relied on the formation of nitrogen oxide in the high-voltage arc. His first publication, written with his assistant Adolf Koenig, begins with a thorough theoretical examination that summarized their first results as follows: "As to using an electrical discharge for the preparation of nitric oxide, our reflections show that in contrast to the current ideas, which we previously also shared, the best results may be obtained, not by using high temperatures and consequently quenching, but by producing cold arcs."[10] Haber and Koenig attempted to substantiate this conclusion in various subsequent papers.[11]

Negotiations between Haber and BASF began soon after their first results were published, and Haber eventually made a firm commitment to the company to carry out further research on nitrogen fixation. He stipulated, however, that he would maintain his independence as a teacher at the Karlsruhe Institute of Technology.

Haber and Koenig wrote an extensive report on the state of the field of oxidation of atmospheric nitrogen in 1910.[12] They described the industrial advances as well as the scientific work, especially the processes developed by Otto Schönherr, BASF's further work on them, and the transfer of the results to the plant in Norway. Haber also gave a lecture to the Chemical Society in Heidelberg, "Obtaining Nitric Acid from the Air," and gave a similar lecture to the Karlsruhe Scientific Club.[13]

Haber's work on nitrogen fixation led him into a field of considerable interest to the major chemical corporations, and he inevitably came into ever-increasing contact with these firms. The chemical departments of the Karlsruhe Institute of Technology had also formed close relationships with the rising chemical firms in the Baden area, both because of their proximity and because of the highly technical direction of their work. BASF in particular sought closer cooperation with the institute. Haber's senior colleague Carl Engler was among the first; he had maintained good connections with BASF since the 1890s, and he tried to make a connection with Haber attractive to them. In a letter to the management he advised against delaying a contract with Haber too long, "for with his restlessness and his drive to achieve something in the area of nitrogen oxidation, he no doubt will get offers from other parties, and I can only repeat that it would not be good, considering the mighty undertakings in Norway, if this worker were to hire himself out to others."[14]

In early February 1908 August Bernthsen of BASF visited Haber, and after further negotiations two contracts relating to collaboration were drawn up on 6 March 1908.[15] These contracts obliged Haber to make all results of his work known to BASF immediately.

The experiments and papers on the oxidation of atmospheric nitrogen continued into 1910. Koenig moved to BASF and there at first also continued work in this field. In 1909 Haber registered the first patent, which BASF then took over. It covered a process for producing nitric oxide using electrical discharges and manipulating experimental conditions so that the electrical effects rather than the thermal effects dominated.

In his Nobel Prize lecture in 1920 Haber said of this method of oxidizing atmospheric nitrogen that it had certainly been an industrial success where hydroelectric energy could be exploited. But it had not spread as widely as it had promised in the early 1900s. "Blocking its further development is the realization that using a kilowatt hour of energy will result in a mere 16 grams of nitrogen being converted to nitric acid, whereas a complete conversion of electrical into chemical energy would produce an amount thirty times greater."[16] Haber's own process for capturing usable nitrogen from the atmosphere by synthesizing ammonia far upstaged this earlier work.

## The Ammonia Equilibrium

Haber first began to explore synthesizing ammonia when Otto and Robert Margulies, owner and managing director, respectively, of the Austrian Chemical Works (Österreichische Chemische Werke) in Vienna approached him, probably in 1903, about the project. They asked whether it would be feasible to use catalysis to combine large quantities of nitrogen and hydrogen to form ammonia. Haber must certainly have known of Ostwald's papers in this field, for he now wrote Ostwald that "an Austrian firm . . . has recently written repeatedly" to him on this matter and continued:

> I answered them by pointing out the low cost of producing ammonia as a by-product of coke plants. Pointing this out did not lessen this company's desire to pursue the preparation of ammonia along these lines. Now a foreign colleague . . . has told me that you . . . have studied this question and have taken it as far as working out a technically feasible method.[17]

Haber obviously was unaware that Ostwald, not being successful, had abandoned this work two years earlier. He asked Ostwald whether "it would be acceptable if I were to direct the Austrian firm to you. I am thinking that you may possibly wish that a respectable company with a strong capital base should take over the technical execution."[18] Haber also probably did not know that Ostwald had negotiated with Hoechst and BASF three years earlier. How Ostwald answered Haber is not known.

The encouragement of the brothers Margulies, however, motivated Haber to study the ammonia equilibrium. The Austrian company supported this work generously. His investigations, which he published in 1905 jointly with his assistant G. van Oordt, were, as Haber himself later wrote in a letter to BASF, "a kind of expert opinion that I gave the gentlemen and that they regarded highly because it had the effect of restraining them from investing large amounts of money in the preparation of ammonia."[19]

What might Haber's thoughts have been at the beginning of this investigation? He must have conjectured that continual ammonia synthesis could take place during the simultaneous formation and reduction of metal nitrides in the presence of the gases nitrogen and hydrogen, with the solid phase acting as a catalyst. Whatever the mechanism, it should be possible to determine the maximum yield obtainable from the ammonia equilibrium. Haber therefore investigated this equilibrium first.

Haber clearly understood the positive effect of pressure. But he still used ambient pressures in his first experiments, as that allowed him to use a simpler experimental set-up. Haber and van Oordt passed the gas mixture over iron, which they prepared from iron oxalate, at 1,020°C. Haber remarked about their results "that one could obtain a greater yield of ammonia if one only had a catalyst." Apart from this "the temperature was too high to allow large yields of ammonia."[20] But Haber felt that basing an industrial process on the direct synthesis of ammonia was hopeless. He informed the Margulies brothers of his negative results and dropped the subject in favor of the atmospheric oxidation of nitrogen.

Matters might have rested there, but in the autumn of 1906 Haber received a letter from Walther Nernst, who had read Haber and van Oordt's publications. Their results, if used to calculate the ammonia equilibrium, did not seem to fit his heat theorem. When Nernst's assistant Friedrich Jost tried a similar experiment at 50 atmospheres, the results were closer to Nernst's expectations.[21] Haber, with his new assistant, Robert Le Rossignol, immediately started to check the values obtained previously. Le Rossignol had just come from England, where he had worked with William Ramsay, who had studied the synthesis of ammonia more than twenty years earlier. He first worked with Haber in electrochemistry, then turned to the topics that would later bring him considerable success.

On rerunning Haber's original experiments using a more exact means of determining the yield of ammonia, Le Rossignol got results that were indeed closer to Nernst's but still too high for his calculations. Both teams reported their various results at a meeting of the German Bunsen Society in May 1907, where they came under intense discussion. Nernst rejected Haber's latest values as not exact enough and could not resist giving his younger colleague some "homework": "I would like to suggest that Professor Haber now use a method that must give really precise results, in view of the large yield." Haber vehemently defended the exactness of the data he had presented, which were later confirmed. Nernst finally ended the discussion with the words

Then perhaps I may just note one fact that is of general technical interest. It is regrettable that the equilibrium tends even more to the side of much-reduced formation [of ammonia] than has been assumed up to now because of Haber's highly erroneous data, for one could really have thought of producing ammonia synthetically from hydrogen and nitrogen. But in fact the conditions are even less favorable; the yields are about a third of what was previously expected.[22]

This summary was generally accepted at the time.

For Nernst this conclusion was not without significance. He had thought to adapt the ammonia synthesis, whose scientific basis had been worked out, on an industrial scale, and he had become a consultant to the Griesheim Chemical Works (Chemische Werke Griesheim). But when he heard the industry's opinion—that producing ammonia in more than negligible amounts at high temperature and high pressure was impossible—he quickly lost interest in this question—too early, as was soon to become clear.[23]

Haber was offended by Nernst's opinion as well as by that of others and felt his reputation had been damaged. As usual his mood affected his health. His wife wrote Abegg that "Fritz is again suffering from his old sickness: stomach, digestion, nerves, skin problems—all of which weaken him."[24] But Haber did not give in. Without delay he began on a new and decisive determination of the ammonia equilibrium with Le Rossignol.[25] This time they worked at a pressure of 30 atmospheres. They published results that confirmed the earlier values obtained at normal pressure. The apparatus they used was simple in design and admirably suited to its purpose. However, the data they obtained did not really improve the prospects for industrial application of the synthesis.

### The Challenge of the Ammonia Synthesis

Haber and the assistants who worked with him on ammonia synthesis now faced a major challenge. They must have asked themselves whether they should turn to another field because of the great obstacles and difficulties. Or was there a solution to these overpowering problems? One difficulty was that of carrying out the reaction in a vessel under a pressure of at least 100 atmospheres, if not twice as high. At just this time Haber heard of an industrial process that was being set up to liquefy air at a pressure of 200 atmospheres. Further, a process worked out by M. Goldschmidt for making sodium formate from caustic soda and producer gas (a mixed commercial gas) under pressure was introduced during this time. These developments strengthened Haber's conviction that high-pressure synthesis of ammonia was possible.

Haber had first to purchase a compressor that could produce such high pressures. Support from BASF gave him the funds to do so. Moreover, the institute's workshop was so equipped that the mechanics could manufacture any special parts needed. Le Rossignol helped build the apparatus. During the project he developed the seals needed to maintain the required pressures in the experimental chamber. In particular, he and the mechanic Friedrich Kirchenbauer developed the conical valve that later came into general use in high-pressure technology and was protected by patents and registration of the designs. A small department specializing in high-pressure work thus grew within the institute and became the nucleus for the large-scale development of high-pressure industrial syntheses—the synthesis of ammonia and of methanol and the production of benzene from coal. Haber could not have established such a department without Le Rossignol's engineering skills and Kirchenbauer's cleverness and ability. Haber knew this and later often praised them both and thanked them for their support, as in his Nobel Prize lecture.

These collaborators next built an apparatus that worked on the principle of continuous circulation. It was constructed so that the product ammonia could be separated from the circulating stream of gas reactants without the pressure of the gas mixture being reduced. Also the heat produced in the ammonia synthesis was transferred to the new gases entering the reaction chamber via heat exchange.

As stipulated in the contract drawn up on 6 March 1908 with BASF, Haber reported his results in various letters to and discussions with the company management. In a letter dated 12 October, Haber mentions an earlier visit to BASF in which patents were discussed. This discussion resulted in the application for a patent under the file number B.51088 IV/12k, granted as German patent DRP 235421. The final text reads:

> Process for synthetic production of ammonia from the elements, whereby suitable amounts of hydrogen and nitrogen are continually reacted to form ammonia using a heated catalyst, and the ammonia is removed. This process is carried out under constant pressure, and the heat from the ammonia reaction gases is transferred to the ammonia-free gas mixture newly entering the reactor.

This patent was called the "circulation patent" in the correspondence and discussion. It can be considered the base patent for the supplementary patents submitted later.

Even before the submission of this patent, however, Haber and his assistants made another discovery that was to accelerate their progress. In March 1909 they found a surprisingly good catalyst, the rare metal osmium. As a catalyst, osmium allowed the reaction to reach a high rate at temperatures around 550°C, and thus ammonia concentrations of about 8 percent by volume could be obtained relatively easily in a short period at a pressure of 175 atmospheres. This higher yield led Haber to conceive of using a cooling device to separate small quantities of liquid ammonia from the reactant gases.

When in early 1909 the experiments succeeded and ammonia dripped out of the apparatus, Haber immediately called his colleagues. Max Mayer reports: "I still remember well how Haber came over to me and said, 'You have to see how the liquid ammonia is pouring out.' "[26] Staudinger too recounts: "Suddenly Haber came to me and shouted 'Come down, there's ammonia.' He had a vessel with a long capillary and in it was about 1 cm³ of ammonia; I can see it still. Then Engler joined us. It was fantastic."[27]

Haber reported his success to BASF on 23 March 1909.[28] He did not find it easy to convince the management of the significance of his discovery. The department at BASF that was to deal with the invention was quite skeptical, and its first response to Haber's letter disappointed him greatly. The department director, August Bernthsen, said quite bluntly that he could not believe the process was practical, for it still needed a temperature of about 600°C. Though BASF had submitted the high-pressure patent, the management thought that no steel tube, regardless of its thickness, could withstand the high temperatures and the pressure of 200 atmospheres. Carl Bosch was of the same opinion.

But Haber was not satisfied with BASF's opinion, and he asked Engler, who was a member of the board of directors of BASF, to act as mediator. Engler wrote personally to the general director and chairman of the board since 1907, Heinrich von Brunck. The matter was discussed at the highest level, with Brunck, Bernthsen, and Bosch representing BASF. Bernthsen still had misgivings, even after receiving Haber's most recent report on his experiments and a more detailed description of the impressive advances. He asked Haber what pressure would be necessary. When Haber answered, "Well, at least 100 atmospheres," he cried out, shocked, "100 atmospheres! Just yesterday an autoclave at 7 atmospheres exploded on us!" The professors and assistants present at the meeting were disappointed by Bernthsen's reaction. Then Brunck intervened and asked Bosch for his comment. Bosch expressed a highly courageous and momentous opinion: "I think it can work.

I know exactly what the steel industry can do. We should risk it."[29] At this, Brunck decided to increase support for Haber's experiments.

Now Haber and his assistants could continue their work. All agreed that osmium, despite its effectiveness as a catalyst, could not be used on a major industrial scale: it cost too much, and the available supply was too small. They therefore searched for a more favorable catalyst and eventually found uranium. Though many chemists had worked on catalytic effects, Ostwald among them, Haber's work showed for the first time that certain "special" substances have a specific catalytic effect. Alwin Mittasch, who worked on catalysts for the ammonia synthesis after Haber and later investigated catalysis for BASF, said in a lecture to the German Chemical Society in 1925: "A new catalyst is frequently discovered when one breaks through the barrier of prejudice and learns to use substances for a specific catalytic purpose that were previously ignored for this purpose."[30] Here Mittasch specifically mentions Haber's use of osmium and uranium for the synthesis of ammonia.

Using uranium as a catalyst solved a basic problem in the synthesis of ammonia. With the apparatus that had been developed, the catalysts that had been discovered, and the recirculation of the reactant gases, a concentration of ammonia could be reached that finally made industrial-scale production feasible.

Haber and BASF agreed that if a demonstration in Karlsruhe proved successful, BASF should carry out further experiments with the same apparatus in Ludwigshafen. The demonstration in Karlsruhe, in which several experiments were carried out, took place on 1 and 2 July 1909. Bosch, Mittasch, and BASF's chief mechanic Kranz were present. For the first experiment Haber wanted to demonstrate the new pressure reactor, 0.75 meters high, which contained almost 100 grams of osmium powder. Le Rossignol was at first skeptical whether the demonstration would succeed, and he was proved right: one seal did not hold at the high pressure, and the experiment had to be deferred for several hours. Bosch did not want to stay that long, so he instructed Kranz to assist with the repair and asked Mittasch to wait for the next experiment. Bosch then returned to Ludwigshafen, to Haber and Le Rossignol's great disappointment. The second experiment succeeded, and Mittasch witnessed ammonia flowing out of the apparatus. Extraordinarily impressed and completely convinced, he reported the positive result to Bosch.[31]

Heinrich von Brunck was now convinced that Haber's ammonia synthesis could work. He decided on immediate and generous support. Bosch was given unusual authorization to accelerate the scaling up of the process at Ludwigshafen. Karl Holdermann, in his biography of Bosch, describes Bosch's work and that of his assistants at length.[32]

Over the next few months an intensive collaboration developed between Haber's ammonia laboratory and the group that Bosch established. Bosch selected as his main assistant a young engineer, Franz Lappe, from the staff at BASF. Lappe approached his new assignment energetically and optimistically. He had studied materials science under Carl Bach at the Stuttgart Institute of Technology, training that soon proved highly pertinent. Mittasch directed the chemical work, especially the search for a simple, cheap, and efficient catalyst. He was assisted by, among others, the chemist Georg Stern.

The patent department at BASF made clear the need to "absolutely protect every improvement in this field" and asked Haber to send the documents required for patent applications. By 21 July, Haber had sent the formulation for a "supplementary" patent as well as two further submissions, the "external heat patent" and the "diffusion patent." In the first, according to the patent, "a metal body that is externally heated is used as the reaction chamber. This can be protected from chemical change by, for instance, protective coating." The second patented the possibility "that one unite in one vessel hot areas of ammonia formation with cold areas of ammonia liquefaction," thus achieving a more favorable heat exchange.[33]

These last two ammonia patents were submitted under Le Rossignol's name as well. He left Karlsruhe at the end of July 1909 and after a brief sojourn on the Channel Islands took a position with the Auer Company in Berlin. Haber's connections with Auer intensified during this period. He had turned down various professorial appointments at other universities, as he was still bound to Karlsruhe by further work on the ammonia synthesis. He continued to search for more favorable catalysts and proposed that manganese, for example, might be suitable; but further experiments did not confirm this hypothesis. Earlier experiments had also established that platinum, palladium, iridium, and ruthenium had no catalytic effect on the ammonia synthesis.

After the exciting month of July, Haber took a holiday at Pontresina, the Swiss health resort. He was exhausted and suffered from stomach pains. He wrote to Bosch from his hotel to check on the progress of the ammonia work, which consisted of following up on Haber's experiments with osmium and uranium as catalysts. Nothing particularly outstanding showed up. A series of other elements and compounds were tested, but they did not reveal any specific catalytic effects either. Bosch informed the BASF patent department of the results on 11 September. Bosch and Haber visited each other and discussed, among other things, the necessary pretreatment of uranium to achieve a longer catalytic effect. In January BASF reported to Haber:

> Now that our experiments in the area of producing ammonia from the elements, which you started, have reached a partial conclusion, we take this opportunity of informing you of the results. . . . We have managed to find that iron works as a catalyst; with respect to ease of use and cheapness, it cannot be equaled by any other, and using it produces yields as great as those with uranium and osmium.[34]

Haber was surprised. On the day after he received the letter, he wrote:

> I am extremely happy that Dr. Bosch and his assistants have succeeded in . . . making such a great advance, and I congratulate him and you. But it is remarkable how in the course of things new special features always come to light. Here iron, with which Ostwald first worked and which we then tested hundreds of times in its pure state, now is found to function when impure. It strikes me again how one should follow every track to its end.[35]

### The Final Announcement

As the precise catalyst was worked out and the process came ever closer to production, BASF endeavored to make sure that as little information as possible reached the public about the progress of the synthesis. This did not suit Haber, who as a scientist ideally wanted to publish his results as soon as they were confirmed. After much back-and-forth, BASF finally allowed Haber to make his overall results known, so long as he did not reveal information about the details.

On 18 March 1910 Haber gave a lecture to the Scientific Union (Naturwissenschaftlichen Vereinigung) in Karlsruhe, "Making Nitrogen Usable"; a shortened version was published in *Zeitschrift für Elektrochemie*.[36] In it Haber first discussed the "extraordinary need for bound nitrogen, mainly for agricultural purposes and to a much smaller extent for the explosives industry and the chemical industry." He mentioned the quantities of saltpeter imported from Chile and the fixation of nitrogen by plants, and he treated in more detail the oxidation of nitrogen and the energy problems that had to be solved to bind nitrogen in this way. He briefly mentioned the Frank-Caro process, which he described as a "multistage and therefore comparatively complicated process that has not yet proved its economic feasibility." And then the decisive turning point in his talk came with the sentence, "In contrast, there is the preparation of ammonia through direct combination of the elements nitrogen and hydrogen." After noting that this achievement had previously been thought impossible, he continued: "Work carried out in the Physical Chemistry Institute of the 'Fridericiana' in Karlsruhe has disproved this assumption." In the course of the lecture Haber described how the high-pressure process worked in combination with the circulation of the gases and mentioned osmium and uranium as "transfer agents." Finally, he declared,

> These experimental results appear to ensure the basis for a synthetic ammonia industry . . . The Badische Anilin- und Sodafabrik in Ludwigshafen has successfully continued further from this basis, which I have described here, so that the high-pressure synthesis of ammonia from its elements can now be included among the processes on which agriculturalists can pin their hopes when they . . . search for new sources of the most important substance they require.[37]

Haber's lecture hit the experts like a bomb. Within days many individuals and companies approached Haber to offer collaboration in the industrial use of the process.

Even BASF's misgivings about the effects of a public announcement on the ammonia process had not prepared them for the flood of inquiries and the sensation that Haber's lecture caused in professional circles. When he asked how he should distribute reprints, they replied that they had no interest in sending out further reprints. "The less that the process . . . is talked about in the next years, the less attention that is paid by those interested as to whether the technical realization is going to succeed, the more likely it is that we can win an advantage over the competition in the technical use of the process, and this will also be to your advantage."[38]

The extensive correspondence between Haber, BASF, and various parties interested in his work shows that Haber was sometimes unhappy with all this secrecy. His ammonia laboratory was forced to remain barred to unauthorized entry. This restriction led, if not to tension, then to certain animosities in the institute.

Haber now directed his activities more and more into other research fields, with the result that he felt less and less attached to his chair in Karlsruhe. Nevertheless he was very comfortable there. In Karlsruhe he had become a respected personality, his relationships with Engler and Bunte had become familiar and close, and he had moved into a lovely large apartment. One could live well in Baden's quiet capital city, although Haber felt little of Baden's coziness. During this time he was filled with energy and creativity; he could not stand still, and he could not appreciate the value of a well-deserved rest.

One could ask what Haber's life would have been if he had stayed in Karlsruhe or been called to Zurich. But his drive toward new frontiers, along with matters brewing in the nation's capital city, Berlin, decided his future. This well-known physical chemist and highly respected creator of the remarkable ammonia synthesis was about to sail into storms that neither he nor any of his contemporaries could have foreseen. These storms also ended his first and most brilliant scientific and personal period, as Richard Willstätter would later remark.

## Patents

The path to Berlin opened up for Haber only two months after his lecture to the Scientific Union in Karlsruhe. The next chapter describes fully the steps leading to the establishment of the various Kaiser Wilhelm Institutes in Berlin and Haber's experiences there; only the influence of his move on his relationship with BASF will be treated here.

The first discussions about the leadership of the new institute in Berlin took place in May 1910, but the decisive negotiations took place in September. After Haber had informed Franz Alexander Böhm, Baden's minister of education, about these discussions, he wrote a confidential letter to Bernthsen, at BASF. He described what was going on in Berlin—the German emperor's intention to found institutes for pure research and to convert the Imperial Institute for Chemical Technology (Chemisch-Technische Reichsanstalt) into such an institute. He then continued:

> The second such institute to be created is one for physical chemistry and electrochemistry. Whereas Beckmann's institute [the Institute for Chemistry, of which Ernst Beckmann was director] is to be built and maintained on public funds, the Institute for Physical Chemistry and Electrochemistry is to be built and equipped by a donation of three-quarters of a million marks given to the Prussian state by the chairman of the board of directors of the

Deutsche Gasglühlicht Aktien Gesellschaft [German G
Privy Councillor Koppel.                                    mpany],

Haber went on to describe further outcomes as he saw them
would presumably resign from his position in Karlsruhe towat he
1911. He then discussed the effects of his future change in pd of
contractual agreements with BASF: "As this change will happthe
the course of our current contract, I regard myself in duty bdng
loyalty to inform you of it early."[39]                          f
Haber and his assistants completed the remaining work on the c
of ammonia during the time he had left in Karlsruhe, and over the 1
he finally made an effort to publish it. The work had been carried out
by various assistants in Karlsruhe (and later in Berlin), and part of it w
subject of their dissertations. Haber sent these papers to BASF wit.
urgent request that permission for publication be granted as soon as 1
sible. There arose a lengthy correspondence in which the patent departm
of BASF repeatedly objected to single passages or details and request
changes. These papers were finally published consecutively in 1914 and 191,
in the *Zeitschrift für Elektrochemie* under the title "Investigations on Ammonia: Seven Communications."[40]

Haber had to invest a lot of time and energy in dealing with the various
patent applications and answering the objections from various parties, as his
copious correspondence with both the BASF patent department and the
German Patent Office shows. A large group of opponents raised objections,
based mainly on the work that Nernst and Jost published in 1907, in which
nitrogen and hydrogen were combined under high pressure for the first time.[41]

The Hoechst Dyeworks submitted a nullity suit, or claim of invalidity,
against the patents on the grounds that the catalytic formation of ammonia
under pressure had already been discovered. They also maintained that there
was no chance that the supplementary patents could be successfully applied
and hundreds of thousands and millions of marks would be spent without
the faintest hope of putting them into practice. The patents were therefore
of no technical interest.

Considering how far BASF had already advanced, this nullity suit might
seem very puzzling. It shows, however, that despite Haber's lecture in March
1910, BASF had succeeded in keeping their further successes secret. Now
Haber and BASF were faced with a dilemma—how to engage in legal proceedings against this nullity suit and at the same time not give anything
away about how far along their process was.

eived the claim of invalidity on 9 September and asked BASF
o be done. BASF requested a transfer of the patents, to which
eed. They now remembered at BASF that Nernst had already
th the objections. They approached him again with the request
give an expert opinion. Nernst promptly visited BASF.[42] In a later
ASF formulated the questions that Nernst was to answer:

1. Are the declarations given in patent 238450 correct?
2. Could these results have been predicted from publications known to you
   that were available before the establishment of the patent?[43]

Nernst carried out various experiments with equipment and iron cata-
sts put at his disposal by BASF in order to formulate his opinion. In a
eport on his experiments Nernst stated:

> As the result of the many and varied experimental results, carefully tested in
> all ways, I cannot but express my active conviction that patent document
> 238450 deals with results of a completely new type, and the declarations
> therein form a solid experimental foundation for an extremely important new
> technical process. For this reason it seems to me without a doubt that the
> invention described in the patent under discussion is to the fullest measure
> worthy of the protection given by the granting of a patent.[44]

Nernst's change from sharp critic to well-wishing supporter of Haber was
amazing.

In February 1912 BASF sent Nernst's opinion to Haber with the remark
that Nernst would not be invited to the face-to-face negotiations at first,
but that the firm anticipated his appearance in court.

In the meantime Hoechst had obtained an expert opinion from Ostwald.
Ostwald stated that the process in the patent was purely extrapolation from
low pressures to higher ones, and that the result obtained was to be expected
as not only scientifically probable but as scientifically certain. The surprise
on the part of some of those involved could only be explained by their inability to see ahead. Ostwald went on to say that claims beyond the limits of
what is economically possible are no reason for issuing a patent. The application contained not even the hint of a discussion on new methods for overcoming eventual difficulties. These difficulties would have to do with
apparatus, that is, they would be engineering problems.[45]

Thus the expert opinion of the old master of physical chemistry clashed
with that of Nernst, his former assistant. Their personal relationship was in

no way affected, however, and they remained on good terms with one another even after Ostwald left his position in Leipzig. Ostwald also later actively supported Nernst when the latter and Emil Fischer established the Imperial Chemical Institute (Chemische Reichsanstalt).

Two days before the case was scheduled to appear before the national court in Leipzig, the participants for BASF—Haber, Nernst, Bernthsen, and Bosch—met and expressed their lack of confidence. They judged their position as weak and unfavorable.[46]

The negotiations on Hoechst's nullity suit before the national court took place as planned on 4 March 1912. Representing Hoechst were Richard Weidlich and a patent attorney named Müller-Berneck; BASF was represented by Haber, Bernthsen, Bosch, and Julius Abel, with Nernst joining later. First all claims and counterclaims were presented. Weidlich provides the following description of the negotiations in his memoirs:

> It was very doubtful what the decision of the department for claims of invalidity [*Nichtigkeitsabteilung*] would be, and Ludwigshafen was very concerned, as Bosch had said to Privy Councillor [Adolf] Häuser the evening before the case. During oral argument, to my surprise, Nernst appeared arm in arm with Haber, and after Bernthsen had given only a brief reply to my thorough justification for our suit, my principal witness, Nernst, whose fundamental contributions to the ammonia synthesis I had just praised, made a passionate speech in which he explained that his work had had no technical relevance and his results were of scientific interest only. Only Haber had created the prerequisites for a technical success by investigating new pressure ranges. If chemical entrepreneurs had not had any interest in his, Nernst's, work, that was understandable. However, had such an entrepreneur rejected Haber's process, then he would have had to have been blind. The decisive effects of Nernst's speech were evident, and I, too, was impressed, so that I whispered to Müller-Berneck, who was accompanying me, that we could go home.[47]

Thus, on 4 March 1912 at 3:33 P.M., Bernthsen, Bosch, and Abel telegraphed to the management at BASF, "Hoechst's nullity suit against our $NH_3$-pressure patent rejected, and they are to pay costs."[48]

Several years later a chapter in Haber's relationship with BASF occurred that was not pleasant for either side. According to the contract of 1908 (modified in 1913), Haber was to receive 1.5 pfennigs for every kilogram of ammonia that was produced by high-pressure synthesis. This inventor's payment was considerable, and by the mid-1920s BASF had paid Haber several million marks. Difficulties arose shortly after the war. Haber was worried that his property or his income, or both, would be confiscated because of the charge brought against him of being a war criminal. A change in the contract was therefore worked out according to which Haber was to receive only 0.8 pfennig per kilogram, with his losses to be made up later. The vague formulations in this contract, which were necessary to avoid arousing the attention of the confiscating authorities, led to different interpretations of Haber's entitlement and to disagreement between the parties.

Haber's original relationship with BASF was remarkably close, however, in keeping with the 1908 contract. He had to present all his results to BASF, even though BASF's financial donations to his institute in Karlsruhe were not very high in return. He first reaped greater financial gain when his patented invention in the ammonia area raised production considerably. Of course, Haber had also been paid for such other activities as giving expert opinions and carrying out negotiations. The connection between Haber and BASF was quite unusual, with both good and bad times. But in spite of all the ups and downs they produced an offspring that, although it suffered from obvious growing pains, reached a size that none would have predicted.

## Bosch's Achievement in Scaling Up the Synthesis

Between 1910 and 1913 BASF completed the technical development of Haber's process and established the first full-scale production plant, an amazing achievement by Carl Bosch and his colleagues. Bosch was thirty-five years old when he was assigned to scale up the ammonia synthesis. His direct chief was Heinrich von Brunck, who not only was technical director but also had been chairman of the board of directors since 1907. Brunck was a brilliant chemist. His extraordinary talent at organizing, his spirit of enterprise, and his willpower contributed to BASF's development into one of the largest international chemical companies. He was also known for being lucky in his choice of employees—after first interviewing them thoroughly.

Bosch had already distinguished himself on previous assignments. He was not a man of routine: he often jumped over bureaucratic hurdles, brought new ideas into the projects he was given, and took care of the many details so critical in developing a new process. As a chemist and foundry specialist, one experienced in building apparatus, he combined several multifaceted, solidly based types of knowledge. He had learned to deal with large

*BASF's Oppau Works in January 1914. This first ammonia factory went into operation in 1913.*

quantities of gas over the many years of his work on the formation of nitrides. Brunck could not have chosen a better person for the task to come.

Bosch took on the task, undeterred by the opinions of others. At the time chemists and engineers did not think that a process with such requirements could be carried out. He had to find a simple, cheap, and efficient catalyst; a way to produce sufficient quantities of pure hydrogen for the synthesis; a way to scale up the synthesis from laboratory-sized equipment to technical apparatus; a way to control the high pressures and temperatures; a material for the equipment that would maintain its mechanical stability under the conditions of the reaction; and measuring devices to check up on the operating parameters.

As noted earlier, Alwin Mittasch and his assistants had succeeded in finding a cheaper and readily available catalyst. Mittasch realized that certain additives that themselves had little or no catalytic effect increased the catalytic activity of metals. On the basis of these observations, he proposed that the search for suitable catalysts should proceed on what was at first no more than a working hypothesis—but one he thought so important that he entered a specific date for it in his laboratory book—24 February 1909.[49] The program he assigned to his research group stipulated that they carry out experiments with a specified number of elements, together with numerous additives; test the catalytic substances at the high pressures and temperatures that Haber had used in his experiments; and carry out a very large number of experimental sequences.

Apparatus had to be created for this multiplicity of experiments, and it had to be easier to use than Haber's. Mittasch's assistant Georg Stern designed a much more convenient set-up, and Mittasch's laboratory became a center for catalysis research. By the beginning of 1912 about 6,500 experiments with 2,500 different catalytic substances had been carried out, and an intensive search for even more favorable catalysts continued until 1919. By that time 10,000 experiments had been performed and 4,000 different catalytic systems examined. These long experimental series became a paradigm for screening procedures in chemical research.

Producing ammonia from the elements on an industrial scale also required developing an efficient and economic process for producing the nitrogen-hydrogen mixture required for the reaction, in particular the major reactant, hydrogen. Bosch investigated several processes in the course of scaling up the synthesis, but all had seemingly intractable shortcomings.

Wilhelm Wild, a student of Nernst's, found a satisfactory solution. He subjected water gas to a catalytic transformation with steam. Water gas, essentially a mixture of hydrogen and carbon monoxide, becomes a mixture of hydrogen and carbonic acid in the presence of substances containing iron oxide. The reaction requires no additional heat; in fact, so much heat is released that it can be used to produce a considerable part of the steam required. The conversion of carbon monoxide is almost quantitative, doubling the amount of hydrogen. In addition, the carbonic acid produced in this reaction can be used to produce fertilizer salts. Wild demonstrated his process to Bosch and convinced him of its great superiority. Bosch then devoted considerable effort to ensuring that this technique could be carried out without problems.

Production of nitrogen posed no essential difficulties. It was produced by the Linde process through the liquefaction of air and the separation of the various components. After the nitrogen was produced in the Linde plant, it was mixed in the required proportion with hydrogen from Wild's process.

Now the last traces of carbon monoxide had to be removed from the gas mixture. While trying to solve this problem, Bosch remembered that he had used a copper solution to remove carbon dioxide at the factory in Höllriegels-kreuth, Bavaria. This method, however, would not work in apparatus made of iron, which would have to be replaced with more expensive metals. This relatively minor component of the technical development of the ammonia synthesis caused great difficulties. A small crisis occurred when the management of BASF reproached Bosch. Downcast, he finally instructed the young chemist Carl Krauch, who later became the general director of IG Farben, to add all likely substances to the copper solution and see if one of them made the solution resistant to iron. Krauch set up several experiments with various substances and went off on his summer holidays. When he came back, all samples except one had decomposed: to that sample he had added ammonia. Through this simple trick (and others used later) the group was able to keep the iron from decomposing the copper solution and thus to put the method into industrial production.[50]

Developing production-scale engineering equipment that would stand up to the requirements outlined above also gave rise to special difficulties. In the summer of 1910, Bosch set up a high-pressure laboratory and a plant to prepare 400 kilograms of ammonia per day. Instead of small laboratory ovens, larger units were used, with at first 1 kilogram of catalyst. But there were unexpected breakdowns. The larger converters held out for hardly more than three days, and then they burst. When the hydrogen suddenly erupted under high pressure, it ignited spontaneously in fires and explosions.

Examination of the torn converters showed that the wall of the pressure vessel had apparently lost its flexibility, owing to an unknown cause. This destruction of the steel often spread and could not be arrested, until finally the intact part became too thin and the wall gave way because of the interior pressure.

Bosch was now helped by his experience in the foundry. He took a section from a sample of damaged steel and examined it by a technique then unknown in chemical technology, that of metallurgic etching. He thus discovered that the steel inside, where it came into contact with the gases, exhibited a zone of lighter coloring. Bosch's explanation for this was that the steel contained a dark, carbon-containing perlite, which was dispersed within the basic material of pure steel. The perlite had disappeared from the lightened interior of the tube, and the structure was destroyed when cracks formed. That is, the iron had become decarbonized. Further investigation showed that the hydrogen had combined with the iron to form a brittle alloy, similar to the combination of carbon with iron that forms brittle iron carbides. The stability of the iron was further reduced because during decarbonization a reaction between hydrogen and carbon formed methane; under high pressure this was retained within the structure of the iron, increasing further the stresses on the material. Attempts were made to solve the problem through a variety of changes in construction, including lining the converter with an inner sheath of copper and silver. But these all failed. Finally, Bosch hit upon the idea of using soft, almost carbon-free iron as the material for the interior, since it could not decarbonize. Further, the hydrogen that diffused from the interior into the iron at high temperatures had to be made harmless; otherwise it would accumulate under the steel outer coating and again attack it. Here, too, Bosch found a surprising solution. The steel coating was pierced with thin bores, which did not reduce its stability but through which the hydrogen could escape into the open. Ernst Schwarz, one of the later directors of BASF, thought "that it was this inspiration, which came to him without reflection or calculation, that made the very large scale synthesis of ammonia possible."[51] And Bosch said of his constructional inventions in his Nobel Prize lecture in 1931, "The solution appeared simple and was in fact so, but yet the entire development of the process depended on it to a greater or lesser extent. Today, after twenty years' experience we know that hydrogen still attacks unprotected iron at temperatures even below 300°C and sooner or later causes breakdown at points where frequently they would not have been expected."[52]

The construction proved to be safe in operation and usable for practically unlimited periods. Bosch later used alloyed steel as a construction material. Experiments showed that alloys with chrome, molybdenum, and tungsten gave great stability and complete protection against hydrogen. The experience gathered in this search for cylinders that could withstand high pressures was later of great value to the steel industry.

Bosch and his assistants had now gained an advantage over their rivals, both domestic and foreign, that helped them in future challenges, as, for example, in scaling up the synthesis of methanol or the process of coal-to-oil conversion first developed by Friedrich Bergius. This technological advantage also allowed the German chemical corporations that joined to form IG Farben to remain at the forefront of the world chemical industry, even after the losses sustained during and after World War I.

## Later Successes of the Haber-Bosch Process

Further development of the Haber-Bosch process during the twentieth century is not without interest. It was a long way from the first production plant at Oppau near Ludwigshafen in 1913 to the worldwide adoption of the process. From the beginning the major aim was to produce fertilizer and to increase agricultural yields. Significantly, those who worked in this field, Mittasch among them, also worked on plant physiology. Mittasch's investigations on fertilizers constituted an important contribution to agricultural research.

There were setbacks to the agricultural applications when World War I broke out. It became difficult to produce fertilizer when the pyrites imported for the production of sulfuric acid were no longer available. And at the end of 1914 the Ministry of War demanded considerable expansion in ammonia production by the Haber-Bosch process, but as a precursor of nitric acid, which was used to produce explosives. The site first selected for this expansion was Oppau, which had a plant already running, but Leuna, a small village near Merseburg in eastern Germany, was chosen instead. Military reasons, among others, drove this decision, but the rich supply of water from the nearby river Saale and the proximity of abundant deposits of brown coal and gypsum also played a part.

All details were settled by January 1916, and the plans for setting up

TABLE I. Nitrogen Production per Harvest Year during
World War I

| Type of Production | Tons of Nitrogen | | |
|---|---|---|---|
| | 1915–16 | 1916–17 | 1917–18 |
| Gas and coke works | 90,000 | 100,000 | 100,000 |
| Calcium cyanamide industry | 20,000 | 58,000 | 66,000 |
| BASF | 24,000 | 64,000 | 105,000 |

SOURCE: Walter Eucken, *Die Stickstoffversorgung in der Welt* (Stuttgart/
Berlin: Deutsche Verlagsanstalt, 1921).

the plant were ready by March. In April, BASF and the imperial secretary
of the treasury agreed that BASF should establish a plant with an annual
production of 36,000 metric tons of ammonia by the end of the year. BASF
received a subsidy of 12 million marks and was required by special agreement with the Ministry of War to make its entire output available to the
military administration at a fixed price.

Building continued throughout 1916, although it was considerably hindered by difficulties in supply and by the cold winter. Finally, in April 1917,
the first converters were fired. In autumn 1916 further planning increased
the annual production by 13,000 metric tons. Further expansion was necessary by the end of 1917, which made Leuna the largest ammonia plant in
the world. Table 1 shows how the distribution of nitrogen production from
various sources shifted during World War I.[53]

Shortly after the war the ammonia plants in Oppau and Leuna were
quickly converted to mass production of fertilizers (ammonium sulfate, for
example).[54] Production reached around 350,000 metric tons of fixed nitrogen by 1925, and three years later it had almost doubled to 640,000 metric
tons. Thereafter German production of fertilizer was overtaken by that of
other countries, and, half a century after the construction of the first ammonia factory in Oppau, the world production of fixed nitrogen using the high-
pressure catalysis method invented by Haber and Bosch was 12.7 million
metric tons. Of this, German production accounted for only about 10 percent. Production of nitrogen by other methods (saltpeter from Chile, coke
works, and calcium cyanamide) had reached a worldwide level of only 1.6
million metric tons over the same period. Table 2 shows the differences
between a 1,000-metric-ton ammonia plant in 1940 and one in 1970.

TABLE 2. Comparison of a 1,000-Metric-Ton
Ammonia Plant in 1940 and in 1970

| Plant Statistics | 1940 | 1970 |
|---|---|---|
| Number of reactors | 21 | 1 |
| Number of compressors | 16 | 1 |
| Space occupied (m²) | 35,000 | 7,500 |
| Energy expenditure (gigajoules/ton NH₃) | 92 | 33 |
| Catalytic stages | 2 | 8 |

SOURCE: B. Timm, "The Ammonia Synthesis and the Heterogenous Catalysis: A Historical Review," *Proceedings of the 8th International Congress on
Catalysis, West Berlin, 2–6 July 1984* (Weinheim: Verlag Chemie, c. 1984), 17.

The development of the ammonia synthesis is an unfinished story. Many
questions remain, particularly about the structure of the catalysts and the
mechanism of formation of the ammonia molecule. Remarkably, a better
catalyst than the one Mittasch found in 1910 has never been discovered.

# Endnotes

[1] Fritz Haber, "Über Hochschulunterricht und elektrochemische Technik in den
Vereinigte Staaten" (On university education and electrochemical technology in the United
States), *Z. Elektrochemie* 9 (1903), 291–303, 347–370, 379–406, 514; and R. S. Hutton,
"Notes and Recollections of Professor Fritz Haber," MPG, Dept. Va, Rep. 5.

[2] Fritz Haber, "Gewinnung von Salpetersäure aus der Luft" (Obtaining nitric acid from
the air), *Z. Angew. Chem.* 23 (1910), 684, and especially 685.

[3] H. Pauling, *Elektrische Luftverbrennung* (Electrical combustion of the atmosphere)
(Halle, 1929).

[4] See British patent no. 266602 (1904); see also Trevor I. Williams, *A History of Technology,* Vol. 6, *The Twentieth Century* (Oxford: Clarendon Press, 1978), 521.

[5] Wilhelm Muthmann and H. Hofer, article in *Ber. Deutsch. Chem. Ges.* 36 (1903), 438.

[6] Walter Eucken, *Die Stickstoffversorgung in der Welt* (The world's nitrogen supply)
(Stuttgart/Berlin: Deutsche Verlagsanstalt, 1921).

[7] Wilhelm Ostwald to the management of BASF, 12 Mar. 1900, Archiv der Berlin-
Brandenburgischen Akademie der Wissenschaften, Berlin, reg. no. 3562.

[8] Wilhelm Ostwald, *Lebenslinien: Eine Selbstbiographie* (Lifelines: An autobiography),
Vol. 2, Chap. 12 (Berlin: Klasing, 1926).

[9] Ibid.; Grete Ostwald, "Wilhelm Ostwald: Encounters with BASF," *Die BASF* 13:4
(1963), 207; and Karl Holdermann, *Im Banne der Chemie: Carl Bosch, Leben und Werk* (En-
thralled by chemistry: Carl Bosch, his life and work) (Düsseldorf: Econ Verlag, 1953).

[10] Fritz Haber and Adolf Koenig, "Über die Stickoxydbildung im Hochspannungsbogen"
(On the formation of nitric oxide in a high-voltage electric arc), *Z. Elektrochemie* 13 (1907),
725. Haber's earlier opinion appears in Fritz Haber, *Thermodynamik technischer Gasreaktionen:
Sieben Vorträge* (Thermodynamics of technical gas reactions: Seven lectures) (Munich:
R. Oldenbourg, 1905), 251.

[11] E.g., Fritz Haber and Adolf Koenig, "Über die Stickoxydbildung im Hochspannungs-bogen—II" (On the formation of nitric oxide in a high-voltage electric arc—II), *Z. Elektrochemie* 14 (1908), 698.

[12] Fritz Haber and Adolf Koenig, "Oxydation des Luftstickstoffs: Zusammenfassender Bericht für die Zeit 1907 bis 1909 (Oxidation of atmospheric nitrogen: A report and summary for the period from 1907–1909), *Z. Elektrochemie* 16 (1910), 11.

[13] Haber, "Gewinnung der Salpetersäure aus der Luft" (cit. note 2), 684; and Haber, "Über die Nutzbarmachung des Stickstoffs" (On making possible the utilization of nitrogen), *Verhandlungen des Naturwissenschaftlichen Vereins in Karlsruhe* 23 (1909/10), 20–25; *Z. Elektrochemie* 16 (1910), 784.

[14] Carl Engler to the management of BASF, 19 Jan. 1908, MPG, Dept. Va, Rep. 5, 2069.

[15] Contract between Fritz Haber and BASF, 6 Mar. 1908, MPG, Dept. Va, Rep. 5, 2055.

[16] Fritz Haber, "Über die Darstellung das Ammoniaks aus Stickstoff und Wasserstoff" (On the preparation of ammonia from nitrogen and hydrogen), Nobel Prize lecture, 2 June 1920, published in *Naturwissenschaften* 10 (1922), 1042. See also *Nobel Lectures in Chemistry*, ed. the Nobel Foundation (Amsterdam: Elsevier, 1966).

[17] Fritz Haber to Wilhelm Ostwald, 23 July 1903, Archiv der Berlin-Brandenburgischen Akademie der Wissenschaften, Berlin, reg. no. 1037.

[18] Ibid.

[19] Fritz Haber to the management of BASF, 19 Feb. 1908, MPG, Dept. Va, Rep. 5, 2069.

[20] Fritz Haber and G. van Oordt, "Über die Bildung von Ammoniak aus den Elementen" (Preparation of ammonia from the elements), *Z. Anorgan. Chem.* 47 (1905), 42.

[21] Walther Nernst, "Über das Ammoniakgleichgewicht" (The equilibrium of ammonia), *Z. Elektrochemie* 13 (1907), 521; and Friedrich Jost, "Über das Ammoniakgleichgewicht," *Z. Anorgan. Chem.* 57 (1908), 414.

[22] Alwin Mittasch, *Geschichte der Ammoniaksynthese* (History of the synthesis of ammonia) (Weinheim: Verlag Chemie, 1951), 68, note 6.

[23] Ibid., 48.

[24] Clara Haber to Richard Abegg, 23 July 1907, MPG, Dept. Va, Rep. 5, 921–926.

[25] Fritz Haber and Robert Le Rossignol, "Bestimmung der Ammoniakgleichgewichtes unter Druck" (Determination of the equilibrium of ammonia under pressure), *Z. Elektrochemie* 14 (1908), 181.

[26] Johannes Jaenicke, report on a conversation with Max Mayer, 9 Nov. 1958, MPG, Dept. Va, Rep. 5.

[27] Johannes Jaenicke, report on a conversation with Hermann Staudinger, MPG, Dept. Va, Rep. 5.

[28] Fritz Haber to the management of BASF, 23 Mar. 1909, MPG, Dept. Va, Rep. 5, 2079.

[29] Alfred F. Nagel, *Stickstoff* (Ludwigshafen: BASF, 1969), 21; see also "Alfred König und Fritz Haber," in *Die Technische Hochschule Fridericiana Karlsruhe: Festschrift zur 125 Jahresfeier* (Festschrift for the 125th anniversary) (Karlsruhe, 1950), 64.

[30] Alwin Mittasch, "Bemerkungen über Katalyse" (Remarks on catalysis), lecture given to the German Chemical Society on 21 Oct. 1925, published in Mittasch, *Von der Chemie zur Philosophie* (From chemistry to philosophy) (Ulm: J. Ebner Verlag, 1948).

[31] Mittasch, *Ammoniaksynthese* (cit. note 22), 77.

[32] Holdermann, *Im Banne der Chemie* (cit. note 9), 70ff.

[33] German patents, registration file code H47701 IV/2k and registration file code H48062 IV/12g.

[34] BASF to Fritz Haber, 13 Jan. 1910, MPG, Dept. Va, Rep. 5.

[35] Fritz Haber to BASF, 14 Jan. 1910, MPG, Dept. Va, Rep. 5.

[36] Fritz Haber, "Über die Nutzbarmachung des Stickstoffs" (Making nitrogen usable), *Verhandlungen des Naturwissenschaftlichen Vereins in Karlsruhe* 23 (1909/10), 20–23; and Haber, "Über die Darstellung des Ammoniaks aus Stickstoff und Wasserstoff" (The synthesis of ammonia from nitrogen and hydrogen), *Z. Elektrochemie* 16 (1910), 244.

[37] Haber, "Nutzbarmachung des Stickstoffs" (cit. note 36).

[38] BASF to Fritz Haber, 19 Oct. 1910, MPG, Dept. Va, Rep. 5, 2085.

[39] Fritz Haber to August Bernthsen, Ludwigshafen, 28 Sept. 1910, MPG, Dept. Va, Rep. 5, 2094.

[40] Fritz Haber and coworkers (names for each paper are given in parentheses after the page number), "Untersuchungen über Ammoniak: Sieben Mitteilungen" (Investigations on ammonia: Seven communications), *Z. Elektrochemie* 20 (1914), 597; 21 (1915), 89 (Setsura Tamaru [ST], Ch. Ponnaz), 128 (A. Muschke), 191 (ST), 206 (ST, L. W. Oeholm), 228 (ST), 241 (H. C. Greenwood).

[41] See note 21.

[42] Alwin Mittasch, internal memorandum to Carl Bosch, MPG, Dept. Va, Rep. 5, 444.

[43] BASF to Walther Nernst, 30 Sept. 1911, MPG, Dept. Va, Rep. 5, 444.

[44] L. Suhling, "Walther Nernst und die Ammoniaksynthese nach Haber und Bosch" (Walther Nernst and the Haber-Bosch ammonia synthesis), in *Naturwissenschaft und Technik in der Geschichte: 25 Jahre Lehrstuhl für Geschichte der Naturwissenschaft und Technik am Historischen Institut der Universität Stuttgart* (Science and technology in history: 25 years of the Chair for the History of Science and Technology at the University of Stuttgart) (Stuttgart: Verlag für Geschichte der Naturwissenschaften und Technik, 1993), 343.

[45] Wilhelm Ostwald, expert opinion, 25 Feb. 1912, MPG, Dept. Va, Rep. 5, 444.

[46] BASF memorandum, 8 Mar. 1912, MPG, Dept. Va, Rep. 5, 444.

[47] Richard Weidlich, "Erinnerungen" (Memoirs), ms. given by Dr. E. Fischer to Johannes Jaenicke, deposited 14 May 1956, MPG, Dept. Va, Rep. 5, 1509.

[48] Telegram from Bernthsen, Bosch, and Abel to management of BASF, 4 Mar. 1912, MPG, Dept. Va, Rep. 5.

[49] See B. Timm, "The Ammonia Synthesis and the Heterogenous Catalysis: A Historical Review," *Proceedings of the 8th International Congress on Catalysis, West Berlin, 2–6 July 1984* (Weinheim: Verlag Chemie, c. 1984).

[50] Holdermann, *Im Banne der Chemie* (cit. note 9), 113–114.

[51] Ibid., 95.

[52] Carl Bosch, "Nobel Prize Lecture, May 21, 1932," in *Nobel Prize Lectures: Chemistry, 1922–1941* (New York: Elsevier, 1966), 209.

[53] See Ausschuss zur Untersuchung der Erzeugungs- und Absatzbedingungen der deutschen Wirtschaft (Committee for examining the conditions of production and turnover in the German economy), *Die deutsche chemische Industrie* (The German chemical industry), (Berlin: 1930), 149ff.

[54] B. Timm, "50 Jahre Ammoniaksynthese" (50 years of the ammonia synthesis), *Die BASF* 13:4 (1963), 174, footnote 6.

*Chapter 6*

# Establishing
# the
# Kaiser Wilhelm Institute
# in Berlin

*Fritz Haber and Richard Leiser at the demonstration of the marsh gas whistle.*

*Previous page: Kaiser Wilhelm Institute for Physical Chemistry and Electrochemistry, 1912.*

From 1905 on, three leading chemists—Emil Fischer, director of the Institute for Chemistry of the University of Berlin; Walther Nernst, director of the Institute for Physics of the University of Berlin; and Wilhelm Ostwald, director of the Institute for Physical Chemistry in Leipzig—had planned to establish a research institute to be named the Imperial Chemical Institute (Chemische Reichsanstalt). The idea was modeled after the Imperial Physical and Technological Institute (Physikalisch-Technische Reichsanstalt), which had been founded by Wilhelm Förster, Hermann von Helmholtz, and Werner Siemens in 1887. Fischer and his colleagues founded the Imperial Chemical Institute Association (Verein Chemische Reichsanstalt) for financing this plan by collecting money from industry and by getting assistance from the Prussian government. They succeeded in getting more than one million marks from industry and interested scientists, but the Prussian Ministry of Finance refused to spend any money on the project.[1]

In 1908 the idea was taken up again but modified: now a research organization working in various areas of science was to be founded. The new objectives for this organization, later called the Kaiser Wilhelm Society (Kaiser-Wilhelm-Gesellschaft), were set by Friedrich Schmidt-Ott and Hugo A. Krüss, both of whom held appointments in the Prussian Ministry of Public Worship and Education (Kultusministerium), and by the respected theologian Adolf von Harnack.[2] Emil Fischer gave the money collected by the Imperial Chemical Institute Association to build an institute for chemistry within the new framework. As part of that institute he wanted to establish a department of physical chemistry that would absorb about one third of the annual budget. The Prussian Ministry of Finance created difficulties over the financing, however.

The complicated negotiations over financing the projected institutes, the Institute for Chemistry in particular, began in 1910. August Trott zu Solz, the Prussian minister of education (*Kultusminister*), felt that private donations alone could not cover the operating costs. A dispute began over state participation, and the state authorities remained unforthcoming. The situation had still not been clarified by September 1910. In the meantime the celebration of the hundredth anniversary of the founding of the University of Berlin in October 1910, the date set for announcing the new research society, was approaching. Kaiser Wilhelm II was scheduled to make a speech inaugurating the society, to be named after him, and to make a call for private donations. He was also to emphasize that the new institutes should be supported with state funds. But as late as 13 September Theobald von Bethmann-Hollweg, the head of the Imperial Office of the Interior, was still unable to decide whether to provide such assistance.[3]

At a conference four days later the situation changed completely.[4] Leopold Koppel, a philanthropist of long standing, now arrived on the scene. In 1906 he had created a fund to promote intellectual exchange between Germany and other countries, with one million marks capital. On short notice Koppel now declared his readiness to fund an entire Kaiser Wilhelm Institute—for Physical Chemistry.

## Haber's Road to Berlin

Leopold Koppel was a Jew who had converted to Christianity upon his marriage. He came from Saxony, where he had founded an independent banking company. In 1891 he moved to Berlin to continue his banking business and there cofounded the Auer Gaslight Company (Auer Gasglühlicht Gesellschaft). He also owned several well-known hotels.

Fritz Haber consulted for the Auer Company in several areas. Koppel had attempted to get Haber to join his company, but he had declined. In order to get Haber to Berlin, Koppel adopted a different strategy. He made it a condition for his donation that Fritz Haber should become the director of the institute, a condition that was accepted after intensive negotiations. Haber first heard of Koppel's intentions in May 1910, but then heard nothing further about the matter until the end of June, when Koppel approached him to ask what his conditions were for accepting the offer. Haber sent a copy of these conditions to Emil Fischer, noting in the accompanying letter that in formulating them he had incorporated suggestions made by Schmidt-Ott. Haber also explained that he should consider that "my present position guarantees me full satisfaction and a secure and agreeable place on the teaching staff. Twice during the last three years people here have worked with great energy and personal warmth to keep me here on occasions when a change from my current position to another job was a serious possibility." Haber must have been referring to appointments offered to him in Zurich and Vienna. He continues, "I therefore cannot and will not move to an appointment elsewhere if it were to be a second-rank position under the conditions given."[5]

The essential points of Haber's conditions were as follows.

- In his capacity as director of the new institute, a tenured position as state official and status equal to the director of the Institute for Chemistry.

- A guarantee of a sufficient operating budget and complete independence in the use of these funds and in the choice of subjects to be investigated.

- The right to decide on the equipping of the institute and to choose employees and assistants, plus simultaneous membership in the Royal Prussian Academy, and appointment as professor of the University of Berlin.

- An annual salary of 15,000 marks, with various other benefits (widow's pension, orphans' pensions, official director's villa, etc.); a mutually acceptable agreement on questions concerning patent litigation and payment to inventors, and the right to be active as a consultant and to offer expert opinion.

- Transfer of his assistants Gerhardt Just and Richard Leiser from Karlsruhe, who were also to receive appointments as privatdocents at the University of Berlin and a combined salary of 9,000 marks. Just was to represent Haber in his absence.

On 30 June, Haber sent Schmidt-Ott a copy of his letter to Emil Fischer as well as the conditions he had formulated. Among other things, he wrote:

> I trust that Your Honour will support the view that, according to experience, research can only be carried out successfully if the directorship of the research station . . . is not subject to the influence of colleagues outside. Success arises from inspiration, and ideas cannot be discussed with colleagues before they have been worked through, but only afterward, because they are often

based only on intuitions and not on rational grounds. In addition, no one likes to talk to colleagues outside the institute about scientific efforts that have not yet matured to a finished result because this can easily endanger the intellectual property rights. If the research is directed not toward new insights but toward a quantitative working through of received ideas, then the situation alters greatly, with scientific imagination giving way to scholarly handicraft. As valuable as the latter is, I take it as certain that the new institutes will not be aimed in that direction.[6]

Here Haber raised a question that is still pertinent—whether research is to be funded by the state or by private funds. Financial backers now ask researchers to formulate an exact description of their intentions. They then estimate as closely as possible what costs this research will incur. But even when a research proposal is based on solid foundations, it is often impossible to predict where it will lead. Around 1910 donors gave researchers a remarkable amount of freedom to realize their ideas. Koppel in fact insisted not only that the researcher should have a share in any profits arising from his research but that all people working in the privately funded institute should also have a share. These are the progressive ideas that Haber took up and explained in his letter.

In order to inform the Karlsruhe authorities, Haber sent a communication to Franz Alexander Böhm, Baden's minister of education. He wanted "to report on negotiations that took place under the leadership of Privy Councillor Friedrich Schmidt in the Prussian Ministry of Education in Berlin on Friday afternoon and Saturday."[7] The date of the letter was 17 September, the same day that Leopold Koppel officially made known his donation for the physical chemistry institute, thereby providing the final incentive needed to found the Kaiser Wilhelm Society.

Another year was to pass, however, before Haber was officially able to take up his new post in Berlin. There were various reasons for this delay. Engler tried to keep Haber in Karlsruhe as long as possible. Even after the leaving date, 1 October 1911, had already been fixed, Engler pleaded with Haber to remain one more year, until 1912. But Haber had in the meantime become so occupied with building his new institute in Dahlem that he was not prepared to postpone his departure further.

Haber was also concerned that the Karlsruhe institute remain well provided for despite the transfer of his closest assistants, Just and Leiser, to Berlin. He succeeded in getting BASF to donate important pieces of apparatus to that institute. For his successor at Karlsruhe he suggested his friend Georg Bredig, who one year earlier had left Heidelberg to direct the Laboratory of Physical Chemistry and Electrochemistry at Zurich's Swiss Federal Institute of Technology. Besides Bredig, the Senate of the Institute of Technology in Karlsruhe considered as Haber's successor Max Bodenstein, professor at the Institute of Technology in Hannover, and Max Trautz, who had succeeded Bredig in Heidelberg. On 14 June 1911 the senate decided on Bredig.[8]

Haber moved with his family to Berlin, where they set up temporary lodgings in an apartment in Dahlem, since the construction of his government residence had not yet begun. There was a grand farewell celebration at the institute in Karlsruhe. The *Zeitschrift für Elektrochemie* published a special issue full of fun and jokes. A contribution titled "Yearning" is reproduced here:

> Do you know the land where the potatoes grow,
> Where the pumpkins' light leaves a glow,
> Where the wind of free research blows,
> And soon into giant trees the laurel grows?
> Do you know the land? Thither oh thither
> Would I travel with you, O my master.
>
> Do you know the house? French is the roof,
> Each part of it is vibration proof.
> And thither he whose life is long
> On the underground will travel along.
> Do you know it indeed? Thither oh thither
> Let me travel with you, O my master.
>
> Do you know that work and its demanding weight?
> The researcher's path leads through error to light.
> But after the heavy torment of the job
> One can recover in the cozy pub.
> Do you know it indeed? Thither oh thither
> Leads our path: Let us travel, O Haber.[9]

Several of the Karlsruhe assistants did travel with Haber. He took not only those whose transfer he had negotiated, Just and Leiser, but also such others as Setsuro Tamaru and H. C. Greenwood. His companion in the ammonia synthesis, Le Rossignol, also went to Berlin, but to the Auer Company.

By December 1911 the minister of education, August Trott zu Solz, proposed Haber as full honorary professor at the philosophical faculty in Berlin, then appointed him soon after.[10] Thus Haber became a professor of the university from which he had received his doctorate twenty years earlier. Eventually the kaiser granted him the title *Geheimer Regierungsrat* (privy councillor) for his "outstanding scientific work and the exceptional knowledge and dedication for the great task for which the Kaiser Wilhelm Institute has been created and which has been entrusted to him."[11] Fritz Haber was later also nominated a member of the Prussian Academy of Sciences.

After leaving Karlsruhe, Haber often thought with both pleasure and melancholy about that part of his life and the achievement that had allowed him to rise from a simple *Assistent* to a full professor and one of the most acknowledged scientists in the area of physical chemistry. He continued to feel connected with Karlsruhe's Institute of Technology and his former institute within it. He retained his admiration and affection for his previous superiors, Hans Bunte and especially Carl Engler. It was a great joy for Haber that his friend Georg Bredig was his successor, and through this connection Haber kept in close contact with Karlsruhe.

## Building the Institute, Its Opening, and the First Publications

Late in 1910, when Fritz Haber was certain he would be named director of the Institute for Physical Chemistry and Electrochemistry in Berlin-Dahlem, he became closely involved with the design of the external appearance of the building, the layout of the rooms, and their fitting out. He also thought it important to attract the first researchers and assistants to the institute and to set them up as quickly as possible to carry out experiments in provisional laboratory rooms.

The authorities of the domain of Dahlem had not yet made the land for the two planned institutes available, but this did not disturb Haber. He began to study a variety of domestic and foreign institutes and asked for advice from colleagues in industry, especially at BASF, in order to decide quickly on the requirements for the rooms and laboratories in the institute. A concentration of workrooms, the ability to exchange ideas and inspirations, and scaling up of lab results in "semitechnical" units, which were placed outside the labs in a pilot plant—that was the concept. These ideas were modern, even by today's standards.

While at Karlsruhe, Haber traveled to Berlin monthly, whether to attend meetings or later to view the site for the institute and to discuss details with architects and builders on-site. Construction of both institutes, Haber's and the chemical institute, began in the summer of 1911, even though the land was not formally transferred from the Ministry of Agriculture until November 1911.[12] The rough brickwork was finished in July 1912, whereupon the construction of the interior was begun. Most of the work was completed within three months.

Both buildings, as well as the official residences erected later, partly survive today, although somewhat changed, in the Thielallee and Faradayweg in Berlin-Dahlem. The efforts of the building official, Ernst von Ihne, to unite aesthetics in the exteriors with the requirements of scientific work are striking. For example, the roofs were decked with Thuringian slate, and the building facades were painted gray so that no colored rays, which could be perceived as distracting to the investigations, could enter the workrooms.

Haber's institute was opened just eleven months after construction began, a remarkable achievement considering that the building had a volume of 18,000 cubic meters and a working floor space of 2,500 square meters. Pressure from the imperial court had played a considerable part in procuring rapid construction. No wonder the kaiser was anxious to take part in the inauguration of both institutes.

This official grand opening took place on 23 October 1912, on the same occasion as the opening of the Kaiser Wilhelm Institute for Chemistry. A special program for the festivities was put out in which "detailed directives for the course of the ceremonies were specified . . . in consideration of the presence of His Majesty."[13]

The ceremony, including formal orations and lectures, took place in the library of the Institute for Chemistry. The kaiser made a short speech, mentioning a matter that concerned him especially. On 8 August 1912 he had been a guest of the industrialist Gustav Krupp at the Villa Hügel shortly after a powerful explosion of marsh gas and coal dust occurred at a coal mine, and the whole atmosphere of the meeting was greatly affected by the serious accident.[14] The kaiser now continued:

> Because of the terrible catastrophes that have occurred in recent years in our coal mines, I approached the chemical industry via the head of the Civil Cabinet of Essen, first turning to the institutes of technology, and requested that they submit papers to me and make suggestions as to what preventive measures the chemical industry could take to protect the people working underground. I am thinking of harmless chemical preparations that through

some noticeable change could clearly make the foremen and workers aware of impending danger.[15]

After the opening ceremony a tour was conducted through both institutes. Haber, already apprised of the kaiser's proposal, took this opportunity to show him and the accompanying dignitaries the gas interferometer that Fritz Löwe had developed at the Carl Zeiss Works. This instrument was already being used to measure marsh gas, but it had the drawback of being stationary, not portable. The kaiser's interest led Haber and his assistants not long after to carry out research on a device that could go into the mines.

A small staff was gradually assembled. In 1913–14 the institute had a staff of about five scientists, ten technicians, and thirteen unpaid assistants. As noted above, Gerhardt Just, who was head of a department and worked on the Volta effect that occurred during the emission of electrons, came from Karlsruhe. On Haber's recommendation he received the title of professor. Also from Karlsruhe were Richard Leiser, who remained only until the spring of 1914; Setsuro Tamaru, who stayed with Haber despite the offer of a professorship in Japan; and A. Klemenc, who, like Tamaru, continued working on the ammonia equilibrium.

This was a period of continual change for both the assistants and Haber. Apartments had to be found, and, for those moving from the provinces to the national capital of Berlin, they were not exactly cheap. Haber himself was not able to move into his official villa next to the institute until 1913. Richard Willstätter built his house adjacent to Haber's soon after, and here their previous acquaintance turned into a genuine friendship.

The workrooms were also moved several times, depending on the progress in construction. At first, scientific investigations were carried out in the laboratories at the Imperial Physical and Technological Institute. Then it became possible to move into the first rooms in the new institute. It was well into 1913 before the institute could be run and the scientific work carried out comfortably.

And what of "that work and its demanding weight," as the poem "Yearning" put it? Work with Just in Karlsruhe on the emission of electrons in chemical reactions had already led Haber into a field that reflected the changes occurring in physical chemistry just before World War I. The period of classical physical chemistry seemed to be ending. Nernst's heat theorem had resolved problems in thermodynamics insofar as they concerned chemical equilibria. Researchers, including some at Haber's institute, were still working on extending the application of the theorem—on its behavior near absolute zero, for example. But the first signs of the triumphant entry of quantum ideas and atomic theory were increasingly apparent. These newer concepts allowed researchers to use statistical methods not only to describe chemical equilibria at a more fundamental level than was possible with the calculation of chemical constants, but also above all to get closer to the actual chemical events. A similar trend toward problems at the atomic level became noticeable in Haber's work at about this time.

Haber was thus occupied with the cutting-edge questions of advanced chemistry. He did not become set in his ways and interests but shared the same professional curiosity as the younger generation of researchers. That is one reason he was so admired by his assistants in Karlsruhe, a situation that did not change in Dahlem. His scientific work mirrors the development of physical chemistry during his lifetime. His influence depended just as much on his scientific success as on the perfect fit between his own career and the spirit of the times.

Thus it is certainly more than a coincidence that in 1911 the first publication by the Kaiser Wilhelm Institute for Physical Chemistry was a paper by Fritz Haber dealing with ultraviolet and infrared characteristic frequencies of crystals and the connection between heat of reaction and quanta of energy.[16] Though the results of this paper have since become obsolete, except for an interesting empirical relationship observed in a crystal's characteristic frequencies, it still shows that Haber was thinking about a quite new area that would decisively determine the direction of the newly founded institute. The war intervened, however, so it was eight years before he was able to return to some of these ideas and bring them to maturity.

In the few years before the war Haber's institute continued to investigate other problems already studied in Karlsruhe besides the ammonia equilibrium. One paper that received special public attention dealt with a marsh gas (methane) detector for use in coal mines—the kaiser's recommendation.

After Haber had demonstrated the gas interferometer at the opening of the institute, various experiments using the device were carried out in coal mines in Derne, where Haber and Leiser were supported by a *Bergassessor* (a junior mining official) named Beyling. Löwe from the Zeiss Works also helped with the experiments.[17] It was found that to measure marsh gas the apparatus needed to be easier to use, and attempts were made to adapt the equipment. It was, however, really a measuring device and not the warning device that the kaiser had specified.

Up to this time the miner's lamp had been used as a warning device.

When the wick in the lamp was screwed down, an experienced observer could recognize the corona of light that appears when more than 1 percent methane is present. This corona grows in strength and clarity as the explosive level is approached. Since an open flame is extremely dangerous in confined areas where methane might be present, Humphry Davy, the lamp's inventor, fitted it out with a wire grating through which methane could enter the lamp to burn inside; this device prevented the flame from reaching the surrounding atmosphere. This safety lamp was used in almost all coal mines at that time, but defective lamps frequently allowed the flame to get out, and the mining authorities had therefore considerably restricted the lamps' use.

Haber and Leiser now tried another direction, to which Haber alluded in a letter on 12 December 1912 to Hugo Krüss at the Ministry of Education. Although the research was far from complete, Haber wanted at least to tell Krüss about it privately.[18] Now that he had carried out a variety of successful experiments with chemical detectors, he was beginning to develop an acoustic detector. He noted in his subsequent publication on marsh gas detectors that miners are more accustomed to acoustic signals like whistles or bells.[19]

Haber's new detector relied on the fact that filling a pipe with different gases results in different tones when the pipe is blown. This phenomenon is especially striking when two wind instruments tuned in the same way are filled separately, one with air and one with gas, and are then played. The idea had been suggested to mine owners forty years earlier, but until Haber's demonstrations they had rejected acoustic detectors.

A year after his institute opened, Haber presented his results before the annual general meeting of the Kaiser Wilhelm Society in the presence of the kaiser. He demonstrated his results and how the marsh gas whistle worked. At the end of his presentation he pointed out that the whistle "has an immediately apparent advantage as well as one conspicuous disadvantage in comparison to the safety lamp. . . . The advantage is its unconditional safety in marsh gas, but the disadvantage is its higher price of manufacture. A long testing time is required to see whether it is robust enough during use in mines over considerable periods."[20]

However, the outbreak of war in 1914 and postwar conditions meant that it was 1924 before the marsh gas whistle was successfully produced in quantity. But there was a problem: the pipes could not be tuned so that they held exactly the same tone when the same gas was blown over them, and the whistle was therefore not entered into a 1924 competition for marsh gas detectors.[21] Thus the only portable marsh gas detector in use continued to be the old safety lamp, which was used until 1964, when it was substituted by detectors based on the principle of the burning heat of methane.

# Endnotes

[1] Jeffrey A. Johnson, "The Chemical Reichsanstalt Association," Ph.D. diss., Princeton University, Department of History, 1980; and Johnson, *The Kaiser's Chemists: Science and Modernisation in Imperial Germany* (Chapel Hill/London: University of North Carolina Press, 1990).

[2] *Fünfzig Jahre Kaiser-Wilhelm-Gesellschaft zur Förderung der Wissenschaften 1911–1961: Beiträge und Dokumente* (Fifty years of the Kaiser Wilhelm Society, 1911–1961: Essays and documents) (Göttingen: Generalversammlung der Max-Planck-Gesellschaft, 1961); and Bernhard vom Brocke, "Die Kaiser-Wilhelm-Gesellschaft im Kaiserreich," in *Forschung im Spannungsfeld von Politik und Gesellschaft,* ed. Rudolf Vierhaus and Bernhard vom Brocke (Stuttgart: Deutsche Verlags-Anstalt, 1990).

[3] Theobald von Bethmann-Hollweg, memorandum to Minister of Education August Trott zu Solz, 13 Sept. 1910, Geheimes Staatsarchiv Preussischer Kulturbesitz, Berlin-Dahlem, Rep. 76 Vc, Sect. 1, Tit. XI, Part IX, No. 12, Vol. I, Bl. 91–93.

[4] Memorandum on the 17 Sept. 1910 conference from the minister of education (*Kultusminister*) to the minister of finance, 14 Nov. 1910, copy in Geheimes Staatsarchiv Preussischer Kulturbesitz, Rep. 76 Vc, 2T XXVIII, Lit. A No. 108, Vol. I, 22–33.

[5] Fritz Haber to Emil Fischer, 29 June 1910, MPG, Dept. Va, Rep. 5, 1795.

[6] Fritz Haber to *Oberregierungsrat* (privy councillor) Dr. Schmidt, Berlin, Ministry of Education, 30 July 1910, MPG, Dept. Va, Rep. 5, 1793.

[7] Fritz Haber to *Geh. Oberregierungsrat* (privy councillor) Böhm, Ministry of Education, Baden, 19 Sept. 1910, MPG, Dept. Va, Rep. 5, 851.

[8] Handwritten note in answer to a letter from the Rector and the Senate of the Technische Hochschule Karlsruhe to the Ministry of Education, 13 June 1911, MPG, Dept. Va, Rep. 5, 1585.

[9] *Z. Elektrochemie,* (Special issue in honor of Haber's leaving Karlsruhe), 17 (1911), 485–544.

[10] Prussian Minister of Education August Trott zu Solz, to His Majesty the Kaiser and King, 24 Feb. 1911, MPG, Dept. Va, Rep. 5, 1660.

[11] Letter stating Haber's appointment to *Geheimer Regierungsrat* (privy councillor), MPG, Dept. Va, Rep. 5, 1660.

[12] The Minister of Agriculture and Building Inspector Guth to the minister of education, 14 Oct. 1911 and 11 Nov. 1911, Geheimes Staatsarchiv Preussischer Kulturbesitz, Berlin-Dahlem, file on the KWI for Chemical Research, Rep. 76, Ve, Sect. 2, Part 23, Berlin Lit. 1, No. 109-1.

[13] *Fünfzig Jahre KWG* (cit. note 2), 146–155.

[14] Mines assistant (*Bergassessor*) W. de la Sauce to Johannes Jaenicke, 6 Dec. 1954, MPG, Dept. Va, Rep. 13, A 336.

[15] *Fünfzig Jahre KWG* (cit. note 2).

[16] Fritz Haber, "Über den festen Körper sowie über den Zusammenhang ultravioletter und ultraroter Eigenwellenlängen im Absorptionsspektrum fester Stoffe und seine Benutzung zur Verknüpfung der Bildungswärme mit der Quantentheorie" (On the solid body as well

as on the connection between ultraviolet and ultrared characteristic frequencies in the absorption spectrum of solid material and its use in relating the heat of formation to the quantum theory), *Verhandlungen der Deutschen Physikalischen Gesellschaft* 13 (1911), 1118–1136.

[17] Fritz Haber to Mining Superintendent (*Bergrat*) Bernhardt, 11 Feb. 1913, Staatsbibliothek Preussischer Kulturbesitz, Berlin-Dahlem, file KWG, record file, 27. 1.

[18] Fritz Haber to Hugo Krüss, 1 Dec. 1912, MPG, Dept. Va, Rep. 13, 1802.

[19] Fritz Haber, "Über Schlagwetteranzeige" (On detecting marsh gas), *Naturwissenschaften* 1 (1913), 1049.

[20] Ibid.

[21] De la Sauce to Jaenicke, 13 Jan. 1955, MPG, Dept. Va, Rep. 5, A 336.

## Chapter 7

World War I

*Fritz Haber in his captain's uniform, 1916.*

*Previous page: Kaiser Wilhelm II in 1912, at the inauguration of the Kaiser Wilhelm Institutes for Chemistry and for Physical Chemistry and Electrochemistry. Visible behind the kaiser are Adolf von Harnack (right) and Emil Fischer.*

I N HIS BIOGRAPHY OF KAISER WILHELM II, MICHAEL BALFOUR WROTE about power and morality, and specifically about the conflict between duty to one's country and duty to humanity, during World War I:

> Insofar as men had hitherto looked beyond their own country, they had mostly taken the coincidence of these two duties for granted. . . . To suspect that the ends of one's national community are at variance with the good of mankind is productive of so much indignation to the average individual and of so much agony to the sensitive one as to make it infinitely tempting to assume that the two objectives coincide and that, in serving the nation to one's best ability, one is also serving humanity. . . . So upright and Christian a man as [Friedrich] Naumann declared that "our faith in nationalism and our faith in humanity are for us two sides of the same question."[1]

## From Peace to War

The condition of the population of the German empire—a nation that had undergone astounding changes economically, socially, and politically—explains the complacency of its citizens, especially that of the greater part of the intellectual elite in the period before 1914. The Social Democratic Party nonetheless increased in Berlin, and in 1912 it received 75.3 percent of the votes. There was talk of a "red Berlin," and the Social Democrats stated that "Berlin belongs to us." But this "red" majority had no influence on the dominant social and governmental system. The world of scholarship, too, was almost untouched by it. Instead, the university, the institute of technology, and the ever-increasing number of scientific institutes in Berlin basked in the kaiser's grace. The minister of education, August Trott zu Solz, deflected rhetorical attacks by such members of the Imperial Parliament (Reichstag) as Karl Liebknecht, a member of the Social Democrats' left wing, with no great effort.

Fritz Haber had already established an important place for himself in the community of scholars in Berlin. His connections to the university, to the Academy of Sciences, and to the Ministry of Education strengthened, and he began to participate in efforts to attract more reputable leading scientists to Berlin.

Haber was involved, though indirectly, in the transfer to Berlin of Albert Einstein, whom he had first met in 1909 at a scientific congress in Karlsruhe. In 1911, after Einstein took up the chair of physics at the German University in Prague, he attended the first Solvay Conference in Brussels. The Belgian chemist and industrialist Ernest Solvay had arranged this conference at the urging of Walther Nernst. Solvay was interested in developing a new theory he had in physics, and Nernst had advised him that a conference with leading European physicists would allow him to present his theory. At this conference Einstein met many of the high-ranking physicists of the time, including Henri Poincaré, Marie Curie, and Paul Langevin from France; Ernest Rutherford from England; and Nernst, Max Planck, and Heinrich Rubens from Germany.

After meeting Einstein, Nernst and Planck on their return took on the difficult and delicate task of bringing him to Berlin. Such an exceptionally good offer was made to Einstein that he agreed to become a Prussian state official, even though he was an individualist and democrat who found the Prussian ideals of life—dominated by the fulfillment of duty and unconditional service to king and country—quite incomprehensible.

Haber was involved in the many deliberations over the form such an offer should take. While on holiday in Pontresina he wrote Hugo Krüss, reminding him of a conversation they had had in 1912 on the topic of moving Einstein, and formulating his thoughts in greater detail. The grounds he gives in his summary of the reasons for bringing Einstein to Berlin are of particular interest:

> For me [a decisive reason] is that the development of theoretical chemistry, which, since the days of Helmholtz, has been trying successfully under the leadership of van't Hoff to appropriate the achievements of the theory of thermodynamics, generally has reached this goal, and now tries to subsume radiation theory and electrochemistry. This fundamental task can be incomparably advanced by the admission of Mr. Einstein to the circle of our institutes. It is quite a rare coincidence that not only does such a man exist but also that his age [thirty-four years] and his life circumstances are favorable

*Richard Willstätter, in 1915.*

for his transfer, and his character gives me the firm conviction that there will be a fruitful relationship.[2]

Einstein was not the only candidate Haber worked for. He also gave Willstätter friendly advice before he was appointed to the Kaiser Wilhelm Institute for Chemistry. In June 1911 he wrote from Karlsruhe to Willstätter in Zurich. "I beg you to let me know if there is anything I can do in your interest. Although I am not exactly a man of great influence in Berlin, as one can imagine, I still have occasion to say a word that will be heard, and if such a word can help bring you to Berlin soon, then I will make a double effort to say it in the right place and in the right way."[3]

Willstätter was then teaching at the Swiss Federal Institute in Zurich, and his colleagues included many old acquaintances of Haber's, such as Georg Lunge, Lunge's student Ernst Berl, Alfred Werner, and Georg Bredig. Bredig had been appointed to Zurich after Haber rejected their offer of a post there. It seems that Haber felt drawn to Willstätter even when he was still addressing the latter as "highly honored colleague." The changing terms of address show how quickly a lifelong friendship developed between them. The next year Haber wrote to his "Dear Colleague," then in 1913 to "Dear Friend," and finally to "Dear Richard." It was to be a friendship based on mutual respect. Willstätter describes his friendship with Haber in his memoirs and mentions his "nobility of character, his goodness of heart, richness of ideas, immeasurable and limitless drive to work."[4]

In a 1911 letter Haber expressed his antipathy to preparative organic chemistry, Willstätter's field: "The whole operation is based on mass suggestion: there are so many who can carry out chemical preparations that they mutually convince each other of the usefulness and deep significance of their work, although it is basically an indigestible soup, poor in ideas." But a later remark demonstrates his admiration for Willstätter's research: "Your last paper on chlorophyll gave me back respect and a feeling for the greatness of organic chemical work, and for this I thank you."[5]

Willstätter at first declined the appointment to Berlin because he had been guaranteed only a position as head of a department in Ernst Beckmann's institute, and he felt that this would restrict his work too much. Haber was surprised when he heard of Willstätter's rejection, but he did not give up hope. He wrote to Willstätter that he had "immediately consulted with his friend Engler, who, as a member of the Scientific Advisory Committee of the Kaiser Wilhelm Institute for Chemistry, has a lively interest in the matter. Herr Engler confirmed to me . . . that all people involved have an active wish to bring you to Berlin."[6]

Haber then turned to Emil Fischer and offered his services in clearing up any misunderstandings. Fischer cut short his summer vacation in St. Blasien and traveled with Ludwig Darmstädter, who had made his money in the chemical industry, to Zurich, where both were Willstätter's guests. They were able to persuade him to change his mind, and a month later he met with Beckmann in Baden-Baden, where they together developed plans for the institute.[7] Willstätter accepted the post in the summer of 1911.

When Willstätter came to Berlin, Haber helped him buy a piece of land from the domain of Dahlem. A residence was built for him on the Faradayweg next to Haber's official residence, separated from it by a large garden. Lovely park areas were being created in Dahlem at the time, but a wide plain interrupted only by windmills still stretched toward the south. Dahlem did not become a more densely built-up villa area until after the war. Willstätter relates in his memoirs that Haber also advised him to buy a German shepherd, as the area was fairly lonely. However, the Haber and Willstätter dogs were not on good "speaking" terms with one another. Willstätter describes this situation:

> Unfortunately, the relationship between our dogs took such an unfriendly turn that even our growing friendship was endangered for a time. Mrs. Haber was offended because our dog, Bobbi, barked sarcastic remarks across the fence at her dog, Greif, even in her presence. They were justified, by the way. . . . On the other hand, we were saddened because their nasty Greif jumped over our high fence and severely bit the friendly, if noisy, Bobbi.[8]

Haber's closer relationship with Albert Einstein and his friendship with Richard Willstätter developed in the two years before the war. There was also an active exchange of ideas and opinions with other colleagues, and they met in each other's homes, in the institutes, in the Academy of Sciences, or at special events.

During July and August 1913 Haber was in Karlsbad, recovering from "gallstones and moodiness" in the spa's baths. Even now, after achieving a position that brought him recognition and gave him entrance to the highest social circles, his moodiness was not appeased. He remained continually restless, both at home in the evenings and even on vacation. His lively spirit remained active: Haber was not a person to lean back complacently in the director's seat. He was still ready to take on any tasks the times would set him.

New times were approaching all too soon, and the tasks would be of a kind he could not have anticipated. On 28 July 1914 he applied for a six-week holiday. However, he also wrote: "If the political situation becomes such that our nation is pulled into a warlike entanglement, then I intend to return from this holiday."[9]

Fritz Haber never went on his peaceful vacation. World War I began three days later. Filled with patriotism, citizens everywhere rushed to serve under their flags. Fritz Haber, a noncommissioned officer (*Vizefeldwebel,* or vice-sergeant), also volunteered for war duty, but he was rejected because of his age. Other assignments were awaiting him that were more important for the war effort than marching against the enemy at the front of the field artillery.

## Putting Science and the Economy on a Wartime Footing: Haber's Early Efforts

Neither the scientific institutes nor industry, commerce, and agriculture in Germany and in the other countries involved were prepared for a war as long and as total as World War I. Even as the population, the members of the military, and the administrative authorities were subjected to the turmoil of events, only a few recognized early on the effects of a long war on the economy and on supplies for the army and the population as a whole. The general opinion, firmly held, was that the war would last only until Christmas. That was all the German General Staff had planned for. But Germany's march through neutral Belgium and its advance into France were suddenly checked. When Germany had to resist the Russian invasion in East Prussia, the Allies in the West dug themselves into trenches. The need for equipment and arms increased to an unforeseen degree. Blockades stopped the supply of vital imported goods. Neither the military nor the economy was sufficiently prepared for such a situation.

Numerous German scientists and intellectuals busied themselves with formulating proclamations and justifications, of which the best known was the "Proclamation to the Civilized World" of September 1914, which answered Allied accusations, defended the invasion of Belgium, and denied the ferocity of the German troops. Haber was one of the signatories, together with Adolf von Baeyer, Carl Engler, Emil Fischer, Adolf von Harnack, Walther Nernst, Wilhelm Ostwald, and Richard Willstätter, among others.

Some, however, began to grasp the difficulties of the situation, particularly Emil Fischer among the scientists and Walther Rathenau among the economists. Rathenau was the head of the General Electricity Works (Allgemeine Elektrizitätswerke), director of more than a hundred local and foreign companies, and a well-known author of texts on politics and the economy. Rathenau contacted the minister of war and put forth his opinion that the General Staff was so convinced that the war would be short that it had made no plans for fresh supplies in the event of a long war and had not thought at all about the role of industry. He mentioned Germany's lack of raw materials and listed such important ones as nitrates for explosives, oil, rubber, and various metals: if imports should fail, production of war materials would become extremely shaky. Rathenau went so far as to declare that, by excluding industry from the war preparations, the General Staff had played into the hands of the enemy. To correct the results of the military's short-sightedness, he proposed a system of controls to allow the efficient organization and distribution of strategically important raw materials now barred from import by the British blockade. He also drew up a program to research and manufacture synthetic alternatives to the limited natural raw materials.

Rathenau succeeded in convincing General Erich von Falkenhayn, chief of staff, who had enough authority to carry out these suggestions. He ordered that a Board of Wartime Raw Materials be established inside the Ministry of War, and he appointed Rathenau as its head.

Rathenau quickly filled this office with a select group of scientists and industrialists. The first task facing the new office was to draw up an exact accounting of the situation in raw materials. The results were shattering. As Rathenau had feared, German industry had reserves for less than six months. The great decline of nitrate reserves, in particular, endangered explosives production. So long as the British fleet controlled the sea lanes, there was little chance to stock up from Chile. Were the war to last six more months, a dangerous crisis in the supply of ammunition was inevitable.

To deal with this problem, Fritz Haber was appointed head of the chemistry department of the new board, which soon became known as the "Haber Office." Haber had already worked with Emil Fischer on adapting various research projects to the war economy. Among other projects in his Kaiser Wilhelm Institute, Haber had investigated various substances to replace now-scarce toluene, used as an antifreeze in motor fuel. He found xylene and soluble petroleum fractions suitable as substitutes.

New types of explosives were also investigated at the Kaiser Wilhelm Institute—"a link in the chain of work in progress for military purposes carried out by the institute since the beginning of the war," as Haber stated in a memo of 3 January 1915.[10] Gerhardt Just and Otto Sackur participated in these experiments. During one of the experiments a severe explosion killed Sackur and cost Just his right hand. Haber reported that they were trying to find a more effective preparation to replace an explosive mixture of bromo-xylenes that had been proposed as a lachrymator for use in howitzer shells. Haber had in fact been in the room where the experiments were being carried out just moments before the explosion. It was only because he had been called out of the room that he too was not a victim. He was deeply shaken. He had supported and helped Sackur in a variety of ways, had brought him to his institute from Breslau, and was convinced of his great abilities. He mourned his loss for a long time and mentioned him frequently. Years later he was able to help Sackur's daughter by giving her a position in the institute.

The most important problem that Haber tackled in the first months of the war was the so-called nitrogen question: how could enough sodium nitrate be manufactured as raw material for both explosives and nitrogen fertilizers? Fischer and Haber worked closely together on this problem from September 1914 on. Haber put his excellent connections with BASF to use in solving it.

The first obstacle was obtaining sodium nitrate. The supplies from Chile that were stored in the warehouses of chemical firms, at the Hamburg importers, and for agricultural use were dwindling rapidly. When Antwerp was captured, a large amount was secured from its harbor, but even with this consignment of around 20,000 metric tons, supplies would last only until mid-1915.[11] A commission was set up under the direction of Fischer and Haber to deal with this problem.

Procedures for synthesizing concentrated nitric acid and sodium nitrate had been known for some time, usually relying on one of the various processes for oxidizing atmospheric nitrogen. Another pathway was through the oxidation of ammonia. As described in previous chapters, Wilhelm Ostwald had been working on an ammonia synthesis long before and had studied the oxidation of ammonia as early as 1901. Together with his assistant Ernst Brauer, later his son-in-law, he developed a process that used platinum as a catalyst.[12]

In the summer of 1903 Ostwald first wrote in the newspaper *Schwäbische Merkur* about what had prompted him to do this work. "The significance of bound nitrogen . . . is especially high for both war and peace." He mentioned its agricultural significance and continued:

> There is another agency with a vital interest, the administration of the armed forces. Without saltpeter the best military is almost helpless. . . . Were a war to break out today between two great powers, one of which was able to prevent the export of saltpeter from Chile's few harbors, that ability alone would allow it to render its opponent almost incapable of fighting.[13]

At the beginning of November 1914 the ammunition required by the armed forces rose to 20,000 metric tons of sodium nitrate per month. In a letter to BASF, Haber compiled the following list of the amounts of saltpeter that could readily be made available.

| | |
|---|---|
| BASF | 5,000 metric tons |
| Hoechst | 4,000 metric tons |
| Griesheim | 2,000 metric tons |
| Aussiger Verein[14] | 2,000 metric tons |
| Prussian Railways | 800 metric tons |

BASF had 5,000 metric tons at hand because of its so-called "saltpeter promise." Carl Bosch had visited Berlin in September and found the officers in the Ministry of War woefully ignorant. He then discussed with Alwin Mittasch the progress of experiments to transform ammonia into saltpeter that were already under way in March 1914, and at the beginning of October he made the saltpeter promise: the company offered to build a plant in which, after about six or seven months, 5,000 metric tons per month of sodium nitrate would be produced from ammonia.[15] The essential difference between BASF's procedure and Ostwald's was that BASF used an iron oxide mixture as the catalyst. Ostwald's platinum was considerably more expensive and difficult to obtain during the war, as it came primarily from Russia.

The other manufacturers wanted to use the same process to oxidize ammonia obtained from coke works. Further quantities of ammonia, especially for agriculture, were to be produced by the cyanamide process. Emil Fischer had already carried out negotiations to this end with Nicodem Caro, who stated that more energy would be needed for the calcium carbide ovens.[16] Thus the first steps were taken to increase saltpeter production considerably, but the various promises had first to be converted to fact.

Negotiations over further increase in production and over distribution during and after the war continued through 1915. Toward the end of the year it was finally decided to build a large new plant based on the Haber-Bosch process in central Germany near Leuna, as discussed in Chapter 5. This area was safe from the air attacks that repeatedly threatened Oppau, and as previously mentioned, the location had abundant supplies of water, brown coal, and gypsum. Building began at the Leuna Works in May 1916, and, after some delays caused by the cold winter, the first tank cars with liquid ammonia left the plant on 27 April 1917. To complete this work in less than eleven months under difficult wartime conditions was an extraordinary achievement. In the next few years the works were considerably expanded until they finally became a major center of the chemical industry in central Germany.

At the end of 1914 Haber and Rathenau had a falling out, and Haber gave up his work in Rathenau's office. But he worked on the problem of producing enough nitrogen fertilizer throughout the war. In a report to Rudolf von Valentini, the chief of the kaiser's Privy Civil Cabinet, he praised the industry for managing to cover military requirements, but pointed out that there was still not enough fertilizer for agriculture.[17]

Haber then received an assignment that he chose for himself, although it was to become a heavy charge on him personally and on Germany's reputation throughout the world. He became a pioneer in the use of chemical weapons in World War I.

## The Chemical War and Haber's Role

What is meant by a "chemical war"? The simplest answer is "a war fought with chemicals." But what does "with chemicals" mean? "Chemistry" has after all long been used to kill the enemy. The Orinoco Amerindians extracted curare from the vine *Strychnos toxifera* to poison their weapons. An early written Western source (Sextus Julius Africanus, A.D. 240) recommends poisoning the water, food, and air of an enemy under blockade. The dreaded "Greek fire" of the Byzantines was the product of a chemical process.

Plans for large-scale use of chemicals in warfare were encouraged by the extraordinary scientific and industrial advances of the mid-nineteenth century. In 1862 John W. Doughty recommended the use of projectiles filled with chlorine gas against Southern troops in the American Civil War. The French general Louis-Eugène Cavaignac used poison fog against an Arabian tribe in 1844 in the Colonial Wars in Morocco. In 1845, during the French-Algerian War, the French used smoke to kill over a thousand Kabyles (a Berber tribe) after forcing them into a coal mine. During the Crimean War (1854–56) the British admiral Thomas Cochrane, Earl of Dundonald, proposed creating carbon disulfide from sulfur vapor and red-hot coke and using it to rout the large garrison in the Russian fortress Malakow near Sevastopol. Although well prepared and organized, the plan was not carried out because the military did not believe it would succeed. During this period suggestions were advanced for protection against poison gases. In spring 1854, for example, John Stenhouse, who in 1848 had synthesized trichloronitromethane (chloropicrin), which damages the lungs and strongly irritates the eyes, gave a lecture to the Scottish Royal Society for Science and Arts on his charcoal respirator, the first predecessor of the gas mask.

But the occasional use of poisons during a battle cannot be called "chemical warfare." We take this term today to mean the deployment in full-scale war of highly poisonous substances specifically developed for that purpose with research to determine all the physical, physicochemical, and other scientific facts relevant to and influencing this deployment. This definition covers both the development of techniques that allow deployment of large amounts of such toxic substances and the chemical and technological research on and development of protective devices.

Chemical warfare according to this definition did not exist in the early weeks of the war, but toward the end of 1915 the intensive work directed by Haber—both in his institute and in other precincts of research—made chemical warfare a reality. The research explored with increasing intensity all relevant aspects of the use of irritating and poisonous chemicals as weapons in war. For faster results properly qualified scientists and technicians from various fields had to be welded into an organization of experts able to deal effectively with any problems that might arise. Fritz Haber played a prominent role in setting up this organization and making it effective. He not only pushed forward the research on and development of the chemicals used but also exerted considerable influence on the engineering technology for turning them into weapons and advised on their use in battle.

Besides work on the weapons themselves, a need was growing for fast and effective development of protection against chemical weapons, first Germany's own, then particularly those used later by the enemy; once these protective devices and measures were developed, they had to be distributed to those who needed them. Here, too, Haber, in collaboration with his colleagues and with industry, played a decisive role. It is therefore no wonder that during the war many of his assistants and colleagues and the leading military men admired his organizational talent, persuasiveness, and untiring efforts.

There is no question that Fritz Haber was the initiator and organizer of chemical warfare in Germany. He never denied this. Instead, even after the war, he continued to defend the use of chemical weapons as a feasible means of warfare and to support work in this area.

Many publications have been written on the use of chemical warfare in World War I.[18] Here Fritz Haber's role in chemical warfare is to be considered, using the available reports and documents.

Haber was appointed head of the Chemistry Section in the Ministry of War soon after the outbreak of the war. While he was busy with various assignments, the need to decide whether to use poisonous substances or

*Fritz Haber (right) at the war front, beside his official car.*

irritants against the enemy in battle became more urgent. At this stage of the war, after a first quick advance through Belgium and France, the German armies had been stopped at the Marne, and the war of the trenches and foxholes had begun. Various unsuccessful attempts to take enemy positions by storm demonstrated the superior firepower of the enemy's artillery and machine guns. The German forces then embarked on a strategy of weakening the enemy before and during attacks by deploying chemical agents that acted as irritants or knocked them out. Several proposals were made. Nernst, according to a report by Carl Duisberg "was summoned to headquarters to see General von Falkenhayn after Lieutenant Colonel Max Bauer had conceived the idea of developing shells that contained solid, gaseous, or liquid chemicals that would damage the enemy or render him unable to fight."[19] Nernst reacted positively to this idea.[20]

Soon after, various experiments were carried out at the artillery range at Wahn near Cologne in collaboration with the Bayer Company (Farbenfabriken Bayer), in whose laboratories the shells were filled. The first substance used was dianisidine-chlorosulfonate, readily available through its use as an intermediate in the synthetic dye industry. These so-called N-J shells were used at the end of 1914 in the battles at Neuve Chapelle, and their effects on the enemy encouraged further development. To achieve a long-lasting effect, 15-centimeter howitzer shells were filled with xylyl bromide—the so-called T shells.

Sir Harold Hartley, who worked on chemical warfare in England, reported a conversation he had with Haber after the war in which Haber described being present at the trials for firing T shells.

> [Haber] said that owing to the small area affected by each shell it would be necessary to fire a large number simultaneously to produce any technical effect. He suggested the use of a large number of mortars for this purpose, an idea realised later in the Livens Projector, but he was told that it was impossible to produce them in time to be of use. The employment of gas from cylinders was then proposed in order to get a high concentration and to cover a wide area, the object of the General Staff in using gas being to drive us from our trenches and get back to open warfare. . . . The suggestion of a cylinder attack with chlorine was adopted and Haber was placed in charge of the technical preparation.[21]

Rudolf Knietsch's work at BASF before the war made it possible to liquefy chlorine using compressors lubricated with petroleum. Haber's idea, explained in detail to Falkenhayn and the top military leadership, was to put siphon tubes into steel cylinders, each containing about 20 kilograms of gas. These were then brought to the trenches, where they were positioned and buried in the ground at intervals of about one meter along a continuous front. A lead pipe was screwed into the opening of the cylinders, then brought up over the top of the trench and aimed in the direction of the enemy. When the wind direction was favorable, that is, blowing toward the enemy, all cylinders were opened simultaneously, and the chlorine was released. The liquid chlorine immediately turned into a gas and mixed with the air, forming a yellow-green to white cloud containing about 0.5 percent chlorine at a distance of 50 to 100 meters from the cylinders. Since chlorine is two and a half times as heavy as air, this cloud rolled forward into the enemy trenches and foxholes and forced the enemy troops to flee their positions rapidly. The gas also damaged their weapons with corrosion. The German troops could follow the cloud and penetrate into the enemy positions.[22]

To give Haber the same status as members of the officer corps while he carried out this operation, the kaiser ignored the usual career steps and promoted him to the rank of captain. Haber kept this rank throughout the war. He succeeded in building up an effective organization during his collaboration with the armed forces.

*Preparations for an offensive deploying chlorine gas, World War I.*

Various participants in the planning, organization, and execution of the gas attacks that Haber initiated later reported on their experiences and on Haber's involvement. Franz Richardt, who worked with Haber in Karlsruhe, reported on a special troop for gas warfare (later Pioneer Regiments 35 and 36) that was under Otto Peterson's command and had Haber and Friedrich Kerschbaum as advisers:

> [It] was a unique formation. . . . Any officer selected by Haber, regardless of where he was at the time, was soon transferred by Lieutenant Colonel Bauer to Peterson's organization. . . . Furthermore Haber sought out all physicists and chemists of whom he had heard—where and in which troops they were stationed—in order to draw them to himself through Lt. Bauer. At the time of my arrival there were already, among others, Dr. Kerschbaum, Haber's technical adjutant [who later emigrated to the United States]; Prof. O[tto] Hahn, who later split the atomic nucleus and won a Nobel Prize; Prof. J[ames] Franck [a physicist who later emigrated to the United States and won a Nobel Prize]; Prof. [Hans] Geiger, who later constructed the Geiger-Müller counter; Prof. W[alter] Madelung, [who] later worked at the University of Freiburg in

the area of dye chemistry; and Prof. W[ilhelm H.] Westphal, a neurologist . . . and many others.

This work showed Haber to be a great organizer. One must remember that the generals at the front, who had grown up with the conservative Prussian way of thinking, suddenly had to trust the new idea of chemical weapons. And more than that—everyone, from the general to the last man, had to cooperate enthusiastically.[23]

Westphal remembers:

> My closer relationship to Fritz Haber began when I . . . bumped . . . into the gas regiment in April 1915 at Ypres. I met many who were already good friends of mine and who were there as front-line weather observers, including James Franck, Gustav Hertz [nephew of Heinrich Hertz, the physicist who later investigated excitation and ionization energies of atoms with Franck, for which work they won the Nobel Prize in 1925], Otto Hahn, and Burkhardt Helferich [an organic chemist who worked on the field of natural products; later at the University of Bonn and president of the German Chemical Society in 1956]. This group later grew considerably. Haber frequently visited us on the western front and later on the eastern front. . . . During his inspections of the positions right at the front he often ignored danger so much that we feared for him.[24]

Otto Hahn, whom Haber had known since 1910 and to whom he had even offered a position at his institute, reported in 1955 how he met Haber in Brussels in January 1915:

> Our troop had been pulled back to Brussels because we had suffered heavy losses and had many sick during the battles in Flanders in the autumn of 1914. I received a request from Prof. Haber to meet him in a hotel to talk with him. The appointment was for about 12:00 noon. I came to the hotel and found Haber lying in bed. From his bed he gave me a lecture about how the war had now become frozen in place and that the fronts were immobile. Because of this situation the war now had to be fought by other means in order to be brought to a favorable conclusion. He then gave me a lecture on chlorine gas clouds, which had to blow over the enemy trenches in order to force the enemy to come out of them. I interjected that the use of poisonous substances was certainly universally condemned, whereupon he replied that the French had already tried something similar with shells in the autumn of 1914. [Haber was here referring to the use of tear gas and irritants that had been used in small quantities by the French in September.] We would thus

not be the first to use this kind of weapon. Anyway, in war, methods have to be used that lead to its rapid conclusion.[25]

A section of the front at Ypres in Belgium was chosen. What happened during this gas attack has been described many times.[26] Here a short report from one of the participants, Otto Lummitsch, will suffice.

> The installation for the gas attack front at Langemarck was finished [in mid-April]. On 21 April 1915 we received the news from the commander of our section that his meteorologists had predicted the west-northwest wind required for the attack. We therefore, together with *Geheimrat* Haber, moved as fast as possible into the battle stations we had prepared behind the gas attack front in the Twenty-sixth Reserve Corps and gave the orders for the action that was about to take place.
>
> On 22 April 1915 the wind turned to west-northwest as had been predicted, and on the same day, at about 6:00 P.M., the first gas attack in military history was carried out according to plan. The attack tore open the front for a distance of about six kilometers. Our troops took Langemarck, around which there had been so much fighting, penetrated to the heights of Pilkem without any resistance worth mentioning, except at the flanks. In front of us, only slightly damaged, lay the beautiful old city of Ypres. One could recognize the famous Tuch Hall with the naked eye.
>
> Unfortunately the Supreme Command had not prepared sufficient reserves because they doubted the effectiveness of the new weapon. Otherwise it would have been possible to make a decisive breakthrough.
>
> Naturally, the enemy brought up reserves from all sides, and consequently the general attack on Ypres ordered by the army leadership had only limited success.[27]

It was later difficult to determine how many losses were inflicted solely by the gas weapons. Rudolf Hanslian cites a report of the English General Staff that assumed that about 7,000 victims were poisoned and 350 were killed by the gas during the chemical attack at Ypres.[28] He also argues that having enough troops to break through at Ypres might have effected a tactical success but not the strategic one that would have produced a turning point in the mobile war.

## Gearing Up for the Chemical War: Organization, Production, Defense, and Delivery Systems

Now that the gas attack at Ypres had proved that chemical warfare was a serious form of combat, Haber was promoted to captain. This promotion would not only strengthen his position with the military but would also enlarge his scope of action generally. From the beginning it was clear to Haber and his coworkers at the Kaiser Wilhelm Institute that substantial research—both scientific and technical—was needed to make chemical warfare effective. The institute now reorganized to work on developing and producing gas weapons and the protective measures these weapons would require.

Overall coordination between Haber's institute and industry was secured by putting Bayer's Carl Duisberg on the Kaiser Wilhelm Institute's advisory committee. The committee also included Emil Fischer, who at the beginning of the war worked actively in Rathenau's chemistry section; Walther Nernst, who worked together with Duisberg on irritants and chemical weapons in his institute; and Richard Willstätter, who participated in the development of a filler for gas-mask filters. Carl Engler maintained his connection with BASF through his position on the board of directors.

From February 1916 on, the institute worked only for the military administration, which now paid all its expenses.[29] In 1916 Department W8 of the Ministry of War, which was responsible for coordinating warfare with chemical weapons under Haber's direction, submitted an application to the head of the Ministry of War explaining that "given all its other manifold tasks, this Central Chemistry office can no longer continue to manage the institute directly." The document put forward the motion that

> the whole operation of the institute be converted to a military one while keeping the name "KWI for Physical Chemistry and Electrochemistry" and that the staff currently working at the institute should be . . . put on the staff of the military administration. The Ministry of War—and thus its chemistry section—would, as supervising authority, still control the general direction of the institute on the condition that the position of *Geh[eimer] Reg[ierungs]rat* Captain Haber, head of the ZCh [Zentralen Chemiestelle: Central Chemistry Post], as scientific director of the institute would remain unchanged, as would the positions of the others who had been members of the staff in peacetime.[30]

A complex organization was established at the end of 1916, as surviving documents reveal. To carry out the different complex tasks, nine departments were set up at various locations in Berlin, including Haber's institute and other sites in Berlin-Dahlem. Heading the departments were Reginald Herzog, Friedrich Kerschbaum, Hans Pick, Heinrich Wieland, Ferdinand Flury, Herbert Freundlich, Wilhelm Steinkopf, Otto Poppenberg, and Paul Friedländer. At the end of the war this site for research, development, and testing employed almost 150 academically trained people who had been made temporary state officials, plus around 1,300 noncommissioned officers, soldiers, men and women workers, and additional support personnel working within its framework.

The Institute for Physical Chemistry and Electrochemistry, now the Kaiser Wilhelm Institute Military Institute, had spread far beyond its original building. Even though various temporary buildings and Quonset huts were built on previously empty land, a lot of space in the neighboring Institutes for Chemistry and for Biology was also coopted. No wonder the directors of those institutes complained as their research work was considerably hindered. Yet by early 1917 the expansion had been carried out without too much delay—largely owing to Haber's efforts.

While Haber was directing various actions on the eastern and western fronts, he was also occupied at the Ministry of War with the nitrogen question and other problems important for the conduct of war. As work began on developing and testing chemical weapons and protective devices against gas, Haber also took part in discussions, explanations, and negotiations with the military on the tactics and strategies of gas warfare, on development and production of the chemical weapons, on protective devices against gas, on the many items of equipment that were necessary for gas warfare, and on the purchase of the necessary material.

Reports of Haber's activities in this period give the impression that he was obsessed with the task he had set himself. Everything else in his life was pushed into the background. Wife and family had practically no influence. Indeed, his family as well as his circle of friends and acquaintances seemed to him only further sources of help for advancing his projects. He attempted to interest as many friends and acquaintances as possible in chemical warfare. He ignored everything except war-related work, concentrating almost totally on the field of chemical warfare, which appeared to keep him happy.

The production of chemical weapons developed slowly by stages. During 1915 there was a great deal of improvisation, and many different operations were carried out simultaneously. Haber, for example, concerned himself specially with the planning, preparation, and execution of the gas delivery system. Duisberg at Bayer began work on shells filled with irritants, a project in which Nernst was especially involved. Once protection for the troops against chemical weapons—their own and those that the enemy increasingly used—became urgent, the first contacts were made with the Dräger Works in Lübeck. Protective masks and breathing filters had to be both developed and produced in great numbers. Later Haber proposed that the Auer Company produce the filter inserts, and Duisberg recommended that Bayer produce the gas-absorbing substance. Various firms were approached about gas-mask production. Even well into 1916 no unified organization had been created to coordinate all these tasks. At first Haber was active as an adviser in all aspects, including the use of chemical weapons on the front. And he still was in charge of the research carried out in his institute.

The chemical agents were produced mainly at Bayer, where by 1915 Duisberg had already established close contacts with the military, especially with Bauer, on his own initiative. Duisberg's contacts with Haber also became more frequent and closer. As the demand for dyes for the civilian market declined, Duisberg's plants ceased working at capacity; thus he was interested in using them for military purposes. Because dye intermediates could be used for war materiel, particularly explosives and poison gas, these plants—and those of other firms involved in the dye industry that in 1916 joined to form the IG (Interessengemeinschaft der Deutschen Teerfarben-fabriken: Combine of German Coal-Tar Dye Manufacturers)—were well suited to the purpose.

Once use of shells and mines filled with chemical agents increased, the filling plants had to be expanded and new ones constructed. Subsection 3 of Haber's own department organized this endeavor in close collaboration with the military. The first plants were built by industry, with the state covering the costs: for example, the plant in Dormagen, located on the Rhine opposite the Bayer factories. Haber's department directed the building of the later plants, including Adlershof near Berlin and Breloh on the Lüneberger Heide in northern Germany. These plants were under military control, and almost all the men employed there, though not the women, were members of the armed forces.

It was mainly Haber—with the help of many others, to be sure—who built up and developed this many-faceted organization. He even planned well into the future, suggesting the founding of a special Kaiser Wilhelm Institute for research and development of war technology in peacetime, which will be discussed later.

Since many documents on the research carried out in Haber's institute and its many branches have been destroyed, only an overview can be given. The achievements of 1916 to 1918 are quite impressive, although the research did encounter dead ends. The increasingly military tone of the organization may even have hindered its effectiveness, since many of the scientists and technical people were not used to a strict officer's regime. According to the statements of his employees at the time, Haber seems to have compromised: he was not at all against military ways and understood how to deal with higher officers, but he could also accept the open advice of his assistants when dealing with important decisions relevant to the further work of the institute. Even if he sometimes acted like a dictator, maximizing the work of the institute by allowing department heads and assistants their individual initiative was extremely important to him.

## The Chemical War: Defensive Weapons

As the war progressed, the chemical weapons intended as offensive weapons were increasingly used in defense, hence the need to develop effective protection against the gas, as previously discussed. Defenses against new war technologies are usually found shortly after the technology is introduced.

Even the first pioneer battalion equipped for chemical warfare in early 1915 was also supplied with protective devices against its own chlorine. During the attack on Ypres the general troops were given balls of cotton wool dunked in sodium thiosulfate solution; these were not very effective against the corrosive chlorine gas. The pioneers themselves, who had to handle the chlorine cylinders, received protective oxygen masks—the "Selbstretter Dräger-Tübben" (Dräger's self-rescuer). Similar devices had already been manufactured for quite some time, especially for use in coal mines. They basically consisted of a breathing apparatus, an oxygen cylinder, a potash cartridge, and a breathing tube with mouthpiece, stopper, straps, and nose plug.

Work now began on better equipment. Haber turned first to Bernhard Dräger of the Dräger Works, who made several suggestions for improvements. After wider discussions and various pilot projects undertaken at Dräger, Bayer in Leverkusen, Haber's institute, and (at Haber's suggestion) Auer, the researchers came up with the gas mask with a detachable interchangeable filter. Carl Duisberg recorded the development of the device in several stages in 1916.[31] He noted that at first a "cartridge with one layer" was used as an air filter. Diatomite, previously used as a heat insulator, was the first adsorbent employed. It was produced by burning wood or cork with diatomaceous earth. Next the researches used naturally occurring pumice gravel found in the volcanic region of the Eifel range near Neuwied. This adsorbent was saturated with potash so that it could take up the chlorine. To make the pumice gravel more effective, charcoal powder made from coke was applied to it; this powder also provided protection against such irritants as bromacetone and xylyl bromide.

Duisberg also paid tribute to the "three-layer cartridge" introduced by Willstätter, describing it in detail. The first layer was made of the same material as in the one-layer chlorine filter. The second layer consisted of granulated active charcoal, already used for medicinal purposes, which was made by a new process developed at the Aussiger Verein's chemical works. The third layer again consisted of pumice gravel or diatomaceous earth, here saturated with hexamethylenetetramine and piperazine. The latter chemical absorbed the formaldehyde generated by the former.

Even though an effective air filter was developed in a relatively short time, there were still considerable defects and delays in its production. Haber's correspondence with Duisberg shows that he often had to intervene, dealing with cost overruns, bureaucratic delays, shortfalls of supplies, and various problems with testing the device.[32] But in the end Fritz Haber and his institute, along with various industrial companies—Bayer in Leverkusen, Dräger in Lübeck, and Auer, Schering, and Kahlbaum in Berlin—solved the problem of protective devices for toxic gases quickly and successfully. To be sure, protection always depended on conditions at the front. In a surprise attack, troops could not always put gas masks on fast enough and were sometimes poisoned. At times the concentrations of poisonous chemicals were so high that they penetrated the filters. And finally the gas mask hampered the wearer, causing a natural aversion to putting on the mask, at least among troops not yet experienced with the deadly effects of the toxic chemicals.

How did the introduction of chemical gas affect modern warfare? When Haber formulated the first concepts on chemical warfare, he was convinced that, if carried out with scientific thoroughness, it would have a decisive influence on military strategy. True, for battles fought from fixed positions, as was the case on the western front and sometimes the case in the eastern battle arena, chemical warfare allowed an army to move out again. But Haber had to accept that the method of gas release used at Ypres had not achieved this goal. Moreover, subsequent gas attacks with chlorine and phosgene, or a mixture of both, were only of tactical value. Too many factors—meteorological conditions, discipline of the troops, and the enemies' acquisition of chemical warfare—affected use.

As already mentioned, releasing gas in a cloud was easily affected by weather conditions and likely to deliver too little gas to the target area. An

Englishman, William Howard Livens, recognized that the disadvantages could largely be avoided by a different method. He developed a simple mortar gas bomb in which a container filled with chlorine or phosgene was delivered directly into the front positions of the enemy. These shells had considerable effect.

The original gas cloud and Livens's batteries of mortars were at first complemented and then superseded by yet another method: artillery to shoot the gas. This method became quite precise and by the end of World War I was being used to deliver most of the gas.

## The Chemical War: Mustard Gas

The war effort required an enormous number of gas shells, and a variety of poisonous substances were introduced—for example, phosgene, chloropicrin (trichloronitromethane), the arsenic weapons Clark I and II (diphenyl-chloroarsine and diphenylcyanoarsine), and mustard gas (bis(2-chloroethyl) sulfide). Appropriate gas filling stations therefore had to be set up and operated. The shells were manufactured at munitions factories with an empty space left for the chemicals, which were then inserted into the shells in the filling plants. The space had to be sealed so that the shells could be handled without causing poisoning through leakage. Indeed, a large number of poisoning cases, including some deaths, testify to the danger of the work carried out by the teams in these plants. The plants were organized to minimize contamination by the toxic chemicals, most notably by installing ventilators and by storing the containers with the poisons in separate rooms. But the number of cases of poisoning remained high, and most of the workers directly involved in the filling had to be relieved after a relatively short period.

The first filling plants were built in 1915 in the factories of the chemical manufacturing companies, mainly at Bayer in Leverkusen and at Hoechst. Duisberg describes the filling process in his notes on the activities of the chemical industry.[33] Later the military establishment built its own filling plants, for example, outside of Mancieulles in Saulnes near Longwy in the west and near Warsaw in the east. When munitions were to be filled with mustard gas, the Ministry of War suggested building a plant in Breloh near Munster on the Lüneburger Heide, which was to be supervised by Haber and Kerschbaum. When building was delayed, Haber negotiated with the Kahlbaum Company, a chemical manufacturer.

The first plant for filling chemical weapons—predominantly phosgene, chloropicrin, and a mixture of the two—was built in Breloh at the end of 1916. The plant was called the Klopper Works, after the German code name for chloropicrin, "Klop." More filling rooms were added in mid-1917. Mustard gas was also filled here, and a plant was built at this time for filling with the arsenic compounds Clark I and II.

To help expand these plants further and build more, Haber chose Hugo Stoltzenberg, a chemist and an officer so seriously wounded as to be no longer fit for active service. Stoltzenberg had been a research assistant at the Chemical Institute of the University of Breslau, had married Friedrich Bergius's sister Margarethe, and was active as a scientist in Berlin. After working on chemical weapons first in Haber's institute and then in the filling plant at Adlershof near Berlin, he began working in Breloh in 1917, mostly on mustard gas.

At the end of the year Stoltzenberg wrote Haber "that the work on the mustard gas station has come to an almost complete standstill. The continual bickering between the commander and the building supervisors is to blame for wearing down of will and strength." After giving details of the work, he continued, "Then the frost came, and the building supervisors refused to continue building."[34] In spite of the cold, building did eventually continue; the concrete work was carried out behind a wooden partition using open fires for warmth. Haber announced that he would visit Breloh early in 1918, adding that the mustard gas station had to be finished, otherwise the commander could go to hell. Field Marshal Paul von Hindenburg demanded twenty-five trainloads of mustard gas shells in February, and twelve of these trains had to come from Breloh because Adlershof was partly out of action. A whole battalion of engineers was sent to Breloh to accelerate the building of the mustard gas station.[35]

How dangerous the mustard gas really was first became clear when large amounts were handled in the filling plants. Its effects as an offensive and defensive weapon were already under consideration a year earlier at the beginning of 1917.[36] It was expected that

> the effect of the new chemical weapon . . . would not appear quickly and suddenly. . . . Rather it had a protracted and extraordinarily long-lasting action because of the stability of the material. Even months after bombing, it is dangerous to move on terrain that has been treated with mustard gas. . . . [Therefore] not only offensive tactics but also defensive ones must consider this factor. . . . [To be used effectively], mustard gas shells should always be used . . . crowded very close together and in sharply delineated and clearly

> marked sections of territory. These sections of territory are to be marked as
> treated with mustard gas in the maps of the General Staff and must . . . be
> known to the leadership

so that the troops would not be harmed by their own mustard gas in an
offensive. In defensive actions "trenches, dugouts, streets, wells, barracks
that are to be voluntarily left to the enemy" should be contaminated with
mustard gas.[37]

Once the filling plants had expanded and large quantities of gas shells
became available, the advantages of firing gas shells rather than releasing
a cloud became more apparent. Various tactics were used, but three were
used specifically for attacks. First, gas ammunition aimed at a certain point
would be fired suddenly and all at once so as to achieve the largest possible
concentration. The enemy was to be taken by surprise so that the soldiers
would not be able to don their gas masks in time. A second tactic was shelling to set up a smoke screen of gas over a larger target area. This method,
mainly used with mustard gas, suddenly contaminated an area so that the
enemy could not leave it in time or got caught going in.

The third tactic, high-explosive shelling with gas, was used increasingly
during 1918. When on the attack, the German army launched purely explosive shells and gas-filled high-explosive shells alternately. Attacks by the
German army in the spring of 1918 employed the "rolling artillery fire barrage" strategy, with the infantry following immediately behind the artillery.
When gas-filled high-explosive shells were used with these "rolling fire bar-
rages," one barrage with fragmentation ammunition went directly ahead of
the infantry, while the other, with gas ammunition, went far ahead so that
the troops were not hindered in their advance by the effects of their own gas.

"Shooting to poison" was the main method used for defense. It was not a
sudden gas assault but a quiet and well-aimed assault with mustard gas shells
of low explosive charge. These were shot into territory that was to be evacu-
ated and made it impossible for the enemy to re-enter. Occasionally a similar
tactic was used in offensives to create what were called "yellow areas," to
protect the flanks of the infantry ahead. These areas were avoided by troops
carrying out the offensive and were later fenced off. They were also used in
battles during the retreat in the late summer and autumn of 1918 in order to
form defined defensive zones.

As the war continued, Haber became increasingly concerned that the
enemy would also arm themselves with chemical weapons. After all, the

Germans were dealing with an opponent who also had outstanding chemists and an industry that in the end was in a position to carry out chemical reactions on a large scale. How quickly the English ascertained the new substance the Germans were using in their first "yellow cross" (*Gelbkreuz*) shelling, Lutz Haber reports:

> [Harold] Hartley told me . . . how he was awakened early on that 13 July [the morning after the Germans had first used mustard gas shells at Ypres] and was informed that the Germans had fired a new type of shell that made a "plop"-like sound when it burst. . . . The next day [he] had located some unexploded shells with yellow cross markings. They were defused, taken to GHQ, opened, the contents analyzed . . . and the findings compared with the entry in *Beilstein*. By 16 July they knew what the stuff was, and later analyses added little to this knowledge.[38]

Surprisingly, the French were the first to set up a serviceable process for full-scale production of mustard gas. Haber's fears that once mustard gas was produced it would be imitated soon after were realized when the French began production in July 1918. The French filled projectiles with their bis(2-chloroethyl)sulfide, which they called *ypérite*, and used them as quickly as possible, also delivering them to their allies. By November 1918 they had filled 2.8 million shells. Bombardment with these weakened the German fighting power. As the reserves of gas protection devices dwindled, the troops could no longer be protected effectively.[39]

Plans for 1919 were already being made in the summer of 1918. Both sides assumed the war would continue well into 1919 and made further preparations for chemical warfare. Surprisingly, both the Germans and the Allies placed the main emphasis not so much on the use of gas shells but rather on gas throwers and the gas-blowing process. For example, the Allied front was to be saturated with enormous quantities of gas, or gas cylinders were to be mounted on caterpillar carriers that were to advance under the protection of an artillery barrage and would then release the gas. Additional strategies involved smoke that would penetrate the gas masks and false attacks with fog. After the armistice in November 1918 these preparations were not pursued further, although planning by the military did not cease.

What did chemical weapons achieve in the end? Every new weapon raises that question, and the first answer is that the user of a new weapon hopes for a means of overcoming his opponent, whether through physical menace or through psychological influence. Chemical weapons, however, poison both the body and the person's mental and emotional condition—for both sides. Numerous descriptions report on this combination of effects, with the psychological effect often appearing stronger. For example, particularly in 1918— the last year of the fighting—soldiers on the German western front were threatened with poisoning by numerous chemical weapons, gas alarms became more frequent, and masks had to be donned more and more often. Nerves were stretched to the breaking point, and fear spread.

The moral evaluation of chemical warfare will be discussed in later chapters. The primary aim of this chapter has been to provide an objective description of the gas war developments that Haber led in World War I and of the effects of these weapons on the combatants.

## Peacetime and Collapse

During the war Germany made various plans for expanding and developing its technological "advances" in the new weapons. One such plan was the founding of a Kaiser Wilhelm Fund for the Sciences of Military Technology and the setting up of an Institute for Applied Chemistry and Biochemistry that would be occupied mainly with further development of chemical weapons.

Leopold Koppel approached the Ministry of War on 4 July 1916 with the idea for such a fund.[40] Very likely the initiator of the idea for this fund was Fritz Haber. Both during and after the war he often mentioned cooperation between the military and the scientists—a state that had hardly existed before the war but seemed to him vitally necessary. He surely must have made efforts to preserve the departments he had built up during the war, if not in his institute, then in another agency.

Haber supported further development of chemical weapons even after the war and pointed out in a memorandum that "in peacetime, the development of war weapons should be handed over to the military, but research on the scientific bases of these weapons should be carried out in a new scientific institute, while the Kaiser Wilhelm Institute for Physical Chemistry and Electrochemistry must return to its original aims." He also remarked that "doubts whether solving military problems can be the subject of a free scientific establishment" are groundless "because the institute [that would be newly set up] was not to solve military problems but would be established as an institute of applied science in order to study their scientific basis."[41]

Finally, Haber explained the responsibilities of the proposed institute, mentioning, among others tasks, anti-gas protective devices that could also be used in mining and in industry; work on protective regulations, including general workplace hygiene; development of insecticides; and studies of the relationship between chemical composition and pharmacological effect. He continually referred to the various departments that originated in his institute during the war. It is precisely from this part of the memorandum that one recognizes that Haber was essentially concerned with preserving the war institute he and his department heads had created.

However, the Senate of the Kaiser Wilhelm Society could not come to a decision on whether to open a new institute along the lines that Haber proposed. The strategy followed instead was to establish a special department with its own building that would continue research on gas as part of Haber's institute. The Ministry of War was ready to give six million marks for such research, and the Kaiser Wilhelm Society agreed. Haber actually reached his goal: even though his institute was, in fact, an institute of the Kaiser Wilhelm Society in administrative terms, it was not directly associated with that organization, and its board could therefore make decisions without the approval of the society's senate.

Even as late as September 1918 Haber could not imagine a complete military defeat and the collapse of the German empire. Only when General Headquarters sent a telegram to President Woodrow Wilson asking for a cease-fire did Haber recognize the signs of defeat. His letter to the Ministry of Education on 7 October 1918 makes this clear.

> Because of the course of public affairs, I am writing to you once again about the transfer of the six million marks. In the case of a successful end to the war, public opinion, I believe, would have judged continuation of the work that serves the military gas efforts to be correct and necessary. After the developments of the last few days it seems one must count on an end to the war, totally transforming what we had in mind. It is uncertain what further provisions for armaments will still be regarded as necessary in the next few months. In particular, I do not know if educated public opinion will still accept the use of the six million marks for the original purpose. I can imagine that this money will become a source for criticism that will not be favorable to the institute.... Looking at it from this point of view, the subject seems to me to merit cautious handling as other use is possible as long as the sum is not spent.[42]

Haber apparently had a better view of the situation than the Ministry of War. In a letter to the Ministry of Education on 4 November the Ministry of War maintained its intention of using the money—carefully concealed—

for the original purpose, even after the war was lost.[43] The six million marks from the Ministry of War were indeed still available to the fund's board after the war and were mainly used for maintaining Haber's institute and for work on pest control. Continuing inflation, however, soon caused the money to dwindle, and by 1920 it had been eaten up.

Haber made an effort to carry out slowly and steadily the transition to peacetime research in his institute. But now he had to face an unforeseen consequence of his activities during the war. The Allies placed him on the list of war criminals and demanded his extradition. Haber did all he could to avoid this, and in 1919 he traveled to Switzerland. Other scientists and economists who had also been put on the list, like Nernst or Duisberg, stayed in Germany, however. Haber traveled first to Lucerne, where he joined his second wife, Charlotte, who had preceded him there. (His first wife, Clara, committed suicide in 1915, and Haber had married Charlotte in 1917: see Chapter 9). Haber also encountered Albert Einstein at this time. From Lucerne he went to St. Moritz, while various steps were taken to prevent his extradition to the Allied courts. Haber tried to obtain citizenship in Switzerland, which, according to Charlotte, he received. After he had stayed several months in Switzerland, the Allies withdrew their extradition request, and he was able to return once more to Germany.[44]

He once again occupied himself mainly with reorganizing his institute and with new tasks. A chapter of his life had ended what was for him and for many of his generation a time that brought them to the heights of an uncompromising sense of patriotic duty. Now Haber had to bear the fall from these heights and to put to himself the questions and accusations that would follow him to the end of his life and are still associated with his name.

After the war a lively, highly critical debate took place over chemical warfare and its position in international law. Haber often stood at the center of these arguments. Chemical warfare had already been a subject of international concern for over a century, and there had been much lobbying to prohibit chemical weapons in military engagements. The danger resulting from massive use of poisonous substances in a war had been recognized shortly after the Franco-German war in 1870–71. The first international conference on problems of military law was held in Brussels in 1874; among other topics discussed was the choice of means for injuring an opponent, including the use of "poisons and poisoned weapons" in a military engagement. Although the Brussels conference ended without international agreement, the possible use of poison in warfare spurred diplomatic negotiations over the establishment of an international law.

In 1899 and 1907 negotiations on chemical weapons development were a major concern of the Hague peace conferences, which continued the discussion started at the Brussels conference on "limiting and humanizing unlimited war on land." Several delegates at these conferences had no interest in allowing such weapons to be prohibited. For instance, an American representative contended that it was premature to ban a weapon before it and its effects were known. He maintained that all new weapons are first declared barbaric and are then brought into use.

It took thirty-three years, from the Brussels conference of 1874 to the second Hague conference in 1907, to reach an agreement to prohibit such activities. The Hague Convention on War on Land of 18 October 1907 was signed and ratified by practically all the European states. Article 23 forbade the use of poisonous chemical weapons, with the agreement formulated as follows: "In addition to the prohibitions provided by special conventions, it is especially forbidden: (a) to employ poisons and poisonous weapons; (b) to employ weapons, projectiles, or material calculated to cause unnecessary suffering."[45]

This international agreement, considered part of international law, was signed by Britain, France, Russia, Germany, and others. It did not, however, prevent the use of chemical weapons in World War I. The question of who first broke this agreement, thereby breaking international law, was the subject of mutual reproaches and detailed defense papers and charges both during and after the war. The German participants in the chemical war were finally branded as war criminals.

After the war the German national parliament commissioned a committee to examine the behavior of the German Empire with respect to international law during the war. Within the framework of this investigation a subcommittee dealt with the gas war. This committee sat in October 1923, and its proceedings were later published.[46] Haber was cross-examined as a witness under oath, and the committee then reached a conclusion on the position of international law on the use of gas as a weapon during World War I.

In the course of his evidence, Haber tried to prove it was not the Germans but the French who first used poisonous gases as weapons. He also argued that the use of chemical weapons was not purposeless but was partly decisive in determining the outcome of battle, and that chemical warfare was no more gruesome than other forms of war. Indeed, it was more humane as only a small proportion of those injured died, and, if the troops had had more discipline, they could have used the newly developed protective devices to protect them against serious poisoning.

His arguments were often contradictory. On the one hand he emphasized again and again that the essence of gas warfare was "that its physiological actions on humans and the sensations they cause vary a thousandfold. Every change of sensation in the nose and mouth distresses the mind, making it imagine an unknown effect, and makes a new demand on the moral resistance of the soldier."[47] On the other hand he expressed amazement at the fear that chemical warfare aroused in public opinion and ascribed to this fear the emotionally charged reaction against chemical warfare, its substances, its developers, and its defenders.

The parliament committee accepted the major part of Haber's argumentation. The final paragraph of the committee's verdict reads:

> Neither the German nor the French governments, nor as far as is known, any other power participating in the war or a neutral one raised any protests against the modes of action in the gas war. From this it can be concluded that both sides viewed the Hague Conventions of 29 July 1899 and 18 October 1907 as obsolete and by silent agreement regarded it as annulled. Even accepting this assumption, it remains a fact that the first obvious transgression of an international agreement was on the French side, whereas Germany only followed and thereby merely took a countermeasure as accepted in international law.[48]

Thus the new German democratic state that was formed after World War I accepted Haber's behavior as correct and proper, and he was later able to work freely for his country. But the discussion on the moral aspects of the use of chemical weapons did not flag. Haber was continually pulled into these discussions, and he was to feel the consequences of his wartime activity right up to his death.

Human beings are divided entities, as individuals and in the aggregate. They love and hate, they want a peaceful settlement and they resort to violence. They trust and cannot overcome their own mistrust. Religions and philosophies, ideologies and revolutions have not yet managed to bring individuals and ethnic groups, societies and states into peaceful coexistence. This split nature of humanity is mirrored in the person of Fritz Haber. In his personal life as well as in public he tried to achieve harmony, to mediate, to propitiate—and yet he took part in public violence, and, as will be shown later, in doing so he destroyed personal and family relationships. He tried to promote the development of individuals and of society, and yet even with his intellectual brilliance he could not truly grasp the weaknesses and errors of those living with him or of the society around him. Perhaps it is in this context that Fritz Haber's behavior during World War I and even in the first years after the war can be understood. It is easy to condemn a person; it is much harder to make a fair judgment.

\* \* \*

Today there are still to be found in Breloh the remains of the former gas filling plant in a forested part of the military training area in Münster-Nord. The ruins are hidden under the trees, buried under the remains of new in-stallations built on top of them in 1935, for World War II. Only those who know about them and know the terrain well can find these relics. If you look carefully as you walk through the forest undergrowth, you suddenly see little mounds with cavities that contain the remains of brick walls from the mus-tard gas works of World War I. Where the military railway lines were laid, breaks in the forest can be discerned. Suddenly a piece of track protrudes from the ground. Or one comes across a clearing on what used to be the grounds of the Clark works and finds a burnt-over area with the remains of thick-walled bottles. Such bottles, filled with Clark I and II, were worked into grenades, exactly as described by Duisberg and as shown in the sketches for filling this type of projectile with chemical weapons. Somewhat to the north lies the old experimental shelling range from which filled shells were shot for testing; the target area lies six kilometers away. This old shooting range is still in use today.

Today the area of the former chemical weapons filling stations is closed off. Even today unexploded shells filled with chemical poisons from World War I can be found—not singly but in considerable numbers. If the mustard gas has not come into contact with the atmosphere, it still has the same corrosively poisonous effects. Even more dangerous are the shells filled with tabun and sarin from World War II. All the explosions, planned and un-planned, all the demolition, clean-up work, and operations to destroy the chemical weapons, have not been able to eliminate the remains. The area is still contaminated with such chemicals as arsenic, found in the soil in the form of its oxide. Even after three generations the consequences of using chemical weapons in World War I have to be borne.

# Endnotes

[1] Michael Balfour, *The Kaiser and His Times* (London: Cresset Press, 1964), 424.
[2] Fritz Haber to Hugo Krüss, undated, circa January 1913, MPG, Dept. Va, Rep. 5, 1803.
[3] Fritz Haber to Richard Willstätter, 20 June 1911, MPG, Dept. Va, Rep. 5, 1185.
[4] Richard Willstätter, *From My Life: The Memoirs of Richard Willstätter*, trans. Lilli S. Hornig (New York: W. A. Benjamin, 1965), 377. Orig. *Aus meinem Leben*, ed. A. von Stoll (Weinheim, Germany: Verlag Chemie, 1958).
[5] Haber to Willstätter, 1911, MPG, Dept. Va, Rep. 5, 852.
[6] Haber to Willstätter , 26 July 1911, MPG, Dept. Va, Rep. 5, 852.
[7] Willstätter, *From My Life* (cit. note 4), 204.
[8] Ibid., 201–202.
[9] Fritz Haber to the minister of education (*Kultusminister*), 28 July 1914, MPG, Dept. Va, Rep. 5, 1669.
[10] Fritz Haber, memorandum, 3 Jan. 1915, MPG, Dept. Va, Rep. 5, 1669.
[11] Data in a letter from Lutz Haber to Johannes Jaenicke, 20 Jan. 1964, MPG, Dept. Va, Rep. 5, 173.
[12] Wilhelm Ostwald, *Lebenslinien: Eine Selbstbiographie* (Lifelines: An autobiography) (Berlin: Klasing, 1926), 287.
[13] Wilhelm Ostwald, *Abhandlungen und Vorträge, 1903* (Treatises and lectures, 1903) (Leipzig: Voith, 1904), 326.
[14] Aussiger Verein is the Austrian Union for Chemical and Metallurgical Production (located at Aussig, now Usti).
[15] Fritz Haber to the directors of BASF, 19 Nov. 1914, MPG, Dept. Va, Rep. 5, 2198.
[16] Emil Fischer, memorandum to Senior Executive Autschläger, Kriegschemikalien AG (War Chemicals Co.), 11 Oct. 1914, MPG, Dept. Va, Rep. 5.
[17] Fritz Haber to Rudolf von Valentini, 5 Dec. 1916, Geheimes Staatsarchiv Preussicher Kulturbesitz, Rep. 92, Nr. 6, sheet 11.
[18] Rudolf Hanslian, *Der chemische Krieg* (Chemical warfare), 3rd ed. (Berlin: Mittler & Sohn, 1937; 1st ed., Berlin, 1927); Harold Hartley, "Report on German Chemical Warfare," Public Record Office, WO 33/1079, copy in Stoltzenberg archive; M. Sartori, *Die Chemie der Kampfstoffe* (Chemistry of chemical weapons) (Brunswick: Vieweg, 1940); SIPRI (Stockholm International Peace Research Institute), *The Problem of Chemical and Biological Warfare*, vol. 1, *The Rise of CB Weapons* (New York: Humanities Press, 1971); J. Cockson and J. Nottingham, *A Survey of Chemical and Biological Warfare* (London/Sydney, 1968); S. Francke, ed., *Lehrbuch der Militärchemie* (Textbook of military chemistry), 2nd ed., vols. 1 and 2 (Berlin: Militärverlag der DDR, 1977); L. F. Haber, *The Poisonous Cloud: Chemical Warfare in the First World War* (Oxford: Clarendon Press, 1986).
[19] Carl Duisberg, "Die Reizstoffe für den Gaskampf und die Mittel zu einer Abwehr" (Irritants for gas warfare and means of defense), lecture ms., ca. 1917, Bibliothek Deutsches Museum, Munich, Germany, location no. 3476.
[20] Bauer also mentions this meeting. Max Bauer, "Denkschrift betreffend den Gaskampf und Gasschutz" (Memorandum concerning gas warfare and protection against gas), Bundesarchiv Koblenz, Bauer Nachlass, no. 35.
[21] Harold Hartley, "Report on German Chemical Warfare, Organisation and Policy, 1914–1918," Public Record Office, Kew, WO 33 (A 2715) 1072, pp. 4163-2 and -3.
[22] Bauer, "Denkschrift" (cit. note 20).

[23] Franz Richardt, report, MPG, Dept. Va, Rep. 5, 1494.

[24] Wilhelm H. Westphal, "Erinnerungen an Fritz Haber" (Recollections of Fritz Haber), MPG, Dept. Va, Rep. 5, 1512.

[25] Johannes Jaenicke, memorandum on a conversation with Otto Hahn in January 1955, MPG, Dept. Va, Rep. 5, 1453.

[26] See e.g. Hanslian, *Chemische Krieg*, 8–91; and Haber, *Poisonous Cloud*, 31–35 (both cit. note 18).

[27] Otto Lummitsch, "Meine Erinnerungen an Geheimrat Prof. Dr. Haber" (My recollections of Haber), MPG, Dept. Va, Rep. 5, 1480.

[28] Hanslian, *Chemische Krieg* (cit. note 18), 92.

[29] Ministry of War, Dept. W8, Oct. 1916, MPG, KWG, Dept. I, Rep. 1a, 36, General Administration, 1153.

[30] Fritz Haber to the minister of education, 31 Jan. 1916, MPG, Dept. Va, Rep. 5, 1671.

[31] Carl Duisberg, "Die Tätigkeit der chemischen Industrie während des Krieges" (Activities of the chemical industry during the war), Bibliothek Deutsches Museum, Munich, May 1916, location no. 3476.

[32] Fritz Haber to Carl Duisberg, Aug., Sept., and Oct. 1915, MPG, Dept. Va, Rep. 5, 856, 961, 962.

[33] Duisberg, "Chemischen Industrie" (cit. note 31).

[34] Hugo Stoltzenberg to Fritz Haber, 27 Dec. 1917, Stoltzenberg private archive.

[35] Hugo Stoltzenberg to Margarethe Stoltzenberg-Bergius, 6 Jan. 1918, Stoltzenberg private archive.

[36] Hugo Stoltzenberg, "Über die taktische Verwendung des Losts" (On the tactical use of mustard gas), handwritten memorandum, date unknown (probably early 1917), Stoltzenberg private archive.

[37] Ibid.

[38] L. Haber, *Poisonous Cloud* (cit. note 18), 192. "Beilstein" refers to the reference work *Beilsteins Handbuch der Organischen Chemie*.

[39] Hanslian, *Chemische Krieg* (cit. note 18), 32.

[40] Leopold Koppel to the minister of war, 4 July 1916, MPG, Dept. I, Rep. 1a, KWG, General Administration.

[41] Fritz Haber, memorandum, 18 Sept. 1917, MPG, Dept. Va, Rep. 5, 1616.

[42] Fritz Haber to the minister of education, 7 Oct. 1918, MPG, Dept. Va, Rep. 5, 1680.

[43] The Ministry of War to the Ministry of Education, 4 Nov. 1918, MPG, Dept. I, Rep. 1a, KWG, General Administration.

[44] Based on a description by Charlotte Haber in *Mein Leben* (My life) (Düsseldorf/Vienna: Econ, 1970), 140f.

[45] Quoted from James Brown Scott, ed., *The Hague Conventions and Declarations of 1899 and 1907* (New York/London: Oxford University Press, 1915), 116, 117.

[46] *Völkerrecht im Weltkrieg* (International law during the World War), 3rd Series in the Proceedings of the Subcommittee, vol. 4 (Berlin: Deutsche Verlagsgesellschaft für Politik und Geschichte, 1927).

[47] Fritz Haber, "Die Chemie im Kriege," in *Fünf Vorträge aus den Jahren 1920–1923* (Five lectures from the years 1920–1923) (Berlin: Verlag Julius Springer, 1924), 37.

[48] Scott, *Hague Conventions* (cit. note 45).

*Chapter 8*

# Haber's Research
# on
# Chemical Warfare after World War I

*The chlorine plants under construction in Gräfenhainichen, 1926.*

*Previous page: Building an oven for destroying chemical weapons in Breloh, 1922.*

I N November 1918, shortly after the cease-fire, the National Office for Economic Demobilization (Reichsamt für Wirtschaftliche Demobilmachung) was established, with General Koeth, whom Haber knew from his time in the Ministry of War, as director. Koeth asked Haber to take over the directorship of the office's chemistry section. Haber accepted and worked there for several months. One of the section's aims was to offer advice and help in transforming the chemical industry to suit a peacetime rather than a wartime economy. The process essentially consisted of repealing or relaxing war directives, such as confiscatory measures, rationing, and limitations on import and export, and replacing them with more appropriate directives. Although industry wished to be freed of all obligations as quickly and as completely as possible, its various branches were interdependent. The newly created office therefore had to consider the type and extent of the measures to be taken and the rate of implementation; they then had to examine and discuss these issues with other authorities (e.g., the Ministries of Finance, Labor, and Transportation) and to negotiate with all parties involved. Experience in social conditions, economics, and politics was required more than chemical or scientific knowledge, especially for issues concerning personnel and workers.

In a letter to Carl Duisberg, Haber commented on these goals, stating that it was necessary to give

> official support to the newly re-emerging peacetime industry as if it were a sick person. . . . How should one create goods, maintain the productivity of the country, and employ workers, if one blocks the path of industry? And creating goods [Werte], employing workers, establishing trust again, these are the tasks in the period of demobilization. . . . I myself am carrying out this work, thinking to place it, in compact form, in the hands of the National

Economics Office in February or March. I expect that the Demobilization Office will have been dissolved by then.[1]

His main task was to assist by maintaining an overview of developments, bearing in mind the system of war-economy regulations, and easing the practical transformation as much as possible.

For a while no one anticipated that hunger and political confusion would continue for a longer period, but the blockade maintained by the Allies brought another hungry winter in 1918–19. Children, in particular, died of tuberculosis and influenza, and the system for supplying essentials to the population was frequently on the verge of breakdown. Thus the office in which Haber worked could not be disbanded because it had to solve a tremendous number of problems. Rationing had to be maintained, not only for food and general supplies for the population, but also for many goods that were essential to industry.

The politically uncertain circumstances had a negative effect on production and distribution of goods. The battles between left-wing forces, the reactionary parties, and the troops of the central government, especially in Saxony, Bavaria, Hamburg, and Berlin, often brought the whole supply system to a standstill. In the west the Rhineland, and later the Ruhr area, were occupied by Allied troops. Haber mentions in his letter to Duisberg that he feared that this occupation would draw a line of division right through Germany and would hinder economic exchange, although such exchange was guaranteed by the terms of the cease-fire. He also mentions the concern in Berlin as to whether the Westphalian industry

> has the necessary idealism to hold firmly to the interests of the nation against those movements that promise commercial advantages on seceding from Prussia and forming a new Federation of Rhineland states. An unconditional avowal of loyalty to the nation in the sense of maintaining national unity even at the risk of not doing so well in business [is paramount].[2]

By February 1919 Haber was able to report to Duisberg that he had resigned from his position at the office and had returned to his professional life. He was tired of the work and no doubt much relieved by this resignation, as can be deduced from his comments to Duisberg. He felt that economic life was daily running into new difficulties whose roots were lack of coal, shortage of transportation, labor problems, and lack of raw materials. He continues in his vivid way:

The activity of the government has consisted mainly of pulling at the corners of a blanket that is much too short, sometimes to the right, sometimes to the left, in order to protect a dozen impatient, fidgeting children under it from the worst cold and the worst rowdiness. When that didn't work at all, they cut up the sheets of pictures that are ordinarily called banknotes and that fortunately are held by the majority to be coupons for human happiness.[3]

Haber felt the need once again to concentrate on directing his institute. He recognized that this was in fact his real task, and he wanted to realize the many ideas for reorganization and transformation he had developed during the war.

Nevertheless he did not hesitate to offer his opinion and advice on issues of national importance. In particular, during the 1920s, he supported military leaders in their efforts to keep and develop new knowledge of chemical warfare.

Haber's position is quite understandable. Even during the war he had argued that research on and development of chemical warfare should continue in peacetime. Article 171 in the Treaty of Versailles completely prohibited the use of suffocating, poisonous, and other gases and all similar liquids, materials, and devices as well as their manufacture and importation. This prohibition also covered material used to manufacture chemical weapons and the storage and use of such materials or devices. Haber obviously never publicly supported breaking this prohibition, but he expressed his opinion quite clearly in a lecture, "Chemistry in War," that he gave to officers of the German Ministry of Defense (Reichswehrministerium) on 11 November 1920.[4]

After rejecting the general opinion that chemical warfare was especially inhumane, he added that "gas weapons are definitely no more inhumane than flying bits of metal." He used this argument to conclude that "In the face of this it would not be easy to reach an (international) prohibition of gas warfare on an objective basis." And he mentioned efforts in other countries to continue developing chemical weapons further. He cautioned the officers that it would be "advisable to be as well informed as possible about the military technological characteristics of gas weapons and about the prerequisites for their production."[5]

Such advice could mean only one thing. The officers should participate in the development of chemical weapons, for how could an army learn about the characteristics of chemical weapons if it did not itself carry out experiments? And how could it be well informed about the production of chemical weapons if the officers only read literature and did not test the procedures practically?

In the first years after the war the pressure from the victorious powers and the control on the part of the Allied commissions were so strong and the new republic was so unstable that it could hardly follow advice of this kind. It could only protect what it already had from the confiscation and destructions ordered.

A scenario had to be developed in which they feigned cooperation with the Allied controllers on the one hand but were still able to maintain and even to extend their knowledge of chemical warfare on the other. Haber thus appeared very obliging to the representatives of the Interallied Control Commission and to the members of the Committee on Armament. He welcomed the head of this committee, the French general E. Vinet, and took him around the chemical warfare plants that had been set up in the vicinity of Berlin during the war.

Various documents report on the activities of this commission, including those of Sir Harold Hartley, who had especially close contact with Haber. Hartley taught physical chemistry at Oxford before the war, rose to the rank of general, and finally became controller of the British Chemical Warfare Department.[6] In February 1919 he led the British section of an Interallied committee that visited the occupied German territory. He was impressed by German organization in the field of chemical warfare. Vinet's and Hartley's reports did not, however, satisfy the British authorities, and Hartley was ordered to undertake further investigations, especially of how to proceed with demolition of the production plants for war gases. On this inspection journey, which took place in June 1921, he visited Berlin, Breloh, Munich, and Stuttgart. He held lengthy discussions with Haber (Hartley spoke excellent German) and with Haber's former assistants in the field of gas warfare—Fritz Epstein, Herbert Freundlich, Otto Hahn, and Friedrich Kerschbaum. He also met with Richard Willstätter in Munich, with Erich Regener in Stuttgart, and finally with Duisberg and Walther Nernst.

This inquiry did not occur until almost three years after the end of the war, owing to the strategy of the Ministry of Defense, which either did not answer inquiries at all or did so only after a long delay. Hartley reports that during his visit Haber received him with the words, "Why didn't you come sooner? I wanted to discuss all our documents with you, but there was a very unfortunate fire and they were all destroyed."[7] Fritz Haber's son Lutz finds this story dubious, but it could very well be close to the truth. Haber, together with the German army, had not been idle in the years after the war. It was quite clear to all interested parties that Haber's institute had continued to work in the field of chemical weapons after the war. Decisions had to be made about the fate of the supplies of chemical weapons and the production and filling plants. Moreover, the cease-fire in 1918 did not end the war for either side. The Allies continually threatened to cross the Rhine if the German government did not accept their conditions for peace. New military engagements could still have occurred, in which case the large arsenal of finished and half-finished gas weapons meant a lot to the German military leadership.[8]

In March 1920 various firms approached the National Trust Company (Reichstreuhandgesellschaft), which had jurisdiction, and demanded the return of their rail tanker cars, which still stood in Breloh filled with gas cylinders and materiel. The question was, who could empty the tank cars and clean them so that they could be used for peaceful industrial purposes? The chemicals also had to be either stored elsewhere or destroyed. So the National Trust Company turned to Haber, and he in turn thought of Hugo Stoltzenberg, who had helped build up the mustard gas works in Breloh.

A meeting attended by Stoltzenberg, Hugo Stinnes, and representatives of the Metallgesellschaft (Metal Company) Frankfurt and the National Trust Company, among others, was held that same month in the administration building of the Riedel Company in Berlin. After long hesitation and much persuasion from Haber, Stoltzenberg took on the assignment of managing this project and started work in Breloh in 1920. Under the most difficult conditions, most of the tanker cars could be emptied and cleaned. Many of the chemicals were destroyed by burning, while others were converted to substances for peacetime use.

Haber followed this work with great interest; as Johannes Jaenicke reported later, Stoltzenberg had free access to Haber.[9] Out of this relationship arose a closer cooperation between the Ministry of Defense, Haber, and Stoltzenberg. The first measures they took together were directed at preserving the knowledge and, when possible, the processes and the materials. They were able to preserve the materials only if these could be converted safely for peacetime production, for the work in Breloh was under the strict supervision of the Interallied Control Commission.

While this work was being carried out in Breloh, Haber repeatedly received inquiries from other countries about plant construction and delivery of chemical weapons. These he passed on to Stoltzenberg. Thus delegations from Finland and Sweden visited Stoltzenberg in Munster, near Breloh, but these contacts did not lead to further negotiations. However, in the spring of 1921, "dealings were being quietly initiated concerning the building of a chemical weapons factory for the Spanish state."[10]

Haber also informed the German army, which was interested in this contact. After careful preliminary negotiations Stoltzenberg traveled to Spain in November 1921, but his discussions with leading authorities there did not lead to closure. In January 1922 a commission of Spanish officers visited various places in Germany and met with Stoltzenberg in Munster. A contractual agreement was finally reached.

Thus the help of Haber and the military allowed Germany both to hold on to its chemical warfare knowledge and to gain new expertise. The new knowledge resulted in the improvement of a one-step process for the manufacture of mustard gas developed toward the end of the war in Haber's institute (see Chapter 7). Stoltzenberg had already taken up work on this process again in a small laboratory in Munster; he continued that work in Maranosa, near Madrid, and adapted it as the basis for the manufacturing process there.

Further experience especially with mustard gas was gathered from Spanish battles in North Africa. There, the leader of the Riff Kabyles, Mohammed ben Abd el-Krim el-Khatabi, had defeated the Spanish severely on a number of occasions. The ties between the Spanish, Haber, the Army Ordnance Department (Heereswaffenamt), and Stoltzenberg grew increasingly strong,[11] and the Germans made various deliveries to Spain during 1922 and 1923 from their reserves of chemical weapons. A plant for converting thiodiglycol (Oxol) to mustard gas was finally built in Melilla, in Spanish Morocco. The Oxol was at first delivered from available reserves, but later it was delivered from a plant that Stoltzenberg had set up in his new factory in Hamburg to the German army as well as to Spain.[12] Up to the end of 1922 and into early 1923 the army continued to remain in the background, although Haber continually informed them about Stoltzenberg's activities.

As Stoltzenberg developed various tactics for defeating the Riff Kabyles and presented his recommendations to the highest authorities—including Spain's king, Alfonso XIII, and its dictatorial prime minister, Primo de Rivera—General Max Bauer, who had used all his influence in support of gas warfare, especially with Generals Erich von Falkenhayn (chief of general staff during the war) and Erich Ludendorff, also put in an appearance in Madrid. Considerable experience was gained not only in developing and manufacturing the chemicals but also in deploying them. One focus was delivery by air—not only bombing with gas weapons but also spraying chemicals by a procedure already tested with practice material in Germany by Stoltzenberg and the aircraft manufacturer Junkers.

Stoltzenberg's connections with the Spaniards lasted into the 1930s. Once the revolt in North Africa was subdued, work focused on building up and equipping the plant near Madrid. But in the early 1920s a quite different project dominated the activity of the German army and certain chemical companies—building production plants for the prohibited armaments and testing prohibited weapons systems in the Soviet Union. Here, too, Fritz Haber played an essential role.

In April 1922 representatives of the Soviet Union took part for the first time in a trade and industry conference arranged in Genoa, Italy. The Allies, mainly England, intended that the Soviet Union should present reparation claims against Germany. But the Soviets were not so inclined, especially since the French and the English had previously opposed the new Communist regime in Russia. Instead they negotiated with the German chancellor, Josef Wirth, and with Walther Rathenau, then foreign minister, both of whom were representing Germany at the Genoa conference. Together the Soviet Union and Germany signed the Rapallo treaty, in which both sides renounced any claims for war compensation and agreed to institute diplomatic relations and preferential trade agreements. The treaty also contained secret clauses on cooperation on military technology.

In January 1923 a Soviet commission appeared in Berlin to place a series of large orders for armament material and to request financial assistance from Germany.[13] The Germans agreed to look into the possibility of providing assistance, but they also requested support, and so a further meeting was scheduled in Moscow. Shortly after the Berlin meeting, the head of the Army Ordnance Department, Otto Hasse, approached Haber to ask whether facilities for chemical weapons production could be set up in Russia, and who could handle the project. Haber reminded Hasse of Stoltzenberg, then already working in Spain.[14]

In March, Vladimir N. Ipatieff (1867–1952) arrived in Berlin.[15] A physical chemist who had worked on explosives during the war, he was later appointed head of the Soviet Chemical Committee of Russia's Chief Artillery Commission and played a leading role in chemical warfare. After the war he remained as an adviser on industrial chemistry to the Soviet government. Later he emigrated to the United States and worked on high-pressure processes in petroleum chemistry.[16]

Ipatieff had been officially invited to give a lecture to the German Chemical Society, whose president at that time was Fritz Haber. Haber invited Ipatieff to visit him and discussed with him whether production facilities for chemical weapons could be established in Russia. In his 1946 autobiography Ipatieff reports that Haber suggested Stoltzenberg, whom Ipatieff did not know, as the man to build the plant. Ipatieff added that without Stoltzenberg, chemical weapons would never have been manufactured in the Soviet Union.[17]

After Haber had used his influence with both General Hasse and Ipatieff on behalf of Stoltzenberg, Stoltzenberg traveled to the Soviet Union with a group of experts. The visit lasted from the end of April to mid-May 1923. Both General Wolfgang Mentzel and Stoltzenberg prepared reports on this trip.[18]

Stoltzenberg's first meetings with Ipatieff were made on this visit to Petrograd. They talked about their war experiences and explored ways to use existing supplies of chemical weapons. Further negotiations in Moscow led to the first draft of a contract on constructing a gas factory. On special instruction from Leon Trotsky and Mikhail I. Kalinin, the gas weapons manufactured here were to be supplied to the German army on the same conditions as to the Red Army.[19]

After viewing possible sites, Samara (today Kuybyshev) on the Volga was chosen for a large plant for manufacturing various chemicals used in chemical warfare, and the building began immediately. The main facility was a mustard gas plant, but the site also contained a phosgene plant, a reconstructed plant to manufacture sulfuric acid, and a plant to produce chlorine by electrolysis. The plants were brought into operation one by one beginning in early 1926.

It became clear that it would take quite some time before building was complete in Russia. The German army therefore decided to begin setting up plants to produce chemical weapons in Germany and to fill shells as well. The factories of BASF, Bayer, and Hoechst, which had been involved with gas weapons manufacture during World War I, could not be used because they were situated in zones still occupied by the Allies. Besides, the managements of these companies, which had combined in a cartel then called IG (Interessengemeinschaft) Farben (the predecessor of IG Farben AG), were not prepared to sacrifice their exports for this sort of surreptitious production.

In January 1924 a meeting of the general staff was held to plan the building of a mustard gas factory with a filling station as well as a "green cross" filling station (for phosgene, diphosgene, and organoarsenic compounds). Participants included the then head of the Army Ordnance Department, Major General Wurtzbacher, Major General Haack, Captain (later Field Marshal) Albert Kesselring, and Lieutenant Colonel (later General) Joachim Stülpnagel.[20] The mustard gas factory was to be set up in a district that would not be exposed to enemy air attacks to the same extent as the current industrial plants in western Germany. In order to realize these plans, the army again applied to Haber, who once more turned to Stoltzenberg.[21] After lengthy consideration the site for this factory was also chosen—the former Barbara mine at Gräfenhainichen, between Wittenberg and Bitterfeld. This location in central Germany was chosen for its distance from the area of influence of the Allies, who still occupied the industrial areas along the Ruhr. Here in Gräfenhainichen two plants—a chlorine electrolysis plant and a chlorine alkali plant—were to be erected openly as well as various disguised "oil and refinery plants," which would in reality produce mustard gas by converting Oxol, and two large "storage areas," which would really be filling stations for shells of various types. The relevant "oil contract" was signed in 1924, and building began immediately thereafter.

Over the years 1924 and 1925, however, the political climate began to change. After autumn 1923 Germany's foreign policy lay in the hands of Gustav Stresemann. From the beginning his main theme was the establishment of better relations with the Western powers while protecting Germany's independence and interests. In 1925 Germany's relations with these powers were put on a new footing at the Locarno conference. With the Berlin treaty of 1926, the good relations with Russia that had existed since the Rapallo treaty were solidified. However, the armaments projects that Germany and the Soviet Union had agreed on no longer fitted this new situation.

The army now had to act much more carefully, and the budget planned for further secret military armaments had to be cut back considerably. Both Stoltzenberg and Junkers, having invested heavily in factories in the Soviet Union and central Germany, fell into considerable financial difficulty. In addition, IG Farben now feared competition from Stoltzenberg, since the plants in Gräfenhainichen could also be used for other products. Stoltzenberg went bankrupt, lost his plants in Hamburg, and could only rebuild his company on a much smaller scale through his further activities in Spain and in other countries.

After 1926 Haber withdrew from active participation in the secret production of chemical armaments. This did not mean, however, that he was no longer informed of the further activities of the Ministry of Defense and the Army Ordnance Department. True, in June 1929, Haber complained to the minister of defense that he no longer had any connection with the army, but a memorandum was issued that emphasized that he did indeed have contact with the staff of the Ordnance Department, and appended a list of various posts in this authority.[22] Haber probably wanted even more connections because he was not being continuously informed about the work on "Gasschutzfragen" (gas-protection issues) carried out by various university professors. A week later the Ordnance Department decided that Haber should take part in discussions and experiments on protecting the population, in experiments on new charges for the projectiles (explosives, fog-producing substances, and flammable materials) and in all test firing, among other things.[23] Two weeks later a Lieutenant Colonel Sorsche directed that "according to the suggestion [of the Army Ordnance Department], Professor Haber is in future to be involved as much as possible also in issues related to chemical weapons."[24] Haber's actual participation in these undertakings is not documented.

The university professors who were dealing with protective measures against gas had by 1925 been organized to form a council of scientific workers for the Army Ordnance Department. This council discussed matters concerned with production and testing of chemical weapons, and assignments were decided at regular meetings and their results discussed. Members of this council included two employees of the National Health Authority (Reichsgesundheitsamt), surnamed Beck and Phyl; Ferdinand Flury, who had first worked with Haber and later worked in Würzburg; Albrecht Hase and Max Trenel, representatives of the National Biological Institute who were closely connected with Haber; and Arthur Hantzsch of Leipzig, Heinrich Wieland of Munich, Wilhelm Steinkopf of Dresden, Karl A. Hofmann, and Josef Wirth from the Berlin Institute of Technology, and, as the representative of industry, a Dr. Engelhard from the Auer Company.[25] In addition, Gerhard Jander (whom the army wanted to take over Haber's institute in 1933) attended these meetings from 1929 on. The Army Ordnance Department was represented at these meetings by various high officers and officials under the direction of the head of the department, General Ludwig.

Thus the question posed at the beginning of this chapter on whether Haber participated in the secret preparation of chemical weapons from 1919 to 1933 is answered in the affirmative. From 1919 to 1926 he actively, and then later passively, participated in these secret actions, and he was always informed about the latest events. For him chemical weapons and chemical warfare were no more inhumane methods of warfare than other modern weapons. His opinion was supported by, among others, the German Red Cross at a conference in January 1928 on the protection of the civilian population against chemical warfare, where it was stated that "chemical weapons bring no more danger than incendiary or high-explosive bombs that are thrown from airplanes." However, the Red Cross also stated in 1928 that "the greatest danger lies in a combined attack in which incendiary and high-explosive bombs can render ineffective every conceivable protective measure against chemical weapons."[26]

## Endnotes

[1] Fritz Haber to Carl Duisberg, 30 Nov. 1918, MPG, Dept. Va, Rep. 5, 859.

[2] Ibid.

[3] Haber to Duisberg, 6 Feb. 1919, MPG, Dept. Va, Rep. 5, 860.

[4] See Fritz Haber, "Die Chemie im Kriege," *Fünf Vorträge aus den Jahren 1920–1923* (Five lectures from the years 1920–1923) (Berlin: Verlag Julius Springer, 1924), 35. *Reichswehrministerium* was the term used over 1919–1935.

[5] Ibid.

[6] See, e.g., the papers of Harold Hartley, partly in MPG, Dept. Va, Rep. 5; or E. Vinet, "Les gaz de combat," 12 Oct. 1922, Public Record Office, Kew, WO 188/176.

[7] Harold Hartley, report of a speech at the Royal Society Club Dinner, 14 Nov. 1968, *Notes and Records of the Royal Society of London* 24:1 (June 1969), 112.

[8] Troop Department No. 512/1, 19A 10 II Aug., in re the report of the Troop Department Director to the minister of war on 22 Jan. 1919, Bundesarchiv, Militärarchiv, Freiburg, RH 12-4-v.38.

[9] Johannes Jaenicke to Lutz Haber, 13 July 1960, MPG, Dept. Va, Rep. 5, 170.

[10] Margarethe Stoltzenberg-Bergius, "Wie wir wurden: Eine kurze Entwicklungsgeschichte unseres Unternehmens" (How we began: A short history of the development of our company), part I, handwritten, Stoltzenberg private archive.

[11] See R. Kunze and R.-D. Müller, *Giftgas gegen Abd el Krim: Deutschland, Spanien, und der Gaskrieg in Spanisch-Marokko 1922–1927* (Poisonous gas against Abd el-Krim: Germany, Spain, and gas warfare in Spanish Morocco, 1922–1927), Militärgeschichtliches Forschungsamt (Freiburg: Rombach, 1990).

[12] Ibid.; and Hugo Stoltzenberg diary entries (1922–1924), Stoltzenberg private archive.

[13] Lieutenant Colonel Wolfgang Mentzel (chief of the General Staff), "Report on the trips to Russia," Mentzel Nachlass, Bundesarchiv, Militärarchiv, Freiburg.

[14] Hugo Stoltzenberg, "Visit and Discussion with F. Haber and Flury," memorandum, Jan. 1923, Stoltzenberg private archive.

[15] Lutz Haber, *The Poisonous Cloud: Chemical Warfare in World War I* (Oxford: Clarendon Press, 1986), especially p. 143.

[16] V. N. Ipatieff, *The Life of a Chemist: Memoirs of Vladimir Ipatieff,* ed. X. J. Eudin, H. D. Fisher, and H. H. Fisher (Stanford: Stanford University Press; London: Geoffrey Cumberledge; Oxford: Oxford University Press, 1946). See also Stoltzenberg, "Visit and Discussion" (cit. note 14), 418.

[17] Ipatieff, *Life of a Chemist.*

[18] Mentzel, "Report" (cit. note 13); and Hugo Stoltzenberg, diary entries (Oct. 1922 to May 1923), Stoltzenberg private archive.

[19] Mentzel, "Report" (cit. note 13), 78.

[20] Memorandum on a meeting of the General Staff, 11 Jan. 1924, Bundesarchiv, Militärarchiv, Freiburg, RH-1, sheet 25.

[21] Kunze and Müller, *Giftgas gegen Abd el Krim* (cit. note 11), 118.

[22] Memorandum in the Ministry of Defense (Reichswehrministerium), 3 June 1927; and Dept. Wa B 1 of the Army Ordnance Department, letter to Wa St (Walfenamt Stab: Ordnance Department Headquarters), 18 June 1929; both former Militärarchiv, Nationale Volksarmee, Potsdam.

[23] Ministry of Defense, Testing Office, to Headquarters of the Army Ordnance Department, 25 June 1929, former Militärarchiv, Nationale Volksarmee, Potsdam.

[24] Lieutenant Colonel Sorsche, letter to various posts in the Army Ordnance Department, 25 July 1919, former Militärarchiv, Nationale Volksarmee, Potsdam.

[25] See protocols of various meetings under RH 1 RH 2, Bundesarchiv, Militärarchiv, Freiburg. See also O. Groehler, *Der lautlose Tod* (The silent death) (Reinbeck: Rohwolt, 1989; 1st ed., Berlin, 1978), 78–82.

[26] Report by the German Red Cross to the XIIIth International Red Cross Conference, The Hague, 1928, Bundesarchiv, Militärarchiv, Freiburg, RH 12-4.

*Chapter 9*

# Family
# and
# Friends

*Fritz Haber and Charlotte Nathan after their marriage on 25 October 1917, together with Hermann, Haber's son from his first marriage (in front of the Kaiser Wilhelm Memorial Church).*

*Previous page: Fritz Haber and Richard Willstätter in Klosters, Switzerland, in 1930.*

A S A SCIENTIST, BUT ALSO THROUGH HIS WORK IN PUBLIC LIFE, FRITZ
Haber exercised considerable influence on many who were politically prominent both in his own lifetime and in later decades. Given his own prominence, it is pertinent to ask in turn what influence his origins, family, and
circle of friends and acquaintances had on his motives and actions. Thus
even if it is not always easy for the biographer to answer that question, Haber's
private life—his purely personal affairs—must be examined.

Fritz Haber's family background has already been described. Various
friends and acquaintances, insofar as they relate to his personal career—
especially in the period in Karlsruhe—have also been introduced. To this
era belongs Fritz's friendship and marriage with Clara Immerwahr. The
Immerwahr family, Clara's training as a teacher, and her receipt of a doctorate under Richard Abegg, a close friend of Haber's, were discussed in Chapter 2. Now a closer look at the period of Haber's marriage to Clara makes a
fitting introduction to the more personal side of his later life.

## Marriage with Clara Immerwahr

Fritz Haber and Clara Immerwahr were married in August 1901. Their son
Hermann was born on 1 June 1902. The first years of the marriage were
harmonious. Although in this period the inevitable minor differences of
opinion occurred, all accounts from this time describe a happy couple. Clara
often appeared at seminars in the institute and at the events of the Chemical Society, especially early in their marriage. During the first two years she
showed a lively interest in her husband's work. She wrote to Abegg that her
husband was working on a textbook on thermodynamics, that he was interested in the advancement of a colleague of his friend Georg Bredig, that

Haber formulated his opinion on the appointment of professors, and that she gave lectures on the subject of "Chemistry and Physics in the Household."[1]

This harmonious relationship slowly began to change soon after their son's birth. Clara cared lovingly for her son and spent a lot of time on household work. Many friends and guests who were invited to the Habers' house recalled that she was a meticulous housewife and that her cooking was excellent. But she became more and more a "housewife and mother." She was concerned with every detail in the household, seeing as large problems little things that meant nothing to her husband. A relative's description of the Haber home from this time reports: "Haber often was tense when he came home from the institute. . . . When he was very down and the first thing that his wife did was to tell him about her household problems and her concern about 'Mandel' [Hermann], he sometimes became impatient."[2] Clara's problems typically were worn-out linen, Hermann's sneezing attacks, and the need to entertain guests who turned up suddenly. She wanted to do everything perfectly, which was not always possible when Haber arrived home with unexpected colleagues or guests.

One of Clara's letters to Richard Abegg reveals both her view of life and the reasons for the terrible end of the marriage. She wrote in April 1909:

> What Fritz has gained in these eight years [of their marriage], that—and even more—I have lost, and what is left of me fills me with the deepest dissatisfaction. It was always my view of life that it was only worth living if one developed all one's abilities to reach the heights and experienced as much as possible of what a human life can offer. It was for that reason as well as on impulse I eventually decided on marriage, for otherwise a new page [*Seite*] arising in the book of my life and a chord [*Saite*] of my soul would stay prostrate and barren. But the uplift that [marriage] gave me lasted only a very short time, and even if I must blame some part of the inadequacies on circumstances and on the special disposition of my temperament, still the major part is the oppressive demands Fritz for his part makes in the house and on the marriage, beside which any temperament that does not push even more inconsiderately for its own interests will simply be destroyed. And that is the case with me. And I ask myself whether a superior intelligence really is enough to make one person more valuable than another, and whether a great deal of me that is going to the devil because it didn't get to the right man is really not more valuable than the most important theory in the study of electrons? . . . Everyone should be allowed to go his own way, but in my opinion even a

genius is justified in permitting himself specially cultivated "crotchets" and a sovereign contempt for every rule of normal behavior—even the most every-day ones—only if he is alone on a desert island.[3]

These lines allow a glance into the heart of a woman in despair for herself and for her marriage. Because of her very intelligence, love of truth, and perfectionism, she broke herself on the practical aspects of life at the side of a man who lived for his profession and subordinated all else to it. And the very time of splendor that Fritz Haber experienced in Karlsruhe soon became the time in which the soul of his wife, Clara, darkened. After her death by suicide in 1915, much was spoken and written by relatives and others on whether Clara tended toward depression. Some thought this trait ran in the family because other family members had committed suicide, such as her sister Lotte, married to Fritz Meffert. But there is no need to go so far to find an explanation for her act.

Various relatives and friends described how Clara gradually became "a gray mouse, inconspicuous and nice."

> [She] dressed in rough woolen clothes and always had an apron on. . . . She had no feeling for what would please a man. . . . The child, Hermann, was cared for and pampered in such a way that we made jokes about it. . . . When Fritz Haber was asked one evening where she was after a trip on a steamer on which rain had wet them through, he answered, "She is at home worrying about which relative might have contracted what sickness and how." She was excessively anxious.[4]

When World War I started, the couple became even more estranged. Fritz was hardly ever at home and traveled frequently, and when he was in Berlin, he came home late and left early in the morning for the institute or for meetings. The marriage was apparently destroyed. A friend of Clara's said, "The attrition and wracking of nerves and the difficulties between the couple were not of the minor sort; they were fundamental."[5]

In March and April 1915 Fritz Haber was occupied night and day with preparations for the chlorine gas attack at Ypres. Only rarely did he come to Dahlem for a few days. The attack took place on 22 April, and further actions took place in the following days. Haber traveled briefly to Berlin but had already received orders to travel to the eastern front in early May to prepare gas attacks there as well. On 1 May a reception was held at Haber's villa. It is not known who attended. It has been claimed that Charlotte

Nathan—then a secretary at the German Society of 1914 (Deutsche Gesell-schaft von 1914), which Haber frequented, and later Haber's second wife—was at this social evening in the Haber house, but it cannot be proved.[6] Charlotte describes her first meeting with Haber in her memoirs but does not give a date.[7] It is possible that on this evening, in addition to the other disagreements, Clara expressed her jealousy dramatically, as has been claimed, but there is no evidence. We do not know whether Haber's involvement in gas warfare also came up and whether Clara expressed her despair over it. It has been claimed that she "gave him an ultimatum to break off this activity or else she would commit suicide."[8] Another opinion is that there were "various more or less pathetic interpretations of the suicide, for example, she had begged him to abandon the field of gas warfare. This interpretation is not true."[9]

Clara Haber shot herself during the night of 1 May. She apparently first made a test shot with her husband's army revolver, then shot herself in the heart.[10] She did not die immediately. Her son, Hermann, who heard the shots in the early dawn, found his mother and informed Fritz. There are reports that she survived for another twenty minutes and possibly for several hours.[11]

Before her death Clara Haber wrote several farewell letters, which have not survived. Her suicide was therefore not an unplanned emotional reaction. And here lies the great tragedy, that a person with such a high intelligence, one with such concern for husband and child and one who offered great support for people in need, could no longer help herself. The only solution she saw was ending her life.

A few days later Fritz Haber traveled to the eastern front, as planned. Was his leaving heartless, or was it possibly a flight from the terrible event? It is known that he later felt great guilt about Clara, which he tried to relieve through love and affection for their son, unfortunately not always to the son's advantage.

Clara was buried in the cemetery at Dahlem. Later Fritz decided that she should rest beside him after his death. Her earthly remains were transferred to the Basel cemetery in 1934, and there the two of them, Fritz and Clara Haber, now lie side by side in one grave.

### Fritz Haber and His Son Hermann

As noted, Hermann was born on 1 June 1902. He was well cared for by his mother while he was growing up in western Karlsruhe on Moltkestrasse.

*Hermann Haber in the 1920s.*

There are few reports of his early childhood. Hermann went to primary school in Karlsruhe, and in 1911, when he was nine years old, his parents moved to Berlin-Dahlem. He attended school in Berlin until 1920. He was thirteen years old when the war broke out. As his father's house was near the Kaiser Wilhelm Institute, he observed and experienced what went on there in wartime. Knowing of the many Quonset huts built to house war-related research, especially that on chemical weapons, must have affected his worldview. Certainly father and son saw little of each other during this period. Fritz, who had already become a famous man in Karlsruhe, was someone to be respected and imitated. Clara, who cared lovingly for her son, did not have an easy time with him, particularly in his adolescent years.

Clara's suicide was a terrible experience for Hermann, who heard the shots and found her covered in blood. How does such an event influence a fourteen-year-old, at a critical time in his development?

Hermann remained with his father in the large house next to the institute. His aunts—Else Freyhahn, his father's half sister, and Lotte Meffert, his mother's sister—looked after him. But Hermann was soon to learn about his future stepmother, whom Fritz had been meeting when he was in Berlin. Hermann was certainly one reason why Fritz hesitated to marry again so soon after Clara's death. Fritz was drawn to Charlotte Nathan, who was a strong woman and whom he passionately loved, but he could not make the decision to marry because of Hermann. Charlotte reports that Hermann apparently posed the moral question to his father while they were together on a journey to Freudenstadt in the Black Forest, asking him why he had not yet married his sweetheart.[12] This was the key that opened the way to the official marriage. The wedding took place on 25 October 1917 in Berlin. After a short honeymoon Charlotte moved into the official villa in Dahlem. Charlotte's life with Fritz Haber is described later in this chapter, while here its impact on Hermann is considered.

Hermann lived in his father's house until he was twenty-three. When Fritz was in Berlin, he always tried to make time for his son even though his emotional attachment to his wife influenced their relationship. From the beginning, relations between Hermann and his stepmother were tense.

In her autobiography Charlotte wrote about her husband's son: "Hermann had much of his father's acumen but still more of the pathological disposition of his unhappy mother. I never saw the boy laughing heartily or simply enjoying himself out in the open." As for Charlotte's relationship with Hermann, which affected the attachment between her and Fritz, she wrote:

> My husband and I had our first disagreement about him after only two months of marriage. And our last disagreement was also about Hermann. Between them lay countless frictions. This wore down the bond of our marriage to the point that it finally tore. . . . All my efforts to reach a mutual understanding with Hermann were unsuccessful. Certainly it was partly due to me. I could not give him enough goodness and love. Jealousy over the father and the husband gnawed at both of us.[13]

From these lines one can discern that Fritz Haber often took Hermann's side against his wife. He did this even in situations where agreement between the parents about their behavior toward Hermann would have been more to the son's advantage, including their handling of Hermann's penchant for alcohol, which later became acute at critical points in his life. Charlotte Haber went so far as to call the "Fritz–Hermann relationship" a "mental adultery."[14]

After graduating from high school in 1920, Hermann wanted to study law. But Fritz insisted on his studying chemistry, and the son gave in to the father's wishes. He attended the University of Freiburg in Breisgau in southern Germany and then the University of Berlin, and he obtained his doctorate in the summer of 1925 with a thesis on colloid chemistry supervised by Herbert Freundlich. In the same year he went to work at the Aussiger Verein (see page 34, note 5). The company's general director was Max Mayer, Fritz's friend and his financial adviser. In 1920 Fritz Haber and Max Mayer had jointly purchased the Witzmann estate in the Black Forest, and in subsequent years the families often met at this "desolate farm," as Charlotte Haber called it.

In the mid-1920s Hermann met his future wife, Margarethe Stern, daughter of Richard Stern, one of Fritz's old friends from Breslau. Her brother Rudolf, a doctor who later often gave Fritz medical advice, had brought Margarethe to Dahlem, where she took a job as secretary in the institute, since finances had forced her to give up her studies. Here she got to know Hermann. While Fritz Haber and his wife were on a trip around the world, a genuine romance developed between Hermann and Margarethe, and they soon decided to marry. Neither Hermann's father nor Margarethe's brother was enthusiastic. For Fritz Haber his son's marriage came too early. He had just planned a stay in America for Hermann and at first did not agree to the engagement. Rudolf Stern knew both of Hermann's tendency to drink and also of his sister's tendency toward depression. But finally both men abandoned their resistance. In January 1926 Hermann Haber married Margarethe Stern. It was a relief to the young couple that Fritz soon developed a warm attachment to his daughter-in-law.

After a short honeymoon in the Silesian mountains, the couple traveled to the United States. There Hermann worked in various posts, using his father's connections. He first joined a plant producing zinc at the American Zinc and Chemical Company in Pennsylvania. But at the end of 1926 Hermann went to Washington, D.C., where he worked with a patent attorney. Here he could finally follow his leanings toward law. Fritz also began to question his earlier decision to have his son study chemistry, and he wrote to

Hermann shortly before the move to the patent attorney's office. "I have long held to the thought that your education would make the field of chemistry especially fruitful for you. Now I have begun to waver in this belief."[15] The reason for this change was the refusal of his former assistant, Friedrich Kerschbaum, to employ his son as a chemist.

In 1927 Fritz tried to find a position for his son in Paris. In the spring Hermann joined the International Chamber of Commerce there, but the style of Prussian officialdom that ruled in his department was not to his liking, especially after the quite different lifestyle he had experienced in America. He soon changed jobs and took on several assignments as a patent clerk, in production, and on the staff of a company that manufactured charcoal, a branch of Fabriques des Produits Chimiques de Thann et de Mulhouse. He soon left, although he later went back. So Fritz helped his son again. He took Hermann and Margarethe into his house in Berlin for some time. Their first daughter, Clara (Claire), was born there on 21 December 1928.

In July 1928 Hermann again began work at the Aussiger Verein and stayed there until 1931. During this time he had several jobs, at first as operations assistant and then as operations director for the production of sulfuric acid, pigments, and fluorine compounds. After this he worked in the administrative offices.

But Hermann again changed companies in 1931. His father tried to get him a job with either IG Farben or with his brother-in-law, Fritz Meffert, as a patent attorney.[16] In October 1931, however, Hermann returned to de Thann et de Mulhouse in Alsace. There he became the assistant of Joseph Blumenfeld, the head of that company and of the Société des Produits Chimiques des Terres Rares (Company for Chemical Products from the Rare Earths). Blumenfeld was the brother-in-law of the Zionist leader and chemist Chaim Weizmann, who is discussed further in Chapter 13.

The correspondence between father, son, and daughter-in-law remained warm, but sometimes Fritz was irritated when he did not hear from the "children." He reported to them on his activities and complained ever more strenuously about his poor health. He tried to make his son financially secure, and in 1930 he gave him a considerable sum in the form of stocks. Fritz always delighted in his grandchildren. In 1930 Margarethe and Hermann's second daughter, Agnes, was born; then Marie Anne was born in Paris in August 1934, seven months after Fritz's death.

By December 1931 Fritz was concerned about the decline in political and economic stability in Germany. He had the impression that the German mark was worth only 50 pfennigs in Paris and wrote: "If this is true, then it is naturally the beginning of a quick end, and the Third Reich really does stand just outside the door. . . . When the overthrow comes, the Belgian and the French governments can block entry into their countries, just as Germany can forbid exit."[17] He was concerned about the children of his second marriage, who lived in Berlin at that time, and sought out help in case such a circumstance arose.

Meanwhile Hermann saw difficulties arising in his job, both with his supervisor, Blumenfeld, and in the company as a whole. In May 1932 he wrote to his father, "The questions about . . . my staying in the company and their intentions . . . are a matter for discussion,"[18] and went into detail. Hermann remained in France, and when Hitler came to power in January 1933, Hermann and his home became a refuge for those who left Germany. It later became a refuge for Fritz, who in his last letters from Germany, and then especially from Switzerland and Spain, gave detailed reports to his son about the situation in Berlin. Soon the odyssey began for Fritz Haber that was to end with his death. Father and son were always in close contact, both while Fritz was in Cambridge and during his stays in Switzerland. In between he met Hermann and his family in Paris. In May 1933 Fritz tried to draw his son into an arrangement to help the Jewish assistants he had to dismiss by order of the new German government, an event discussed further in Chapter 13; Hermann participated as much as he could. Hermann also tried to convince his father to bring Charlotte Haber's children, Ludwig (Lutz) and Eva, who were at school in Salem, out of Germany.

When Fritz finally went to England in the autumn of 1933 and stayed for some months in Cambridge, father and son wrote to each other almost every day. Hermann also visited his father in Cambridge, where Fritz's half sister Else Freyhahn was looking after him. They often discussed how Fritz should spend his future.

After much thought and considerable correspondence, father and son met in Basel at the end of January 1934. Either the strain of the journey or the joy of seeing his son again was too much for Fritz, who already suffered from heart disease. He had a severe heart attack on the night of 29 January. Even the support of Rudolf Stern, his friend and doctor, could no longer help him, and he died in Basel in his hotel room.

Hermann had his father cremated, as he had wished, and buried the urn in the cemetery in Basel. Later he also fulfilled his father's wishes to have his mother's remains transferred to Basel and buried in Fritz's grave.

Two events after his father's death show that Hermann had completely broken off connections with Germany, the land of his birth. The first event, which took place in 1935 in Berlin-Dahlem, was a memorial on the anniversary of Fritz Haber's death. This was organized by Haber's friends despite resistance from the National Socialists. Hermann was invited to the memorial by Max Planck, but declined to attend after long deliberation and inner struggle.

The second event occurred one year later. Like so many Jews during this period, Hermann began to take an interest in Palestine, where Chaim Weizmann had planned a research institute to which Fritz Haber had been invited. On 29 January 1936 the Fritz Haber Library was dedicated at the Daniel Sieff Research Institute in Rehovot. The collection came from Fritz Haber's personal library, which the heirs of his estate had donated to the institute. Hermann, who with Chaim Weizmann and others brought the library out of Germany and had it transported to Palestine, was invited to the dedication. He made a short speech, expressing sorrow and gratitude, and mentioned his father's intention of coming to Palestine to help set up the institute.[19]

Hermann Haber remained with his family in France until 1941. He worked with the Société des Produits Chimiques up to the beginning of World War II. Then he joined the Foreign Legion for a short time because he had not succeeded in obtaining the French citizenship that would save his family from internment by the French authorities. When the Germans invaded France, he traveled with his family to the Dordogne, and in 1942 they left France from Marseilles, reaching the Caribbean on a French ship. From there Hermann tried to obtain a visa for the United States, which proved difficult at first. But he was finally successful, and the whole family traveled to New York City, where they were accepted as "friendly aliens." Hermann worked as an independent patent attorney in New York, and the family lived on Long Island. Hermann and his wife received full residency permits during the war, which relieved all financial need. But Margarethe died shortly after the close of World War II, after which Hermann became increasingly lonely and committed suicide at the end of 1946.[20]

Fritz Haber loved his eldest son dearly. When Hermann had difficulties, Fritz helped. When Fritz had to bear sickness, pain, and disappointment, he turned to his son and later to his daughter-in-law. Both helped him in his old age, as he had hoped. Hermann lived through his father's difficult final days, but fortunately Fritz did not have to experience the sad conclusion of his son's life.

## Marriage with Charlotte Nathan

Fritz Haber married his second wife, Charlotte Nathan, on 25 October 1917. The ceremony took place in the Kaiser Wilhelm Memorial Church in Berlin, with Richard Willstätter and Theodor Freyhahn, Haber's brother-in-law, as witnesses. The sermon at the wedding was based on Corinthians I 13:7, which can be called "Praise of Charity": "Charity beareth all things, believeth all things, hopeth all things, endureth all things."[21]

Charlotte, in sharp contrast to Haber's first wife, was not one to endure all things. Her memoirs create the impression of a lighthearted woman who knew very well how to run her own life beside a man who was certainly superior to her in knowledge and mental power. She was intelligent, had charm and humor, and wanted to enjoy life in her own way. Fritz Haber was fascinated by her, probably because she was so different from his first wife, Clara. He felt a healthy love for her, and he was infatuated with her view of life, which was quite unlike what he had known. Her mottoes were not duty, hard work, exaggerated Prussian morals, and rigid codes. She resisted confining her life within too narrow borders, and she knew how to put her view of life across. But in the end her attitudes conflicted with Haber's own convictions, and although they each tried to give the other freedom, they separated after ten years.

Charlotte Nathan, a child of Jewish parents, was born on 1 November 1889 in Berlin. Her father came from Danzig (now Gdansk) and was the son of a municipal plumber. He trained as a merchant and married young, while still in Danzig. After the war of 1870–71 the young couple moved to Berlin. There, after some good years, their financial situation deteriorated. The couple had three children: a son, Leo; a daughter, Paula; and the youngest, Charlotte. Their mother became ill with cancer a few years after the birth of her youngest daughter and died when Charlotte was only eleven years old.

Although Leo and Paula eventually left their father's home, Charlotte remained with him up to his death in 1913. First she wanted to become an actress, but her father was against it. The cost of attending a girls' high school and then studying medicine, as her father wished, was too great a financial burden and in any case would have taken too long for Charlotte.

*Fritz Haber and Charlotte Nathan in 1916.*

She wrote in her memoirs, "I had absolutely no talent for being an ascetic. . . . Life, rather than anatomy, called me."[22]

She attended the Lette Verein, a girls' school that still exists today. She graduated in only one year and at sixteen found her first job at a magazine publisher's, where she worked her way up to the position of head secretary.

She then worked at a secondhand book shop and later moved to an export company, where she was secretary to the management. Other jobs she held were as secretary to the board of directors at the *Vossische Zeitung*, which was then Berlin's oldest newspaper, and at Ullstein Publishers, where she worked with one of the partners, Franz Ullstein. A disagreement with her boss finally took her at the beginning of 1915 to the German Society of 1914. This society was a club in which various personalities from government, politics, finance, science, art, and literature gathered with the aim of giving more public weight to the declaration made by the emperor: "I no longer recognize political parties; I recognize only Germans." The president was Wilhelm H. Solf, who later became ambassador to Japan. The society had its rooms in the Pringsheim Palais on Wilhelmstrasse. Here Charlotte was the manager. She ran the administration, organized the various receptions and meetings, and was, so to speak, general factotum.

The members of the club came from the highest levels of society, and in her memoirs Charlotte names the economist Walther Rathenau; Rudolf Schroeder, a famous writer; Robert Bosch, an industrialist; Max Reinhardt, a famous theater director, first in Berlin and later in New York, and the founder of the Salzburg festival; Frank Wedekind, a dramatist and novelist; and many others. The society remained in existence until shortly after World War I but had little influence on culture and politics. It was more a social meeting place.

This extraordinarily attractive woman met Fritz Haber in a period when he was coming into his own. He felt accepted into the society of prominent people in his fatherland, which he could serve uniquely as a scientist and an officer. This special feeling of coming into prominence did not correspond at all to his private life and the depressed mood in his own house. It is not surprising that he wanted to escape from his sad home to soar again as a man, so to speak. And this is exactly what happened when he met Charlotte Nathan at the club for the first time.

During the last year of the war, which was also the first year of his marriage with Charlotte, Haber was ceaselessly moving between the institute, the gas-filling plants, and various army headquarters to organize chemical warfare. The pair met only in Berlin, and even when Fritz was at home, they saw each other only briefly. Part of a letter Charlotte wrote him contains a description of their family life:

> In my opinion you can't expect a twenty-eight-year-old woman, who hasn't lived a family life for years and still does not—for you can't call it family life

to have breakfast in a hustle and bustle at 8.30 A.M. and supper around 9 to 10 P.M. in the company of a man who's usually flat-out tired—to keep calm and quiet and to live out in contemplation her new married life, the past nine months of which have brought no great joys.[23]

The "nine months" refers to the period of her pregnancy, for on 21 July the Habers' daughter Eva-Charlotte was born in the clinic at the Schiffbauer-damm in Berlin. Fritz needed recuperative leave shortly after his daughter's birth and traveled to Wildbad in the Black Forest. He was exhausted and wrote Charlotte, "They say that it is very tiring to have a child, which makes me think that I'm lying in childbed, not you." He also mentioned that Leopold Koppel was staying in Wildbad for his health at the same time and that Hermann and Willstätter had visited him for several hours. He advised his wife to take good care of herself.[24] But she too had an urge to travel and wanted to go somewhere to recuperate, perhaps in Bad Kissingen or with her husband in Wildbad, as soon as she left the clinic. But Fritz did not agree at all with his wife's travel plans. He wrote her: "It is my urgent and definite wish that you . . . move to Dahlem with our child and that you establish yourself there as befits a mother and wife. . . . I have struggled greatly before I decided on this letter. But I regard it as necessary to write it to you."[25] Charlotte was "angry" about these lines but submitted to his wishes "because this is best for our little one."

This correspondence foreshadows later events in the married life of two diverse individuals: Fritz Haber, the overextended man, who wore himself out for his work and his duties and then finally, exhausted, sought the quiet of a health spa; and his wife, who, since she found it difficult to tolerate life in Dahlem at the side of a man who was constantly tired out from his work, therefore had to keep on escaping to other locales, where she could steal some pleasant sunny days in the company of interesting people. However, the years after the war were generally a good period for the couple. Their son Ludwig-Fritz (Lutz) was born on 12 July 1920, and Charlotte stayed in Berlin for some time after his birth.

She later did enjoy journeys with her husband. They traveled to Sweden and Norway in 1920, when Fritz was awarded the Nobel Prize for 1918 (see Chapter 10), and they visited London in 1923 when Haber was invited to the First World Power Conference. Charlotte was especially enthusiastic about the long trip they made around the world in 1924. That trip alone consumes almost 90 of the 284 pages in her memoirs, a sign of what an experience it was for her and how many lasting impressions it made.

Haber used the trip to strengthen and renew various scientific and scientific-political contacts. After the war Germany's scientific academies and universities were still largely cut off from those in other countries and from the international scientific organizations. Their first destination in 1924 was the Benjamin Franklin Centenary in Philadelphia, attended by scientists from many countries, where Haber went as a delegate representing both the Prussian Academy of Science and Berlin University. They also visited California, Japan, Korea, Manchuria, Shanghai, Hong Kong, Singapore, Indonesia, Ceylon, and Egypt. And after a cruise on the Mediterranean Sea that ended in Genoa, Italy, the couple arrived, after a stop in Ticino, Switzerland, back in Berlin in mid-March 1925.

After Hermann Haber (who lived in the house in Dahlem up to the end of his studies and often joined his father on holiday) married in 1926, Charlotte and Fritz enjoyed a more harmonious family life with their two children. It was, however, overshadowed by Fritz's increasingly frequent maladies. The efforts of the war years, the disappointment of the defeat, and the difficult new beginning in the confusion of the postwar years had taken their toll. He was repeatedly forced to interrupt his work in order to rest.

Then, in early 1927 came an open marital crisis. Charlotte was in Switzerland, where she had taken the children to recuperate from influenza, and she stayed longer and longer. Haber tried in many letters to persuade her to return home. Finally, with a heavy heart, she acceded to his wishes, certainly aware that despite her still great love and admiration for her husband she would not be able to avoid the sharp disagreements aggravated by her self-confident manner.

The final break came soon after. Fritz and Charlotte had first traveled together to Cherbourg; then Fritz had pushed through a lot of work in the summer, which prompted another stay in the sanatorium. The family was supposed to join Hermann and Margarethe in the Black Forest, but the children came down with bad cases of whooping cough, so Charlotte took them to Insel Sylt to recuperate. After the school holidays the children returned to Berlin while their parents finally journeyed to their farm in the Black Forest.

During that stay together, Fritz and Charlotte had a critical disagreement that led to their separation, a disagreement based on their different attitudes to life.

The separation proved final, although the children, who remained with Charlotte, often saw their father, and Fritz and Charlotte occasionally corresponded and saw one another. The divorce was officially granted on 6 December 1927. Charlotte kept the name Haber and in her memoirs emphasizes her continuing inner feeling of connectedness with her former husband. She wrote: "Even 29 January 1934, the day on which Fritz Haber left the earth, which had become a torture for him, even the day of his death did not dissolve our connectedness, but instead strengthened it high above all moods and the disagreements of everyday life. My whole life afterward testifies to this bond and proves it. Even this book makes it clear."[26]

After the separation Charlotte Haber first wanted to move to Switzerland. But she was attached to Berlin and decided to live in a house that Fritz had purchased for her on Fasanenstrasse in Berlin's West End. The children visited their father often in his house in Dahlem; to them he seemed an old man who moved very slowly. They sometimes played chess with him. And when they were on vacation, their father wrote them letters. But when they wanted to visit, they first had to tell his secretary or Aunt Else.[27]

In the early 1930s their parents enrolled Eva and Lutz in a prestigious school, Salem, in southern Germany, which was headed by Kurt Hahn. In December 1932 Charlotte left on a trip to South and North America and did not return until the summer of 1933. She first heard about the upheavals in Germany in April, when she was in Florida.

Staying at Salem had already become problematic for the children. On 13 March 1933 Fritz Haber wrote to his daughter: "I don't believe that anything bad will happen to Herr Hahn."[28] But only three days later Hahn was arrested, as Haber was to discover in a circular sent out from the school. He told his daughter about the arrest and that the circular recommended that a normal routine be followed in the school. (Later that year Hahn took his school to Gordonston, Scotland.) But after the summer holidays both children were removed from Salem.

Without consulting Charlotte, Fritz wrote Lutz that he wanted to take him to England—which did not please Charlotte in the least. In the following months Haber had various misunderstandings and difficulties with his son Hermann on the one side and with Charlotte on the other concerning both the future of their children and financial matters. But in the end Charlotte and her children moved to England, and after the war Eva and Lutz became British citizens. Haber's half sister Else Freyhahn also took trouble over the children in England and gave them support. Eva became a lively woman, enthusiastic about life. She lived in Kenya with her husband for some time but now lives in Bath in southwestern England and leads an active life. Lutz became Reader at the University of Surrey and is the author of two well-known books on the economic history of the European chemical industry. He also published an analysis of chemical warfare in World War I titled *The Poisonous Cloud*. Since his retirement he also lives in Bath.

Charlotte Haber traveled a great deal. She wrote her memoirs, her *Reflections on the Past,* as she named them in the subtitle. She died on 6 December 1978 in Basel, the same city in which her husband had died almost forty-five years earlier.

## Other Relatives and Friends

As seen in Chapter 1, Fritz Haber's family tree had many branches, and many relatives were in close contact with him. He made numerous friendships in his youth that faded with time, and he later took up new friends. We cannot describe all these ties, but three are examined here at length because they had such a strong influence on Haber's personal life and because detailed accounts of them (correspondence, memoirs, and publications) have survived: his friendships with Rudolf Stern, Richard Willstätter, and Albert Einstein.

Haber also maintained his connections with his relatives, as numerous letters and documents attest. His uncle Julius Haber, who had a respected position in the federal court in Leipzig, and Julius's family deserve special mention. Fritz's closest relationship was with Else, his half sister. She married Theodor Freyhahn, the son of the sister of his dearly loved uncle Hermann, to whom Fritz had owed so much in his childhood. Theodor Freyhahn was a doctor and *Sanitätsrat* (an honorary title for German physicians) in Berlin. The two families often met, as did the children. The Freyhahns had three sons: Hans, Robert, and Dieter. Else looked after Fritz's children from early on and often lived in her half brother's house after the death of her husband. After Fritz and Charlotte Haber's divorce she looked after Fritz and finally moved with him to England. After his death she was the main person to help the two children, Lutz and Eva, and to care for them later in England.

Fritz Haber was less close to his other half sisters, Helene, who married Franz Weigert, a doctor, and Frieda, the wife of Alfred Glücksmann, who became mayor of Guben, a middle-sized town in eastern Germany.

Many friendly acquaintances can only be mentioned in passing, while others have disappeared into the shadows of the past. Some connected with

Haber's scientific and professional work have already been mentioned, for example, his assistants in his Karlsruhe period and those in the 1920s in Berlin, as well as such faculty colleagues as Richard Abegg, Ernst Riesenfeld, and Emil Fischer, and his financial adviser and friend, Max Mayer. Others will be described below. Later, in Dahlem, Haber had a closer, trusting relationship with several directors of the Kaiser Wilhelm Society, for example, Carl Neuberg, Max von Laue, and Otto Hahn. His activity in scientific politics in the 1920s increasingly brought Haber into contact with many different personalities in public life, including Friedrich Schmidt-Ott, Friedrich Glum, Hugo A. Krüss, Wichard von Moellendorff, and Wilhelm Solf.

## Rudolf Stern, A Young Friend

Haber developed an especially close relationship with the young doctor Rudolf Stern, the brother of his daughter-in-law. Rudolf Stern was the son of a well-known doctor and university professor in Breslau, Richard Stern, who had an excellent reputation in Breslau society around the turn of the century. Fritz Haber got to know him during his student days. The elder Stern died before the war. Rudolf fought at the extreme front during World War I, was promoted to officer's rank, and was awarded the Iron Cross, first and second class. His terrible experiences during the war turned him into a pacifist.

After the war Rudolf Stern continued to study medicine in Breslau and then carried out several years of scientific work in Haber's institute under Herbert Freundlich. Stern practiced medicine and then became a lecturer at the University of Breslau. He emigrated to the United States in 1938 and practiced medicine in New York City for nearly twenty years. He died there in November 1962. Despite his pacifist convictions, he was a German patriot, like Fritz Haber. His son, Fritz Stern, a historian and professor at Columbia University, calls him, in the foreword to his father's memoirs, a "good European" who would have much preferred to stay in Europe rather than emigrate to America. The foreword continues: "He emigrated . . . leaving his native country, from whose culture and genius he had derived so much, and for which he had done and endured so much." At his son's urging, Rudolf Stern wrote down his memories of Fritz Haber, and Fritz Stern published them after his father's death under the title *Fritz Haber: Personal Recollections.*[29]

Rudolf Stern first met Fritz Haber in 1913, when he was in Switzerland with his father. They met again after the war, in 1921, in the village of Oberschreiberhau in the Silesian Riesengebirge district. This unexpected reunion was to have, as Stern wrote, "a decisive influence on my whole life."[30] Haber was staying in the sanatorium there with Fritz Epstein (one of his main assistants at his institute) and was deeply depressed by the recriminations over his activities during the war, which had flared up again when he was awarded the Nobel Prize. Epstein, Stern, and Stern's wife, Käthe, tried to cheer him up. Haber was grateful for this and was quite taken by the young medical doctor. He offered him a position as *Assistent* in his institute in order to help him through that difficult period. Stern accepted happily and worked from May 1921 to October 1923 under Herbert Freundlich in the field of colloid chemistry. When he reported to Haber on starting his job, Haber gave him the additional job of "house doctor" for the institute. Stern was not pleased, as he had hardly practiced as a doctor, but the medical care he gave in the institute led to his becoming one of Haber's medical advisers.

In the autumn of 1921, on the recommendation of his teacher, the well-known Breslau doctor Oscar Minkowski, Rudolf Stern was named privatdocent for internal medicine. His son, Fritz, was born at the same time. Haber was the boy's godfather and telegraphed: "If a son is given as a reward for the habilitation, then I hope to be able to send threefold congratulations for the professorship."[31]

In January 1926 Hermann Haber and Rudolf Stern's sister, Margarethe, were married. It was a happy celebration. But when Stern visited Fritz Haber in May 1926, he was shocked by the bad state of Haber's health. He noticed how severely the general social circumstances and successes or failures in Haber's work influenced his health, an observation that Haber's close friend Richard Willstätter had also made.

In December 1926 Haber asked Stern to join him on a trip to Monte Carlo, although he was "conscious that he was inflicting a grievous deprivation on [Stern's] wife and children in taking [him] away from them at Christmas." (Haber had recently quarreled with Charlotte.) The trip began with a short stop in Munich, where Willstätter brought a small bottle of French brandy to the train, remarking, "Fritz, I don't dare give you a bigger bottle as you have your doctor with you."[32]

The two friends conducted many serious and happy conversations on this holiday. They were joined after a short time by Leopold Koppel, with whom Haber had also become friends, and the three undertook many expeditions in the area. Koppel, who was an early riser, had usually already walked for hours before Haber and Stern followed him in the car to meet for lunch. Haber was still grateful to Koppel for his strong support before the war. Although by the mid-1920s the institute was financed mainly by the state and by other funds, Haber always called it "your institute" when he was with Koppel. Koppel was still curious to find out what topics were being worked on in the institute and what new findings there were in the fields of physics and chemistry.

After the trip Haber threw himself right back into his work. Stern was continually worried about Haber's health. It was clear to him that Haber suffered from coronary artery disease. When Haber took a holiday for recuperation at Bad Kissingen, he wrote Stern satirical remarks on the various treatments but also confessed that the nitroglycerin Stern had prescribed for him often brought him immediate relief.

In his memoirs Stern also mentions Haber's divorce in 1927 and his opinion that this was a relief for Haber. He wrote that the decision to divorce had been made in the last days of August in Munich and that he and his wife had been with Haber at the time. He commented that "for a man who still lived in the tradition of a high-ranking Prussian official, the thought of a divorce was practically impossible" and that he felt Haber had had great difficulty in reaching the decision.[33]

In 1930 Rudolf Stern left the university for a job at a hospital. He had enough time to visit Haber at least once a month and to consult with the doctor who always treated Haber, a Dr. I. Krieger. The two were able to slow down but not to prevent the deterioration of Haber's health. The political events even before 1933 had an especially negative impact on Haber's general condition. Haber frequently asked his friend to come over and give him medical advice. He wrote Stern in November 1932: "I am filled with the perception that I owe my present recovery to your earlier visits. . . . Permit me to request that you come here when it seems important to me."[34]

The reports on his health that Haber sent Stern from Cap Ferrat in December 1932 were extremely disturbing. And by the time Haber returned to Berlin, the Third Reich was already established, and he was gripped by a deep depression. Stern visited him again in Berlin in May. Haber's heart condition had become so serious that Stern advised him to leave Germany immediately and to try and recover in a Swiss sanatorium. Haber ignored Stern's advice, however, because he still wanted to find satisfactory posts for his Jewish coworkers, who had lost their jobs. Nevertheless he was fully aware of his condition, and he wrote to his friend and doctor in June: "I don't want to complain about my emotional suffering and to express the bitterness that fills me and that, anyway, often breaks out of me instead of my keeping it to myself. I have lived too long."[35]

Haber finally went to Mammern, Switzerland, on the southern end of Lake Constance, and Stern visited him there. At that time Haber was already considering whether he should go to Palestine, but he finally decided to go to England first, although Stern advised him against this because of the unfavorable climate.

On completing his work in Cambridge, Haber traveled to Switzerland and asked Hermann to meet him in Basel. He also asked Rudolf Stern and his wife to come. They arrived on 29 January 1934. When they met Fritz Haber in the hotel, they were shocked by his terrible appearance. Haber could hardly speak for a long period without having a severe attack of angina. Stern tried to cheer him with the prospect of a rest in Orselina, near Locarno, Switzerland. They all retired early in the evening, and shortly afterward Haber had the severe heart attack that led to his death.

Rudolf Stern's memoirs are a moving tribute to Fritz Haber. He felt a deep admiration and friendship for Haber, which is clearly transmitted in his *Personal Recollections*. They are a rich source of information on Haber since Stern draws such a detailed portrait of his older friend.

## Albert Einstein, A Colleague and Friend

A truly extraordinary relationship arose between Fritz Haber and Albert Einstein. Fritz Stern called it a friendship in his contribution to the history of the Kaiser Wilhelm Society and chose the title "Friends in Opposition."[36] But was there really a friendship between them?

The German language uses an unambiguous word for a close friendship, the familiar form of address, *Du;* at least this was the case fifty to seventy years ago. Today Germans use this form lightly. Haber and Einstein did not use this form of address with one another, although Haber later chose to use the salutation "Dear Friend Einstein" in his letters. But he never wrote to "Dear Albert," and Einstein always replied "Dear Haber." Whether the relationship between Haber and Einstein was a friendship or not, it was often astonishingly warm, and Haber especially admired Einstein.[37]

Haber and Einstein became acquainted in 1911, and Haber played a

*Fritz Haber and Albert Einstein in 1914.*

significant role in Einstein's move from Zurich to Berlin in 1914, after which their relationship strengthened. Haber helped Einstein purchase an apartment. When the problem of Einstein's citizenship arose, it was Haber who pointed out that Einstein automatically received German citizenship on becoming a member of the Prussian Academy of Sciences. When Einstein came to Berlin, half of his salary was paid by Leopold Koppel, Haber's great benefactor. Haber may have had an influence on Koppel's decision, though it is not documented; Koppel was asked for help from many quarters.

Einstein moved to Berlin with his wife, Mileva, and their two sons on 6 April 1914. His relationship with Mileva had long been fragile, and by the summer she had moved back to Zurich with their sons. She stayed there after the outbreak of the war and never returned to Berlin. Haber wanted to mediate and made various futile attempts to reconcile the two. But Einstein, who seemed quite satisfied with the situation, had little desire to exert any pressure on his wife. The only difficulty was transferring money to Zurich during the war, though Haber helped occasionally.

World War I changed the close contact that had developed between Haber and Einstein. They held opposing views. Haber agreed with the large majority of his colleagues and acted according to the slogan, "For the fatherland in time of war." Einstein had hardly concerned himself with politics up to the outbreak of the war. He was an individualist who sought freedom to work. For him physics came before what he considered all the other trivialities of life, but the war changed his outlook. He became a convinced pacifist and internationalist and, in diluted form, a socialist. He was one of the few scientists, in Germany and elsewhere, who did not let the war influence his work.

When in October 1914 a letter called the "Proclamation of the 93," signed mainly by scientists and artists, defended the behavior of the German army in Belgium and denounced the accusations of their opponents as lies, Einstein, along with Georg Nicolai, a professor of physiology at the University of Berlin, wrote an opposing piece called "Manifesto to the Europeans" ("Das Manifest an die Europäer"). They distributed it among the scientists in Berlin, but only Wilhelm Forster, the head of the observatory in Potsdam, and a certain Otto Bück signed. These four signatories thus stood essentially alone.

In November 1914 a peace group called the Federation of the Germans (Bund der Deutschen) was founded by Hugo Simon, a banker, and Ernst Reuter, who became mayor of Berlin after World War II (1947–1953). The federation wanted a quick peace settlement and further wars prevented.

Einstein joined this federation. He openly expressed his opposition to the war, especially when he was in other countries, as when he visited the physicists Paul Ehrenfest and Hendrik A. Lorentz in Holland and the writer and philosopher Romain Rolland in Switzerland. His remarks bordered on high treason—after all he still held the position of a state official in Prussia. But nothing happened to him, except that some colleagues expressed their displeasure.

Oddly, the very patriotic Haber, who during World War I invested all his strength in helping his fatherland to victory, did not allow Einstein's political escapades—which he must have known about—to change his high opinion of Einstein as a person and a scientist. He is not known to have remarked on Einstein's extrascientific activities; he apparently even overlooked Einstein's actions outside of Germany. Perhaps Haber recognized the impulsive openness and honesty that Einstein was later to demonstrate in his public remarks and highly respected this kind of behavior, even if his own opinion was completely different. At any rate, although contact between them was now infrequent simply because of their different spheres of work, Haber continued to support Einstein in setting up his physics institute and in personal matters.

The Kaiser Wilhelm Society's Institute for Physics was finally founded in the autumn of 1917. Representatives of the Kaiser Wilhelm Society, of industry, and of the Ministry of Education sat on the board of trustees. Haber was a member of the board of directors, along with Einstein, Nernst, Planck, Heinrich Rubens, and Emil Warburg. Einstein headed the institute, with Max von Laue as his deputy. The rather low budget of 75,000 marks also had to support scientists working in the field of theoretical physics, although this function was later taken over by the Emergency Association of German Science (Notgemeinschaft der Deutschen Wissenschaft), which Haber had helped found.

Einstein had published another important work during the war: "The Foundations of the Theory of General Relativity."[38] It is therefore not surprising that Haber expressed respect for him and his achievements in a letter written in January 1918.[39] Along with many other scientists in the Kaiser Wilhelm Society and the academy, he recognized the significance of Einstein's work. And after the war Einstein was especially important to Germany's world standing. For many years he was almost the only representative of German science who was received and honored outside of Germany. He was also prepared to speak in other countries in support of the transformed Germany, and he hoped for a fundamental change in the state of its affairs.

Einstein was generally praised and flattered while traveling. In Germany, in contrast, opinion was more divided. Planck, von Laue, Nernst, and Haber recognized what Einstein had achieved. For others he was a source of provocation, an intellectual pacifist, and a left-leaning Jew. Einstein declared his loyalty to the new German state by giving his oath to the Weimar constitution in March 1921. But his opponents, among them Ernst Gehrke and Philipp Lenard (Nobel Prize in physics, 1905), gathered together in the Working Group of German Natural Scientists (Arbeitsgemeinschaft Deutscher Naturforscher) and proclaimed that the theory of relativity was part of a Jewish conspiracy. At first Einstein did not seem to take this seriously, but in 1920 a crisis almost ensued over Einstein's remaining in Berlin. Haber tried to keep Einstein in the German capital and wrote to him from Switzerland:

> The papers carry the report that you wish to leave Berlin and Germany. The reasons that the media give [anti-Semitic provocation at a gathering in the Berlin Philharmonia] could not have caused your decision, if you have really made it. If the anti-Semites meet in the Philharmonia in order to take a stand on the common ground of lack of understanding and antipathy against you, then this entente of nonentities cannot have a weight equal to the general admiration that is felt by all serious natural scientists for you.[40]

Haber was "extremely happy" once he was sure that Einstein wanted to stay in Berlin. He informed Einstein of the funding he was trying to obtain for him, both from the government and from the Kaiser Wilhelm Society and Koppel. And he asked Einstein not to make the mistake of "butting in with a refusal. That would be an unfriendly way to treat me." The letter ends with the wonderful concluding sentence: "So scold me, but don't make me angry, because I have to recuperate and must have my way."[41]

In the autumn of 1922 the Swedish Academy of Sciences announced that Einstein was to be awarded the Nobel Prize, which he received in December 1922 in Stockholm. Einstein was now a famous personality. High society in Berlin took him up and invited him to soirees, and he found it difficult to refuse. But he also frequently enjoyed the company of more interesting people in gatherings that included Haber, Fritz Kreisler (who played the violin with Einstein), the painter Max Slevogt, the pianist Artur Schnabel, and Foreign Minister Brockdorff Rantzau. They engaged in many discussions and listened to short talks and musical recitals. Einstein was often seen at Haber's house—usually very plainly dressed. Einstein put very little value on external appearance, and several anecdotes were told at this time about his homely way of dealing with the conventions. Haber, who had quite different views about them, admired Einstein's lack of pretension. When both were in Berlin, they often met in the evening, played a game of chess, and talked. When traveling, they occasionally sent each other postcards, Haber writing in the verse form he often used. He sent the following greeting on a postcard from the Allgäu in southern Germany, writing ironically about himself:

> I walked a whole day—or very near—
> To see Sturmann's cave and the ravine
> But had to leave them both unseen:
> My body's strength denied my desire.
> This is the pain, this is the inner fear:
> Will you persist in what you have begun
> When autumnal storms of life about you run
> And around your steps, cold fogs drear?
>
> When you are young, you lack the stubborn will;
> Life's variety pushes you from goal to goal!
> Too much strength keeps you unsteadfast!
> Nervous turmoil makes you a fool at last,
> The new things you plan take their toll,
> Along paths already trod you must trot still!
> Greetings, Haber.[42]

And from Biarritz he sent the following greeting:

> It seems to me, if you watch over time,
> Waves and people act about the same!
> They keep on coming and make a foam
> They thunder a lot and take up room,
> But if one observes what they bring forth,
> What they leave behind is nothing worth.
> Both waves and people stay the same,
> They have no point, like this rhyme.[43]

A letter from Haber on the occasion of Einstein's fiftieth birthday in March 1929 reflects the ironic way in which the two discussed the world:

> Of the great things I have met with in this world, the significance of your life and your work stir me most deeply. A few hundred years from now the com-

mon man will refer to our time as the period of the World War, but the educated man will connect the first quarter of this century with your name, just as today some think of the end of the seventeenth century in connection with the wars of Louis XIV, while others remember Isaac Newton. We will all be remembered, each and every one of us, to the degree that there is a connection between us and the great events of our time. But in your biography, if sufficiently detailed, I think it will not go unmentioned that you had me as a partner for more or less pointed remarks about the affairs of the Academy and for more or less dreadful coffee. I thus serve my own future fame and continued personal existence in history as I beg you, on your fiftieth birthday, to look after yourself and stay healthy so that I can keep on scoffing and drinking coffee with you, and in quiet times afterward I can feel proud to be counted as one of the circle that in a more intimate and human sense lives with you.[44]

Einstein traveled a great deal from 1929 to 1932. Haber wrote in one of his letters: "I have no idea in which part of the world you are representing German culture at this moment."[45] Haber may have viewed Einstein's travels in this way, but Einstein was certainly not trying to be seen as such a representative. He was too much the individualist, and German culture was taking on an ever more nationalistic quality. He much preferred to play the violin with the Belgian queen, to visit the astronomer and physicist Arthur Stanley Eddington, and to enjoy London's "high society." He spent time in Oxford and traveled to America, where he stayed at the California Institute of Technology in Pasadena. While in Berlin he enjoyed his house at Caputh on a lake outside the city, sailed on the Havel lakes, and worked on his field theory, though he became increasingly pessimistic about conditions in Germany. In November 1932 he again traveled to Pasadena, and in January 1933 he gave a talk on the possible improvement of German-American relations.

After Hitler's rise to power Einstein canceled his lectures in Berlin and at the Prussian Academy of Sciences. In March 1933 he made it known that he would not be returning to Berlin. He traveled to Belgium, handed in his German passport to the German Embassy, and thus canceled his German citizenship. In October 1933 he and his second wife, Elsa, traveled to Princeton, where he remained until his death in 1955.

During this period of frequent travel Einstein and Haber rarely met in Berlin. Haber, too, was often absent from Berlin, either on his farm in the Black Forest, in Switzerland, or giving lectures or attending meetings both in Germany and abroad.

Little of their correspondence has survived. Einstein wrote to say farewell to Haber before he went to Caltech in Pasadena in November 1931. "I decided to go to Pasadena so quickly that I unfortunately didn't have time to say good-bye. My train leaves in two hours. So, by letter, I wish you good times."[46]

But the good times were to end for Haber.

On 6 April 1933, after Einstein had attacked the new regime, mentioning the cruelties against the Jews and calling for a "moral intervention" of other people against the "excesses of Hitlerism," he was expelled from the Prussian Academy of Sciences after considerable controversy.[47] Haber agreed with this decision, and he tried to explain his position in a letter to Einstein:

> If ever a time occurred when I felt all the tortures of conflicting duties and envied you your simple aim in life, which you pursue in accordance with your own individual nature, then that time is now. The Prussian Academy has exchanged letters and newspaper statements with you and is not happy with the result. For the topic of your departure does not die down. . . . Unfortunately these living idolaters have derived from the Christian religion the ineptitude of linking divinity and fallibility. And the predominant opinion of the one side for divinity and the prevailing view of the others that you acted wrongly are the reasons that the matter of your departure does not come to rest. Perhaps it would still go right if only it were clear wherein your offenses lay. According to all information on this matter, it is clear that you have become an enemy of the National Socialist movement and a criminal with respect to Hitler's government, and that honorable mention of you endangers the originator or the disseminator of the remarks. But that you committed an offense by turning against this government while abroad and declaring yourself a voluntary exile has not persuaded a fair number of people. You come to be attacked because you did not defend this government while abroad. But indeed, the others note that for a defense a factual knowledge of the situation is required, knowledge to which you would have had no access or insufficient access while abroad. Yes, and so on. The outcome of this business for you is "many enemies, much honor," but we have to carry the worst part. For our honor has been stained.[48]

A few days later Haber set himself to advance the cause of one of his coworkers to Einstein: "I must write to you once again. For the people who would like to receive your help are many, and I am forced . . . to bother you in individual cases."[49] Haber wrote these lines at a time when many Jews had been expelled from public service, and he felt that finding jobs abroad for as many as possible was his main task.

It is apparent that Haber did not exclude himself when he wrote Einstein that "our honor has been stained." How Haber's feelings and actions must have swayed and changed. The inner conflict this created for Haber, the German patriot and Jew, during the first months of 1933 must have caused tremendous distress. Einstein knew about Haber's inner strife and wrote to him:

> I am amazed at the unintelligent behavior of the Academy, less so at the lack of moral stature (this latter I already knew about). I can imagine your inner conflicts. It is similar to having to give up a theory that one has worked on all one's life. It is not so with me, because I never for a moment believed in them. I hope that soon I can write to you at some other place.[50]

Einstein naturally meant some place outside Germany. In August, Haber wrote from Paris.

> I am here traveling through Paris to Santander in Spain, where there is a meeting organized by the Universidad International de Verano. What I shall do afterward is uncertain. My life plan was set so that I would occupy my position as director of the Kaiser Wilhelm Institute until 30 September and then would choose a lifestyle and work befitting my years and my no longer perfect health, if this were offered me. I cannot say that I have been showered with attractive offers. . . . Three times now I have received an invitation to go to Palestine and there enter into closer relations with the University in Jerusalem. The first time was through [Chaim] Weizmann, the second time through a Professor [Abraham Shalom] Yehuda, whom I do not know [a supporter of the director of the Hebrew University, Rabbi Judah Magnes], and the third time here in Paris, again through Mr. Weizmann. . . . For me, Mr. Weizmann is a person who has commanded my fullest respect and good opinion since our afternoon stroll along the Unter den Linden, when you expressed your unconditional admiration for him. Since then differences of opinion have arisen between you. . . .
>
> Perhaps I should try and describe the situation in Germany to you. But I assume that you have daily contact with informed people. The provision for German scientists who have had to yield to the law on *Berufsbeamtentum* [racial laws regarding employment in the public service] is being interpreted to Aryan colleagues abroad who are trying to help—for example, [Max] von Laue and [Fritz] Schlenk—as a crime. The support for a limited number of prominent scholars that comes from abroad makes the overall situation only more terrible. I was never in my life as Jewish as now.[51]

Einstein answered Haber immediately, writing to him in Santander: "I was very happy to receive such a detailed and long letter from you, and

I was especially happy that your earlier love for the blonde beast has cooled a little. Who would have thought that my dear Haber would approach me as the advocate of the Jewish, even the Palestinian, matter!" At the end of the letter he returns to Haber's situation:

> I hope you will not return to Germany. It is no true business to work for an intelligentsia consisting of men who prostrate themselves on their bellies before common criminals and even sympathize to a certain degree with these criminals. They could not disappoint me, because I never had any respect or sympathy for them, apart from some individuals (Planck is 60 percent noble and Laue 100 percent). I wish for nothing more strongly than for a truly human atmosphere for you in which you can be happy again (France or England). But the nicest always (for me) is contact with a few cultivated Jews; a few thousand years of civilized history do mean something after all! As you now will not be returning to "Teutonia," I hope to meet you soon under a milder sky. Good times for you until then, and warm greetings to you and your Hermann.[52]

Einstein and Haber never did meet under a milder sky. When Haber died in January 1934, Einstein wrote to Hermann in sadness and in gratitude for his dead friend and supporter of days gone by.

Thus a really friendly relationship existed between Fritz Haber and Albert Einstein, from their first encounter in 1913 up to Haber's death. It was a relationship based on mutual respect and admiration for the achievements of the other. The achievements lay in quite different areas, both in their scientific work and in their efforts in public and political life. At the end of "Friends in Opposition," Fritz Stern wrote about their relationship:

> Einstein was proud to be a Jew, just as Haber was proud of being a German. It is an honor to both men, and especially to Einstein, that the distress that the other's position must have caused each of them to feel did not seriously hinder their friendship. It remained with a deep, mostly unexpressed inconsistency in questions of human existence and intensity. . . .
>
> For both men the scientific environment was the deepest form of nourishment. They came and discovered a place of human decency and kept this alive, an oasis even up to the time when Hitler was destroying everything that was valuable and even destroyed the innocence that had been the prerequisite for this deep connection.

Stern concludes with words from Einstein's eulogy at the grave of Rudolf Ladenburg, a friend of both Haber and Einstein:

For beings of our sort, being limited to the "I" is inconceivable, both for bare existence and for an awareness of life. The "I" leads to the "you" and to the "we"—a step that makes us what we are. And still the bridge that leads from the "I" to the "you" is subtle and uncertain like the whole adventure of life. If a group of people joins together to form a "we" that forms a harmonious whole, then the highest is achieved that people as creatures can attain.[53]

## Richard Willstätter, A Good Friend

Fritz Haber and Richard Willstätter had already crossed the bridge from "I" to "you" to form a close and durable friendship before the war, and they continued to secure this bridge after the war. In an account of the events leading to Willstätter's appointment at the Kaiser Wilhelm Institute for Chemistry in Berlin, Willstätter described his friendship with Haber, noting his "noble mind, goodness of heart, wealth of ideas, and his boundless, extravagant drive."[54]

Richard Willstätter was Jewish like Haber, Rudolf Stern, and Albert Einstein. Why were most of Haber's friends, even those in his youth, such as Max Warburg and later Georg Bredig, Jews? Was it the attitude toward life, childhood experience, a common spiritual attitude? Although Haber was not attached to Judaism, and indeed had severed himself from it early on during his stay in Jena, there may have been an unconscious feeling of belonging together that is difficult to explain.

Friendships and close relationships are fragile structures, and to be of long duration they must have a common point of reference, an unconscious force of attraction, a mental bond that cannot rip even in times of crisis, through lengthy physical separation and interrupted contact. Haber often mentioned this sort of friendship, particularly in his letters to Richard Willstätter.

Willstätter's forebears were Jews who had lived in Karlsruhe since 1720. There were several rabbis in the family. His grandfather, Meier (Maximilian) Willstätter, was a doctor who practiced in Karlsruhe and the surrounding towns and villages. Richard's father—who was born in 1840 and died in 1912—was a cloth merchant, at first in Karlsruhe. To seek his fortune, he went to America without his family and was separated from them for quite a long time.

Richard Willstätter was born in 1872. He spent his earliest childhood in Karlsruhe, the tranquil city of residence of the Grand Dukes of Baden. In

1883 Richard's mother moved to Nuremberg with the children, while their father went to America. The move was like an "expulsion from Paradise" for the young child.[55] At first, as Willstätter tells it, he was a sickly little stay-at-home. But, in spite of many illnesses, he graduated from secondary school in Nuremberg. He had already chosen chemistry as a profession, just as Fritz Haber had, and he had carried out experiments in a small laboratory at home since his fourth year of high school.

The study of chemistry took Willstätter to Munich in October 1890. Adolf von Baeyer was the outstanding personality, as head of the Institute for Chemistry there. Willstätter chose to undertake chemical research. He did his doctoral research with Alfred Einhorn on derivatives of cocaine and worked closely with Baeyer. His habilitation was on the tropine group.[56] In 1902 he was appointed associate professor after Johannes Thiele received a professorship at Strasbourg. Research on quinine followed his first investigations of chlorophyll, which mainly dealt with methods for separating and identifying its derivatives.[57]

In August 1903 Willstätter married Sophie Leser, daughter of the political economist Emanual Leser, who lectured in Heidelberg. Their son, Ludwig, was born the next year, and their daughter, Margarethe, was born later in Zurich. Sophie died early and tragically in 1908 from protracted appendicitis.

Willstätter was appointed professor at the Swiss Federal Institute of Technology in 1905. His major work in Zurich involved the isolation and constitutional analysis of chlorophyll and the study of how it worked.[58] He began his work on plant pigments in Zurich and continued this work intensively in Berlin at the Kaiser Wilhelm Institute for Chemistry with Arthur Stoll and others.

His account of life in Dahlem and of his connection with Haber gives an interesting illustration of their relationship at that time.

> Haber, who was helpful and let me know his friendly intentions [toward me] from the first day on, helped me acquire some land from the domain of Dahlem adjacent to his official residence and large garden. Forty-first Street, later Hittorf Street, ran between us, and the front was continuous with that of the institutes. Since Haber was well acquainted with the director of the royal domain of Dahlem, we acquired some influence in naming the streets of that section. It is thus no coincidence that my house was located on Faraday Way.
> . . . Parks were laid out in our immediate neighborhood, which softened the harsh north wind; to the south extended a broad plain studded with wind-

mills. It was not until I moved away, in fact in the postwar period, that the face of Dahlem changed, with unbroken rows of little houses on the [domain] lands.[59]

The chemistry of natural products remained Willstätter's primary area of research, and he later worked for years on enzymes. He received the Nobel Prize in 1915 and went to Munich the same year, where he became a teacher much admired by his students. But in 1924 anti-Semitic incidents occurred that made clear the attitude of the authorities and the professors at the university. Willstätter drew his own conclusions and resigned from his professorship. He declined to teach at any other university, but continued his research.

It is remarkable that Willstätter remained in Germany until 1939. In spite of all the unpleasantness, he found it hard to leave the beautiful house he had bought in Munich in 1925, his few but good friends, and his work. Several loyal coworkers helped him continue the work on enzymes and on such new adsorption substances as silicic acid. He continued to publish his results and gave lectures in Germany and abroad. He was also active, often at Haber's request, in many organizations: He gave expert opinions for the Emergency Association of German Science and at meetings of the Prussian Academy of Sciences. He gave a hand at the Deutsches Museum and traveled to Berlin to meetings of the German Chemical Society and to various committees.

In his free time Willstätter occupied himself with art and the theater and with traveling. Here his inclinations fitted in with those of Haber, whose travels occupy several pages in Willstätter's memoirs. Passages from these memoirs illustrate his friendship with Haber quite clearly:

> When I gave up teaching I had more freedom to travel. The most beautiful trips were the ones I took with Fritz Haber; they were hours of friendship in which I came to know and understand his individuality, his noble mind, goodness of heart, wealth of ideas, and his boundless, extravagant drive. . . .
>
> I have many happy memories of earlier travels with Haber. Once we met in the Engadine to travel to Italy. . . . We hurried to Genoa to spend some of our vacation in Florence, but got to Rome by mistake. Haber was lecturing to me on the symmetry conditions in penta-erythritol according to [Karl] Weissenberg, and so we had passed Livorno without changing trains. Now I attempted to interrupt the physicochemical observations with a remark to the effect that the ocean was on the wrong side. Haber was indignant at the distraction and continued to discourse on the modifications of van't

Hoff's theory. I interjected that the ocean was definitely in the wrong place. Haber returned to this world, and I was barely able to restrain him from pulling the emergency brake. So we went to Rome, and our baggage went to Florence. . . .

Once we went to Ragusa by way of Traù [Dubrovnik], that Venetian jewel, and Spalato [now Split]. It was a beautiful Easter Sunday, and a warm trip across the Lapad peninsula. Haber was expounding a new theory that the energy liberated in a reaction initially adheres to the single molecules produced in the reaction, and that it is transferred from these primary particles to suitable molecules on collision with the latter. These considerations have fruitful applications in the explanation of combustion processes. Haber did not merely lecture; his method was to rehearse concepts with which he was still struggling, over and over again. He read and learned by ear and made little use of his eyes, in nature and with people. Unfortunately he thought I was being unjust and spiteful when a cry of delight escaped me at a view through to the Adriatic. However, when we arrived late in the overcrowded dining room and had to wait for food and drink, he detained the headwaiter by the coattails as he hurried past us to ask him, "Could you bring me a coffin? And how much is a cemetery lot in Dubrownik?"[60]

Willstätter's memoirs also describe his visit to the August 1933 conference at Santander:

This was one of the last times I saw Fritz Haber. We had met in Paris but had had to travel separately. Furthermore, like the majority of our colleagues, he stayed only a short time, while my obligations required a longer stay. I recall this time we spent together with a heavy heart. It stands before me now like a hideous *danse macabre.*

Haber's life hung by a slender thread. He took his lecture very seriously indeed and worked on it with me until late at night, despite the fact that there was no audience other than the handful of colleagues whom courtesy forced into the hot little lecture room, though most of them understood no German. One of the few listeners who spoke German used to go to sleep whenever he was not speaking himself. My poor friend took his medication before his appointed hour, but even so he could not escape one of his heart spasms; he broke off, took the nitroglycerin he kept in readiness, and gasping and shaking, brought his lecture to some sort of conclusion.[61]

It seems astonishing that Haber lectured to such an empty room. However, as indicated by a letter from Haber's friend Julio Kocherthaler, his lecture may not have been advertised in the original program.[62]

Willstätter described his friend, and his life and career, in several lectures and papers. His contribution to the festschrift of *Die Naturwissenschaften* on the occasion of Haber's sixtieth birthday, where he describes his friend's scientific development, deserves special mention. In a short passage he characterized Haber's approach to work:

> His greatness lies in his scientific ideas and in the depth of his searching. The thought, the plan, and the process are more important to him than the completion. The creative process gives him more pleasure than the yield, the finished piece. Success is immaterial. "Doing it was wonderful." His work is nearly always uneconomical, with the wastefulness of the rich. Haber knew his weakness, and complained about his own lack of purpose in a letter to me from Pontresina (August 1921), "when I suddenly jumped up between the soup and the roast to hurry up a snow-capped mountain in unnailed shoes at high noon and then had to turn back at the snow line." We should misjudge this scientist seriously if we were to judge him only by his harvest. The stimulation of research and the advancement of younger scholars become ever more important to him than his own achievements.[63]

A letter from Haber to Willstätter, written in 1929, provides a special demonstration of Haber's close feelings for his friend. It also shows a broad recognition of his own behavior in this and the following period, just as it was later depicted by his children:

> I write . . . in remembrance of the incomparable overestimation and unchanging affection that I have received from you with pride and joy, with thanks and embarrassment. Humans are so many-sided, and in old age they are crusty, like bread browned in the fire, distrustful and temperamental. But you, with the gentle sincerity of your indulgent gratitude, have broken through all the hard crust and made me happy. Now my life is so bound up with yours that I can spend weeks and months in great inner turmoil without exchanging ideas with you and without expressing my feeling of connectedness. But as soon as there is a turning point, or something causes me to stop, the need arises to reach you and to ask when we will see each other again, talk together again, argue again, and as much as I can, make a life out of the course of days by meeting again.[64]

Apart from their feelings of being bound in friendship, the two exchanged again and again experience, scientific knowledge, and discussions of current technical and scientific problems and those of scientific organizations.

In 1931 Haber spent a long time in Munich as a guest of Willstätter's. They were working on the problem of oxygen radicals and their uptake by enzymes at the time. Afterward they sent letters back and forth on this and on other scientific questions—on various approaches and on equations for the course of the reactions (for example, on the reduction of peroxidase and the role of catalase in this process).[65]

Willstätter celebrated his own sixtieth birthday in 1932, and a festschrift of *Die Naturwissenschaften* was published for that occasion also. Haber wrote the introductory passages, remarking ironically:

> We honor our great chemists on their red-letter days in the confined circle of our profession and related professions. That circle never succeeds in doing them full justice because it excerpts a specialized sort of towering ability one-sidedly out of the picture of the whole personality. The true insights that keep the name of their creator living on in printers' ink on textbook paper through generations suffice for human greatness only if they derive from a personality whose mental range and spiritual richness are not inferior to that great professional ability. I, at least, do not want to dedicate these congratulations on behalf of the profession to anyone on his sixtieth birthday whose claim to that privilege rests only on his understanding of his subject.[66]

Haber could not have foreseen the extent of the shocks he and his friend would receive during the very next year. By February 1933 he still did not seem to have grasped the consequences of Hitler's rise to power. That is clear from a letter he wrote to Willstätter at the end of the month. Even though he mentions "an absence of tranquillity in view of the future," he is mainly referring to an impending meeting in Spain and does not know how he can travel there without his sister Else.[67] In March the letters that Haber and Willstätter exchanged dealt only with professional subjects. But once the emergency laws and the notorious Law on the Restoration of the Civil Service (which ordained the dismissal of all Jewish civil servants) were announced in May 1933, Haber submitted his resignation. He then wrote to his friend, after meeting him in Munich:

> In the meantime I have spent the time in agonies that come partly from the soul and partly from the body. Perhaps contributing to them is that I can no longer imagine how I can ever again get to work and to be effective. I am bitter as never before, and the feelings of irritability inside me increase daily. I have been German to an extent that I only now perceive fully, and I feel an unprecedented disgust in that I can no longer work well enough to dare take up a new position in another country. I admire the composed tranquillity with which you bear up against the pressures of these times.[68]

He informed Willstätter during the summer that his resignation had been accepted as of 30 September 1933, and he remarked: "[I] am herewith free to think about how I will arrange this last chapter of my life. A lot of things are brought to a close more simply than I had thought."[69]

During his odyssey through various countries in 1933 Haber met his friend in Switzerland, in Paris, and later, for the last time, in Santander, as described above. Only three of Haber's letters to Willstätter from this period remain, all of them written during his sojourn in Cambridge. In one he informed Willstätter that he would travel to Paris on 25 December. And he makes a remark that shows how downcast he felt—but also how grateful to his hosts:

> Personally, I have two wishes: one concerns morphine and the other NaCy [sodium cyanide]. Presumably you will not want to make easier my struggles to get hold of these reserve supplies for old age. I feel exceptionally well here. I enjoy the kindliness, namely that of [William Jackson] Pope, but I would have to begin my life anew were I to regain the sense of an existence that is complete. The life's work I have lost is for me irreplaceable.[70]

Although Willstätter knew how sick Haber was, it must have been a shock for him when he heard of his friend's death in Basel. He immediately traveled there and met Fritz Haber's half sister Else, his son Hermann, and his friend Rudolf Stern. He spoke a few moving words at his friend's graveside.

For some time Willstätter maintained extensive correspondence with Hermann; their contact ended shortly before World War II began. Willstätter's last surviving letter, which he wrote in exile in Switzerland, mentioned the move of Hermann's family to the United States, something often discussed in previous letters.

Of his stay in Switzerland, Willstätter commented: "If I remain healthy, life would be very good here, if only grief and sorrow did not ride behind me in the saddle."[71] This grief—including that for the many relatives and friends who were to be carried off during the war, kept barely alive in the concentration camps, and some of them murdered—weakened his health, just as with Haber, and finally led to his death in August 1942. Thus both friends died in exile in Switzerland, a country where they had many a time spent wonderful days of relaxation together.

Friendships were a wellspring that enriched Haber's life. He could discuss his thoughts freely with his friends, and he got new ideas from give and take. He gave friends advice and help and received both in return. So arose an inner solidarity, one in particular that he was privileged to experience with Richard Willstätter, a gift that carried him through many difficult hours, particularly during the last years of his life.

# Endnotes

[1] Clara Haber to Richard Abegg, 15 Sept. 1901, 18 Oct. 1901, 15 Feb. 1902, and undated, MPG, Dept. Va, Rep. 5, 921–926.

[2] A relative's description in a letter to Johannes Jaenicke, MPG, Dept. Va, Rep. 5, 215.

[3] Clara Haber to Abegg, 25 April 1909, MPG, Dept. Va, Rep. 5, 812.

[4] A memorandum regarding a conversation with Mrs. Noack (daughter of a female friend of Clara Haber), MPG, Dept. Va, Rep. 5, 215.

[5] Ibid.

[6] Descriptions and memories of a coworker of Haber's from 1958, MPG, Dept. Va, Rep. 5, 260, 261.

[7] Charlotte Haber, *Mein Leben mit Fritz Haber: Spiegelungen der Vergangenheit* (My life with Fritz Haber: Reflections on the past) (Düsseldorf: Econ Publishers, 1970).

[8] *Im Frieden der Menschheit, im Kriege dem Vaterland: 75 Jahre Fritz-Haber-Institut der Max-Planck-Gesellschaft: Bermerkungen zur Geschichte der Gegenwart* (For humanity in time of peace, for the fatherland in time of war: 75 years of the Fritz Haber Institute of the Max Planck Society: Remarks on contemporary history) (Berlin: Fritz Haber Institute, October 1986). See also Gerda von Leitner, *Der Fall Clara Immerwahr: Leben für eine humane Wissenschaft* (The case of Clara Immerwahr: A life for a humane science) (Munich: Beck Verlag, 1993).

[9] Noack conversation (cit. note 4).

[10] Descriptions (cit. note 6).

[11] Ibid.; and Charlotte Haber, *Mein Leben* (cit. note 7).

[12] Charlotte Haber, *Mein Leben* (cit. note 7), 112.

[13] Ibid., 119.

[14] Ibid., 121.

[15] Fritz Haber to Hermann Haber, undated, MPG, Dept. Va, Rep. 5.

[16] Fritz Haber to Hermann Haber, 16 April 1931, MPG, Dept. Va, Rep. 5, 889.

[17] Fritz Haber to Hermann Haber, early Dec. 1931, MPG, Dept. Va, Rep. 5, 893.

[18] Hermann Haber to Fritz Haber, 6 May 1932, MPG, Dept. Va, Rep. 5, 1046.

[19] Speech by Hermann Haber at the opening of the Fritz Haber Library in Rehovot on 29 Jan. 1936, MPG, Dept. Va, Rep. 5, 926.

[20] Lutz Haber, conversation with Dietrich Stoltzenberg, 11 Oct. 1989, Bath, Stoltzenberg private archive.

[21] Charlotte Haber, *Mein Leben* (cit. note 7), 113–114.

[22] Ibid., introduction.

[23] Charlotte Haber (from the Schiffbauerdamm Clinic in Berlin) to Fritz Haber (in Wildbad), MPG, Dept. Va, Rep. 5, still unnumbered.

[24] Fritz Haber to Charlotte Haber, postmarked 9 Aug. 1918, MPG, Dept. Va, Rep. 5, still unnumbered.

[25] Fritz Haber to Charlotte Haber, 9 Aug. 1918, MPG, Dept. Va, Rep. 5, still unnumbered.

[26] Charlotte Haber, *Mein Leben* (cit. note 7), 271f.

[27] Eva Lewis-Haber, conversation with Dietrich Stoltzenberg, Bath, 11 Oct. 1989, Stoltzenberg private archive.

[28] Ibid.

[29] Rudolf Stern, *Fritz Haber: Personal Recollections*, Leo Baeck Institute Yearbook 8 (New York, 1969), 70.

[30] Ibid., 75.

[31] Telegram from Fritz Haber to Rudolf Stern, date not readable, MPG, Dept. Va, Rep. 5, unnumbered.

[32] Stern, *Fritz Haber* (cit. note 29), 87.

[33] Ibid., 90.

[34] Ibid., 98.

[35] Ibid., 100.

[36] Fritz Stern, "Freunde im Widerspruch—Haber und Einstein" (Friends in opposition: Haber and Einstein), in *Forschung im Spannungsfeld von Politik und Gesellschaft: Geschichte und Struktur des Kaiser-Wilhelm/Max-Planck-Gesellschaft* (Research in the tension between politics and society: History and structure of the Kaiser Wilhelm/Max Planck Society), ed. Rudolf Vierhaus and Bernhard vom Brocke (Stuttgart: Deutsche Verlags-Anstalt, 1990), 516–551.

[37] On Einstein's life and work see, e.g., Albert Einstein, *Mein Weltbild* (My view of the world) (Berlin: Ullstein, 1959); G. J. Whitrow, ed., *Einstein: The Man and His Achievement* (London: BBC, 1967); Abraham Pais, *Subtle Is the Lord: The Science and the Life of Albert Einstein* (Oxford/New York: Oxford University Press, 1982); Albrecht Fölsing, *Albert Einstein: Eine Biographie* (Albert Einstein: A biography) (Frankfurt: Suhrkamp Verlag, 1993).

[38] Albert Einstein, "Grundlagen der allgemeinen Relativitätstheorie" (The foundations of the theory of general relativity), *Annalen der Physik* 49:4 (1916), 767–822.

[39] Fritz Haber to Albert Einstein, January 1918, MPG, Dept. Va, Rep. 5, unnumbered.

[40] Haber to Einstein, 30 Aug. 1920 (from Bad Gastein), MPG, Dept. Va, Rep. 5, 861.

[41] Haber to Einstein, undated but about 1920/21, MPG, Dept. Va, Rep. 5, 922.

[42] Haber to Einstein, 2 Sept. 1922, MPG, Dept. Va, Rep. 5, 979.

[43] Haber to Einstein, 1927, MPG, Dept. Va, Rep. 5, 979.

[44] Haber to Einstein, 14 March 1929, MPG, Dept. Va, Rep. 5, 980.

[45] Haber to Einstein, about 1932, undated, MPG, Dept. Va, Rep. 5.

[46] Einstein to Haber, 23 Nov. 1931, MPG, Dept. Va, Rep. 5, 981.

[47] "Dr. Einstein Urges Hitler Protests,"*New York Times*, Mar. 1933, MPG, Dept. Va, Rep. 5.

[48] Haber to Einstein, 8 May 1933, MPG, Dept. Va, Rep. 5, 983.

[49] Haber to Einstein, 11 May 1933, MPG, Dept. Va, Rep. 5, 983.

[50] Einstein to Haber, 19 May 1933, MPG, Dept. Va, Rep. 5, 983.

[51] Haber (in Paris) to Einstein, summer 1933, MPG, Dept. Va, Rep. 5, 983.

[52] Einstein to Haber, 9 Aug. 1933, MPG, Dept. Va, Rep. 5, 983.

[53] Fritz Stern, "Freunde im Widerspruch" (cit. note 36), 550.

[54] Richard Willstätter, *Aus meinem Leben* (From my life), 2nd ed., ed. Arthur von Stoll (Weinheim: Verlag Chemie, 1958); trans. Lilli S. Hornig as *From My Life: The Memoirs of Richard Willstätter* (New York: W. A. Benjamin, 1965), 400. Citations in this chapter are all to the Hornig translation.

[55] Ibid., 24.

[56] Richard Willstätter, "Synthesen der Tropingruppe" (Synthesis of the tropine groups), *Annalen der Chemie* 317 (1901), 204–374; and 326 (1903), 1–128.

[57] Richard Willstätter, "Untersuchungen über Chlorophyll" (Investigations of chlorophyll), *Annalen der Chemie* 350 (1906), 1–48.

[58] Richard Willstätter, *Untersuchungen über Chlorophyll* (Investigations of chlorophyll) (Berlin: Verlag Julius Springer, 1913).

[59] Willstätter, *From My Life*, trans. Hornig (cit. note 54), 216.

[60] Ibid., 400, 402, 403.

[61] Ibid., 414.

[62] Julio Kocherthaler to Fritz Haber, 23 July 1933, MPG, Dept. Va, Rep. 5, 1091.

[63] Richard Willstätter, essay for a Haber Festschrift, *Naturwissenschaften* 16:50 (1928), 1053–1078; reproduced in Willstätter, *Aus meinem Leben* (cit. note 54); quoting from *From My Life,* trans. Hornig, 268–269.

[64] Haber to Willstätter, undated, 1929, MPG, Dept. Va, Rep. 5, 886.

[65] Haber to Willstätter, 19 Oct. 1931, 21 Oct. 1931, and undated, MPG, Dept. Va, Rep. 5, 892, 1200 and 916.

[66] Fritz Haber, "Zum 60. Geburtstag von Richard Willstätter" (For Richard Willstätter's 60th birthday), *Naturwissenschaften* 20 (1932), 601.

[67] Haber to Willstätter, undated, end of Feb., MPG, Dept. Va, Rep. 5.

[68] Haber to Willstätter, undated, April 1933, MPG, Dept. Va, Rep. 5, 1202.

[69] Haber to Willstätter, undated, June/July 1933, MPG, Dept. Va, Rep. 5, 1202.

[70] Haber (in Cambridge) to Willstätter, undated, Dec. 1933, MPG, Dept. Va, Rep. 5, 916.

[71] Willstätter (in Switzerland) to Hermann Haber, 31 May 1939, MPG, Dept. Va, Rep. 5, 1202.

*Chapter 10*

---◆---

# The Nobel Prize
# and
# Succession
# to
# Emil Fischer's Position

*Emil Fischer, circa 1910.*

*Previous page: Fritz Haber's Nobel Prize certificate.*

I N TIMES OF INTERNATIONAL TENSION AND WAR THE SELECTION OF THE
Nobel Prize recipients is accompanied by heightened emotions on the part
of governments, the press, and scientific circles. Such was the case during
and especially after World War I, when many Germans received prizes.[1]

Emotions reached their high point when the prizewinners, who had been
notified during the war but had been unable to travel to Stockholm, were
invited to a prize-giving ceremony in 1920 on Nobel's birthday, 1 June. One
sign of those feelings was who came to the event: all the German prizewinners from 1914 to 1919 attended, but only one of the others, the Englishman Charles Glover Barkla. The French and British publics were
incensed that Haber in particular and Willstätter as well had been distinguished by the award in chemistry, since both had played significant roles in
the mobilization for chemical warfare. Haber had even been included in the
first list of war criminals. When Nernst was awarded the chemistry prize in
that same year, the indignation knew no bounds. The daily press as well as
political and professional journals whipped up waves of accusations against
the Nobel committee.

These accusations, however, did not take into consideration that the suggestions and nominations for the prize were often made some years before.
Thus the award of the Nobel Prize to Fritz Haber was discussed in 1910,
when Friedrich Schmidt-Ott from the Ministry of Education traveled to
Sweden to consult with Svante Arrhenius on the appointment of the director of the Kaiser Wilhelm Institute for Physical Chemistry.[2]

Haber was especially happy about the prize and the invitation to Stockholm. It compensated a little for all he had had to suffer in Berlin after the
war and for the heavy burden of the Allies' accusations, including his listing
in 1918 as a war criminal. A new list in 1920 omitted his name.

Five highly elated German Nobel laureates traveled to Stockholm in 1920 and had a wonderful time taking part in the celebrations associated with the awards.[3]

The speech on the presentation of the prize to Fritz Haber was given by the president of the Swedish Royal Academy of Sciences, Å. G. Ekstrand. He mentioned the importance of the various types of artificial fertilizers and the special significance of minerals containing nitrogen and discussed the possible methods for synthesizing various nitrogen-containing compounds, such as the Frank-Caro process and the oxidation of nitrogen. He briefly summarized Haber's work on the ammonia synthesis, its scaling up by Carl Bosch, the oxidation of ammonia to yield nitric acid by Ostwald's process, and finally the conversion of nitric acid into stable nitrate salts. At the end of the speech he adressed Haber directly:

> This country's Academy of Sciences has awarded you the 1918 Nobel Prize for chemistry in recognition of your great services in the solution of the problem of directly combining atmospheric nitrogen with hydrogen. A solution to this problem had been repeatedly attempted before, but you were the first to provide the industrial solution and thus to create an exceedingly important means of improving the standards of agriculture and the well-being of mankind. We congratulate you on this triumph in the service of your country and the whole of humanity. Please, accept now your prize from the President of the Nobel Foundation.[4]

Ekstrand's laudatory address is remarkable for its omissions: although he described in detail the significance of the ammonia synthesis for agriculture, he made no mention of its significance for the explosives industry, in which Nobel made his fortune. Such remarks clearly would not have been appropriate, particularly since Nobel's will stipulated that the prize "should be awarded to those who in the year just past have brought great benefits to humanity." Haber's Nobel Prize lecture began with the words: "The Swedish Academy of Sciences has seen fit, by awarding the Nobel Prize, to honor the method of producing ammonia from nitrogen and hydrogen. This extraordinary distinction puts upon me the obligation of explaining the position occupied by this reaction within the subject of chemistry as a whole and [of outlining] the road that led to it."[5]

Haber went on to describe in general terms the state of chemical knowledge about this reaction before his work. He then explained the motives that led to his investigations. He mentioned the economic significance of a possible industrial application of the reaction and further described, just as

Ekstrand had done before him, the nitrogen cycle in nature and agriculture in the pre-industrial age. His speech ended with the following glimpse into the future:

> The solution that we found to the problem derives its importance from the fact that very high temperature levels are not used, and that this makes the ratio of coal consumption to nitrogen production more favorable than is the case with other processes. Results are enough to show that, in combination with other methods of nitrogen fixation, which I have mentioned, they relieve us of future worries caused by the exhaustion of the saltpeter deposits, which has threatened us these twenty years.
>
> It may be that this solution is not the final one. Nitrogen bacteria teach us that Nature, with her sophisticated forms of the chemistry of living matter, still understands and utilizes methods that we do not as yet know how to imitate. Let it suffice that in the meantime improved nitrogen fertilization of the soil brings new nutritive riches to mankind and that the chemical industry comes to the aid of the farmer who, in the good earth, changes stones into bread.[6]

This almost prophetic concluding sentence of his Nobel Prize lecture shows how far Haber could see into the future of scientific development. Much effort is now being spent on using bacteria for the very purposes Haber had indicated.

In 1920 Haber almost received another high honor, namely that of becoming Emil Fischer's successor at the University of Berlin. The then "wise old man" of organic chemistry, to whom Haber had grown closer during the war, died in 1919. The incumbent of the chair of chemistry at the University of Berlin held a special place among the professors of chemistry at German universities. To be appointed to this chair was not only high recognition of the nominee's scientific ranking but also a great honor generally. The appointee occupied high status in Berlin society. He could make critical contributions to solving problems in science and could influence the decisions of governmental agencies in ways that would affect the whole country.

Richard Willstätter was chosen first as Emil Fischer's successor, but he declined. This angered Carl Duisberg, the director of the Bayer Company and the president of the Society of Chemical Industry (Verband der Chemischen Industrie), who had supported Willstätter's appointment. Subsequently, a battle ensued over Fischer's successor in which many were involved, especially Duisberg. Apart from Willstätter, the first short list for the appointment included Ludwig Knorr and Carl Dietrich Harries. They both hesitated to accept. Then the government minister responsible for the appointment apparently approached the selection committee and indicated that it was far more important to appoint an exceptional person than a person working like Fischer in the field of organic chemistry. Clearly the minister was already thinking of Fritz Haber. The committee responsible at the University of Berlin—Ernst Beckmann, Gottlieb Haberlandt, and Max Rubner—expressed their opinion in a letter to the minister.

> The faculty greets with the utmost sympathy the suggestion that the question of Emil Fischer's succession should be examined without necessarily considering Emil Fischer's special field of work but rather by trying to gain a personage of quite unquestionable and outstanding consequence. The faculty is convinced that the following suggestion sent to Your Excellency will satisfy these demands.
>
> However, the faculty cannot refrain from once more expressing its conviction that the three persons selected in its first suggestion [Willstätter, Knorr, Harries] were quite the best that the faculty could put forward with regard to the encouragement of organic chemistry in teaching and research, and that the faculty would still not be able to name any better German representatives of organic chemistry today. Under these circumstances the faculty cannot suppress its concern that if, for whatever reason, the suggestion given below should turn out to be unrealistic in the course of the negotiations for the appointment, the chances of winning Professor Knorr or Professor Harries, which are not great now, would be reduced even further.[7]

The opening passage reveals that a difference of opinion on the occupation of the chair already existed among the scholars. Doubts about the suggestions, which followed, had been expressed from various sides. The letter continues:

> With these reservations, the faculty members signing this document propose the present director of the Kaiser Wilhelm Institute for Physical Chemistry in Dahlem, Prof. Dr. Fritz Haber. Even though, at present, he essentially represents physical chemistry, he is originally not a physicist but a chemist and well experienced in the fields of inorganic chemistry and organic chemistry, as proved by a number of excellent publications in these fields. Haber therefore seems clearly able and in all respects excellently qualified to direct the general teaching in the field of chemistry, the most important task of Fischer's institute, whereby his well-known and extraordinary organizational talent will prove useful to the interests of the university.[8]

Haber's appointment would also solve various other problems. First, it would strengthen the currently uncertain position of Ernst Beckmann and counter the speculations about Beckmann's leaving. Second, the old suggestion was raised again of merging the Kaiser Wilhelm Institute for Chemistry with the university. Apart from the university it is not clear who supported this suggestion. The Ministry of Education appears to have been favorably inclined to it, but it seems doubtful whether Haber would have agreed to such a connection after an eventual appointment. It is also not known how the Kaiser Wilhelm Society reacted, but it would probably have strongly opposed such plans. The society's president, Adolf von Harnack, supported Haber's appointment as Fischer's successor, and it seems therefore likely that Haber would not have supported the plan put forward by Beckmann, Haberlandt, and Rubens for incorporating the institute into the university.

When Carl Duisberg learned that Haber was to be appointed Emil Fischer's successor, he was vehemently opposed. Duisberg had a major say in the discussion about Fischer's successor. His connection to Fischer stretched back into the prewar period; they had worked closely together on many questions of inventions and their uses as well as in the politics of science education and the promotion of research. Duisberg from the beginning had supported Fischer's idea of founding a national institute of chemistry, realized when the Kaiser Wilhelm Institute for Chemistry was founded. In fact Duisberg later sat on the board of directors of this institute. He played a decisive role in the Kaiser Wilhelm Society and was a member of its senate from 1917 up to his death in 1935. From October 1920 he was also deputy treasurer. He was director of the Justus Liebig Society for the Promotion of Teaching in Chemistry, an organization founded on Fischer's initiative. Like Fischer, Duisberg was a member of the National Economic Council, and, as the managing director of one of the largest chemical companies in Germany, he also had considerable influence in the chemical sciences.

Duisberg was extremely disappointed when Richard Willstätter declined Fischer's position, and it damaged their relationship considerably. Now Duisberg responded with an emphatic "no!" to Haber's appointment. This led Willstätter, who did not understand Duisberg's behavior toward his friend, to make reproaches, which created an irreparable rift in their previously good relations.

Duisberg repeatedly justified his conduct over Haber's appointment in correspondence with Harnack. He thought that Emil Fischer's chair, the leading chair in organic chemistry in Germany, should retain this orientation. Although his relationship with Haber was good, he found it inconceivable that a physical chemist such as Haber should hold this chair. Duisberg asked Harnack to inform the Ministry of Education about his opinion, "which, as I do not doubt, is that of the representatives of the majority of the chemical industry in Germany." He concluded with the threat: "I fear that were the significance of organic chemistry to be pushed into the background to that extent, it will be impossible or very difficult to raise money for the purpose of supporting chemical research, both now and in the future."[9]

Harnack reacted with great diplomacy to this massive attack and further defended the plan of having Haber succeed Emil Fischer. But Duisberg's influence was so strong that he was able to persuade not only Harnack but also the faculty of the university and the minister of education to drop the plan. This did not end the fighting over Emil Fischer's successor. There was talk of splitting the chair and its resources. Finally, after extensive discussions, in which Duisberg was also involved, Wilhelm Schlenk, an organic chemist from Vienna, was offered the position, and he accepted.

Haber's relationship with Duisberg, which up till then had been good, was greatly strained by these events. True, Haber and Duisberg maintained the appearance of good relations in public and in their work in various societies. Yet it is no wonder that during this period Haber began to consider whether he should leave Berlin. Instead he continued to consolidate his institute and had great plans for expanding the direction of research and other work in the first years after the war. Unfortunately the financial crises in the postwar period prevented these plans from being realized. The next chapter will delve further into this period, delineating the life and scientific work in an institute during a period of radical change in both physics and physical chemistry.

## Endnotes

[1] The prize for physics was awarded to Max von Laue (Germany, 1914), William Henry Bragg and his son William Lawrence Bragg (England, 1915), Charles Glover Barkla (England, 1917), Max Planck (Germany, 1918), Johannes Starck (Germany, 1919), Charles Edward Guillaume (Switzerland, 1920), and Albert Einstein (Germany and Switzerland, 1921), with no prize awarded in 1916. The prize for chemistry was awarded to Theodore W. Richards (United States, 1914), Richard Willstätter (Germany, 1915), Fritz Haber (Ger-

many, 1918), Walther Hermann Nernst (Germany, 1920), and Frederick Soddy (England, 1921), with no prizes awarded in 1916, 1917, or 1919.

[2] Friedrich Schmidt-Ott, *Erlebtes und Erstrebtes, 1860–1950* (Experience and aspiration, 1860–1950) (Wiesbaden: Franz Steiner Verlag, 1952), especially chap. 18, "Kaiser-Wilhelm-Gesellschaft."

[3] Richard Willstätter, *Aus meinem Leben* (From my life), 2nd ed., ed. Arthur von Stoll (Weinheim: Verlag Chemie, 1958); and Charlotte Haber, *Mein Leben mit Fritz Haber: Spiegelungen der Vergangenheit* (My life with Fritz Haber: Reflections on the past) (Düsseldorf: Econ Verlag, 1970), 141.

[4] *Nobel Lectures: Chemistry, 1901–1921* (Amsterdam: Elsevier, published for the Nobel Foundation, 1966), 321 (lightly edited).

[5] Ibid., 326.

[6] Ibid.

[7] E. Beckmann, G. Haberlandt, and H. Rubens to the minister of education, 3 Jan. 1920, Humboldt University, Berlin, Archive of the Philosophical Faculty, No. 1468, folio 208–211.

[8] Ibid.

[9] Carl Duisberg to Adolf von Harnack, after 26 Feb. 1920, cited in H. J. Fechtner and Carl Duisberg, *Vom Chemiker zum Wirtschaftsführer* (From chemist to captain of industry) (Düsseldorf: Econ Verlag, 1959).

*Chapter 11*

# Haber's Institute
# and
# Scientific Work from 1919 to 1933

*Treating a mill with hydrogen cyanide.*

*Previous page: Fritz Haber at the blackboard. Seated are Count Hermann von Schweinitz and Ladislaus Farkas, and Paul Goldfinger stands at the left.*

Q UOTATIONS FROM THE RECOLLECTIONS OF TWO PHYSICAL CHEMISTS
who were deeply involved in the "great period of physical chemistry" that
"began in Berlin at the end of World War I and lasted until 1933" make
an appropriate introduction for this chapter. The words just quoted are Paul
Harteck's, in his retrospective review "Physical Chemists in Berlin, 1919–
1933." About Haber's institute he writes:

> [Haber proceeded] to develop his institute and organize it in such a way that
> it became, without a doubt, the leading institution for physical chemistry in
> those days. Scientists, young and old, and many guests were in contact with
> Haber's institute. . . .
>
> Haber, by his personality, gave tone to the institute. He was wise enough
> to know that one has to give to the group leaders and also to keen young
> members of the institute [the] far-reaching scientific freedom to develop an
> atmosphere of free scientific thinking and enterprise.[1]

Wilhelm Jost gives a similar picture in his review of the first forty-five
years of physical chemistry in Germany. He portrays Berlin as the center of
German physical chemistry and mentions the three most important institutes. First was Nernst's institute at the university, where Franz Simon, Arnold
Eucken, F. A. Lindemann (later Lord Chatwell), and Henry Tizard worked,
and which Max Bodenstein took over in 1923. Second was the group of
physical chemists that Max Volmer gathered around himself at the Charlot-
tenburg Institute of Technology in 1922, which included Ivan Stranski,
Paul Günther, and Eugen Wigner. Above all was Haber's institute, where
Jost singled out James Franck, Gustav Hertz, Herbert Freundlich, Michael
Polanyi, Rudolf Ladenburg, Karl Friedrich Bonhoeffer, and Paul Harteck.
In Jost's opinion,

the decisive factors influencing physical chemistry in Berlin between 1918 and 1933 included not only the availability of these three independent groups of physical chemists but also the additional stimulation from physics, especially theoretical physics. Planck had been there for decades; later came Einstein, and then von Laue. [Erwin] Schrödinger and F[ritz] London came in 1927, and W[alter] Schottky and E[ugen] Wigner returned to Berlin at the same time. . . . There were so many independent scientists in Berlin that the atmosphere for work and the contacts and connections among them were so free . . . that each young man had a chance of being successful with his own ideas. There was much poverty here, but that was really no limitation for truly creative young people. . . . During the 1920s and early 1930s, Berlin provided a unique environment for the flowering of modern physical chemistry and the newly developing theoretical chemistry.[2]

## A New Beginning in the Institute

A chapter of Haber's life came to a close with the end of World War I and the collapse of the German Empire. He now had to accept a fall from the heights to which he had climbed during the war, and he was confronted with questions and accusations that he often found incomprehensible but that weighed heavily on him nonetheless. Many of his actions and reactions immediately after the war can be explained by this situation: for example, his involvement in the Demobilization Office, his further secret activity in the field of chemical weapons, his behavior toward the Interallied Control Commission, his pleasure over the Nobel Prize, and his fear of possibly facing a war crimes tribunal. He grew a beard so that he would not be as easily recognizable when out in public; attacks on prominent people were fairly common in the turbulence of war-ravaged Berlin. He also had to deal with the consequences of his overexertion during the war. His health was broken; he experienced periods of weakness and often had to interrupt his work to take rest breaks.

Considering all these factors, it is amazing that Haber managed to reorganize his institute completely and build up new research departments. Even during the war he had been concerned about what would happen after its end—hence his efforts to fulfill the plans of his patron, Leopold Koppel, for an Institute for Military Science. Of course these plans were out of the question after Germany lost the war. But Haber was not prepared to surrender to the chaos around him. On the contrary, he tried to convert these plans into a peacetime program. The means were available, both in equipment and in financial support. And finally he had to integrate his large staff, still in place in 1919, into a new and appropriate program.

During the war, buildings, facilities, and equipment available in Haber's institute and in others had been commandeered for military purposes. Even if some of this property was no longer usable, the laboratories could still be made operable. The temporary buildings on the institute grounds in which physiological experiments had been carried out on animals during the war had to be torn down because many rooms were in too poor a condition for scientific research. Improvisation was necessary, which was nothing new, since many scientists had become old hands at this during the war.

Haber could not of course keep every one of his workers on, although he took great pains to retain as many as possible. That effort was probably one reason he had such good relations with the Workers' and Soldiers' Council (Arbeiter- und Soldatenrat) established in his institute after the war. He was able to choose the best coworkers from the large group of employees from his own institute and from the others he had directed during the war.

The list of institute members in 1919 is dominated by personalities who later achieved great reputations in physics, chemistry, and physiology. Some worked only as guests; either they did not want to tie themselves down, or Haber could not give them a permanent position. To mention a few: the physicist James Franck, later a Nobel laureate; Gustav Hertz, who worked with Franck and received the Nobel Prize with him; Hermann Mark, later a polymer chemist; the physical and colloid chemist Herbert Freundlich, who was to remain a member of the institute for many years; the pharmacologist Ferdinand Flury; the physical chemist Reginald Herzog; the physiologist Albrecht Hase, who became well known in the field of pesticides; the organic chemist Paul Friedländer; and the physical chemist Karl Weissenberg.

With these people Haber tried to construct a multidisciplinary institute. His previous experience in Karlsruhe and Dahlem had convinced him that to expand knowledge rapidly in many areas, as well as to develop highly specialized technologies and methods, would require increasingly closer cooperation between various disciplines—physics and chemistry, including both physical and physiological chemistry—in order to increase the potential of research. He therefore intended to build up an institute with eight largely independent departments, the first of which would be the departments of physics, directed by Franck, and of colloid chemistry, directed by Freundlich.

*Participants in a seminar with Niels Bohr in 1920. Front row (left to right): Otto Stern, James Franck, Niels Bohr, Lise Meitner, Hans Geiger, Peter Pringsheim. Middle row (left to right): Lenz (first name unknown), Rudolf Ladenburg, Otto Hahn. Back row (left to right): Paul Knipping, C. S. Wagner, Johann von Baeyer, Georg von Hevesy, Wilhelm Westphal, Gustav Hertz.*

These would be followed by pharmacology, under Flury, and theoretical physics, for which he tried to involve Einstein as a consultant.

This period of astonishing development and interdisciplinary cooperation at Haber's institute lasted for only a short time, as the money from the war effort ran dry and inflation consumed the institute's endowment. But for those who had found a haven of work there, this period provided an unforgettable experience. Many of the descriptions from those involved sound almost euphoric. Haber's commitment to interdisciplinary cooperation was exemplary and found its fullest expression in the colloquia he started in 1919, which maintained a worldwide reputation well into the 1930s.

The Haber colloquia were of unusual character and gave Haber an ideal opportunity to make the borders more fluid between physics, chemistry, physical chemistry, and biology. Many guest speakers came from different fields, and the department heads and older scientists from other Dahlem institutes gave lectures. Widely differing themes were discussed, as one said in those days, "from the helium atom to the flea." Every lecture was followed by a passionate discussion, deliberately stirred up by Haber, and scientists from all the represented disciplines had a chance to speak, so that the discussion automatically stimulated interest across specialist boundaries. Haber regarded controversy as a necessary element for the clarification of a problem, and he had a great dislike of dogmatic views. Younger people, who were especially encouraged to participate in the seminars, developed an immunity to authoritarian and dogmatic thinking. At this time scientific knowledge was expanding quickly in all areas, and no one could claim to have the right answers. Haber never shied away from bringing suggestions and ideas into the discussion that shocked some new participants—often deliberately provoking refutation. Some of Haber's ideas that were not realized until later originated in this first period after the war—ideas on pesticides, toxicology, capillary chemistry, and the chemistry of manmade fibers.

But two years after the war ended, a great crisis in the institute cut short this promising beginning. The funds left over from the war were gone, Koppel's endowment was eaten up by increasing inflation, and the state could not help. Industry was still depressed, and the conditions of the Treaty of Versailles were so harsh and the reparation costs so high that the public, the federal and state governments, and business and industry were not easily convinced of the importance of research and development. Through his own deep commitment Haber sought to change that.

## Financial Crisis and Consolidation

For the first two years after the war, Haber's plans for a multidisciplinary research institute were financed, along with other support, primarily by the six million marks that Leopold Koppel had originally donated to support military research. As early as November 1918 provision had been made for the council of the foundation to have command of those funds at their disposal without limitation. Early in 1920, however, financial difficulties began. By October 1919 the treasurer of the Kaiser Wilhelm Society (KWS), Franz von Mendelssohn, had announced that the mark's reduced purchasing power prevented construction of a new building that was planned.[3] When Haber saw the financial crisis coming, he wrote in January 1920 to the president of the society, Adolf von Harnack: "The devaluation of the currency [can] no longer be regarded as a phenomenon that will pass quickly."[4]

Haber attempted to merge his institute with the university.[5] His concern was, above all, to support his closest scientific coworkers, to whom he could not offer much money or respectable titles. He considered various possibilities for raising money for his institute and early on suggested selling the war loans that had been underwritten by the institute's foundation. But all of Haber's efforts to maintain the institute at the size it had reached by 1920 failed. An expansion along the lines planned in 1918 was absolutely out of the question. The ambitious plans had to be buried.

The staff and the costs of running the institute had to be drastically reduced. The number of departments was reduced from six to three, while the number of scientific coworkers and other employees was reduced from forty to twenty-five. Haber tried to employ workers who were as young and therefore as inexpensive as possible and who were happy to find any work at all. The size of the budget sank dramatically from 243,000 marks in 1919 to 65,000 marks in 1923.[6] But, in 1923, even after these drastic measures had been taken and there was a renewed possibility of receiving financial support, Haber still had to turn to the Ministry of Education for an assurance that it would cover the deficit.[7] In this phase of stabilization, from autumn 1923 to July 1924, the issue was one of sheer survival.

Haber was finally successful in persuading the national and Prussian governments to help, in view of the forced reduction in salaries and the modest support in operating costs. One consequence of this support was that Haber's institute was now fully integrated into the KWS, both organizationally and financially. Nonetheless, the Kaiser Wilhelm Institutes themselves, which also received support from sources outside of the society and remained relatively independent, could act according to their own judgment and were never required to reveal fully their finances and their organization to the general KWS administration. As can be seen from many documents, however, Haber remained loyal to the general administration and to the president.

Haber's institute received various donations in the ensuing years. He succeeded, for example, in persuading Koppel to increase the support he had already promised the institute to 15,000 gold marks annually for ten years.[8] Koppel paid this sum up until 1935, by which time Haber had already fled the country and died. Haber himself contributed to the institute the payments he received as a member of the board of directors of IG Farben.

The institute's financial position was more successfully consolidated by 1924, but difficulties arose again and again, especially where new facilities and buildings were concerned. However, although there were some differences of opinion over financing with the general administration of the society, it was still possible to carry out such plans up to 1930.

The Great Depression that began in 1929 hit Germany particularly hard and led to the decline of its economy, enormous unemployment, and considerably reduced income for the state and thus to extremely strict economic measures by the national and the Prussian governments. It took some time before these measures affected the KWS. By repeatedly submitting many memoranda that conveyed the same message in the same terms—that without growing public subsidies there would be no development, that falling subsidies meant an unavoidable catastrophe, and that an external control of finances would affect scientific freedom—the society actually succeeded in increasing its public subsidies up to the fiscal year 1930–31. Only then did fairly steep cuts begin that led, in 1932–33, to a reduction in subsidies to 70 percent of what they had been in 1930–31.[9]

Assistance from both the state and Koppel's foundation kept Haber and his institute relatively unaffected by this renewed financial crisis. Although the number of workers in the institute sank from sixty-one in 1931 to thirty-eight in 1932, his personnel budget was higher in 1932 than in 1931. The reduction in personnel was partly caused by the closure of the physics department after its head, Rudolf Ladenburg, emigrated and went to Princeton.

But let us turn to Haber's work in those fertile years.

## The Work: Pest Control

On 15 February 1917, in the rooms of War Chemicals Incorporated (Kriegs-chemikalien Aktiengesellschaft), a meeting was held about the means to control pests that threatened both agriculture and the storage of agricultural products. Participants included representatives of the Ministries of War, the Interior, and Finance; Friedrich Schmidt-Ott from the Ministry of Education; the minister of agriculture; a representative of the National Biological Institute in Dahlem; Fritz Roessler from the management of Degussa (Deutsche Gold- und Silberscheideanstalt, the German Gold and Silver Refinery); and Fritz Haber. Haber had a particular interest in this meeting. He thought that the field of pest control offered his institute a way to continue its work on chemical weapons, even though the war had ended. As he put it: "The experiences gained in gas warfare must be further pursued and deepened, . . . essentially through scientific research within the framework of a scientific institute." He referred to plans launched concurrently under the aegis of the Foundation for Military Technology and Science that had been established at the end of 1916.[10]

The deployment of hydrogen cyanide, already used in pest control in America, was discussed at this meeting. The Degussa representatives reported in detail on their experiences. As a manufacturer of cyanides the company was very interested in finding a new field of use for their products, and they were supported by Richard Heymons, a professor at the Agricultural College. Heymons was a cofounder of the German Society for Applied Entomology, founded in 1913 on the initiative of the entomologist Karl Escherich. Escherich had visited the United States in 1911 and was impressed by the excellent organization of the Bureau of Entomology and by the varied methods of fighting harmful insects and worms, especially with hydrogen cyanide.[11] He later became the director of the Institute for Applied Zoology in Munich and one of the leaders in the field of entomology until the end of World War II. (Haber and Escherich were to meet later, but there was never any intensive collaboration between these two researchers.)

The important result of this meeting was the founding of the Technical Committee for Pest Control (Technische Ausschuss für Schädlings-bekämpfung), known as Tasch, a government body at first. Haber became its chairman. It was Tasch's job "to preserve through the application of highly poisonous substances for pest control, the high output that has hitherto been maintained in agriculture and forestry, in viticulture, horticulture, and fruit growing, as well as in industry by the destruction of animal pests; to promote human and animal hygiene; and thereby to ward off diseases."[12] Circumstances permitted this ambitious goal to be only partially met at the time.

As the military had the main say during wartime, and as it was basically the military that had taken the initiative in the current program, Haber and the committee set up a military division to carry out pest control. A pest-control battalion—and later special "gas personnel" at the various general commands—were entrusted with the practical aspects of gassing. They applied hydrogen cyanide for the most part, primarily on commercial mills and granaries as well as military quarters. This campaign began in April 1917 and was carried out mainly in the eastern territories.

Flury reported on the work in Haber's institute on the problems of pest control at a meeting of the Entomological Society in Munich in September 1918.[13] He described the problems that arose when hydrogen cyanide and its derivatives were used for gassing barracks, hospital trains, prisoners' camps, enlisted quarters, and other mainly military installations. Of the work done in the institute, he mentioned investigations on improving gas delivery, increasing the safety of personnel by using protective devices, and calculating the amounts of gas residue, as well as on detecting still-dangerous traces of hydrogen cyanide and on the effects of the gas on animal and human skin. Various analyses were carried out on the absorption of gas by bread, drinks, seeds, and milled products. There was also work on the effects of hydrogen cyanide and other gases on such raw materials as metals and dyestuffs as well as on plants, fungi, and bacteria.

Though Tasch had been started to meet war needs, the founding of a non-government body to take over its tasks was already fully under way at the beginning of 1918. Haber had contacted interested industrial sources and had received pledges of one million marks. On 5 October, at a preparatory meeting for the founding of the new company, Haber once again outlined Tasch's activities.[14] He went into more detail about the economic and business side of the undertaking and mentioned that the current business report showed "that an enterprise has evolved that can pay its way economically."

Eventually the German Corporation for Pest Control (Deutsche Gesellschaft für Schädlingsbekämpfung), known as Degesch, was established as a private company. The first paragraph of the company's statutes asserted that "the object of the company's existence is the control of animal and plant pests using chemical means. . . . The company is permitted to carry out all transactions suitable for promoting the company's purpose." This wording was included in order to forestall any restrictions on pest control with highly poisonous substances. Also important is the second paragraph, which states that "the operation of the company is not directed toward profit, . . . rather the company is to follow exclusively a course directed toward the public good."[15]

After the war Haber gave the directorship of Tasch over to Walter Heerdt, who occupied the position until Tasch was dissolved, when he was made director of Degesch. In 1919 the position of National Commissioner for Pest Control was created and placed under the jurisdiction of the Ministry of Agriculture. It existed, however, only for the short period until Degesch was established as an independent company, when the supervision and control of the preparations used in pest control increasingly passed into the hands of the National Biological Institute. Haber filled the position until it was dissolved in 1920.

In May 1920 Degesch, with Heerdt as director, moved to Frankfurt. Haber took a lively interest in its development. He was also concerned that the company become active outside Germany, and in 1929 he initiated a trip by Heerdt and Albrecht Hase that covered Austria, Yugoslavia, Romania, and Hungary. Degesch later developed into an internationally active company with agents in thirty-nine countries, and treatment with hydrogen cyanide became a routine process.

Both the composition of the gas mixture and the procedure used in applying it underwent further development, which was first carried out in 1919–20 in Flury's department at Haber's institute. At first the gas was applied in both Germany and America simply by releasing it from steel cylinders. But the so-called vat process was introduced during the war. That process used earthenware containers (the "vats") in which acids acted upon metallic cyanides, usually sodium or calcium cyanide. First, dilute sulfuric acid was poured into the vats, and cyanide in paper bags was laid next to them. The person applying the gas then added the cyanide to the vats in such a way that he was always moving toward the exit of the room to be gassed. Of course gas masks with appropriate filters were worn, but one still could remain only for a short time in a room that was being gassed, as absorption through the skin was also a danger.[16]

The so-called Zyklon process was later worked out in Flury's department. In this procedure the hydrocyanic acid was stabilized by a carrier substance and combined with a warning indicator. Formic acid was used as the stabilizer, and the indicator was cyanogen chloride, which has a strong odor. This combination was called Zyklon C.[17]

This occupation of Haber's and of the many others also working in this field had one unforeseen consequence that cannot be overlooked. It is indeed macabre and tragic that the Zyklon process started in Haber's laboratory was used to kill countless Jews at Auschwitz and elsewhere during World War II. Among Haber's relatives who died in Auschwitz were the daughter of his half sister Frieda, Hilde Glücksmann, and her husband and their two children.

## Scientific Work in the Early Years after the War

After the war, while Haber was lobbying first for the reorganization and then later for the preservation of his institute, his coworkers and the guests working in his institute developed active programs of scientific research. Haber's own scientific creativity was considerably reduced at this time because of his poor health. In addition, the emergency at his own institute and difficulties in other scientific fields preoccupied him. His efforts to overcome the continual crises blocked the concentration necessary for the scientific tasks facing him. Even so, some of Haber's papers from this period still clearly show his ability to help generate new discoveries.

Haber became more of a coordinator. He gave his workers maximum freedom in the choice and execution of their scientific work, and he showed, moreover, the greatest interest in the topics being dealt with. He often came to his coworkers' laboratories late in the evening to ask about the state of various experiments, and he had various problems explained to him and gave suggestions during hour-long walks either up and down the institute's corridors or out in the open air. He sometimes intervened to give support. One remarkable intervention involved work that was not even carried out at his institute. It also shows how a fruitful collaboration can grow out of a chance meeting.

The occasion was the exchange of ideas that Haber and Max Born had in 1919, which led to the so-called Born-Haber cycle. From the time he came to Göttingen, Born had occupied himself with the structure of and the forces within crystals. The result was his book *Dynamik der Kristalle*, published in 1915. He worked on the structure of crystals, especially those of cubic sodium chloride, with his research assistant Alfred Landé, and he developed a theory in which he stated that the cohesive forces in ionic crystals have electrical origins.[18]

After World War I had ended, once relative quiet had returned to Berlin, Born turned to the chemical deductions to be drawn from his theory of ionic crystals. He calculated the lattice energy, that is, the work that must be carried out by atomic forces to form a crystal from its ions. But there was no experimental way of testing his theory.

One day, while Born was discussing some problems with Franck in his room at Haber's institute, Haber entered and joined in the debate. Born's ideas immediately inspired him with enthusiasm. Born, who had maintained his reserve toward Haber because of the latter's wartime activities, could "not resist Haber's charm," as he wrote in his memoirs, adding: "He was in fact a fascinating personality, full of life and vigour, with perfect yet somewhat old-fashioned manners, clear-minded, fast-thinking, interested in all fields of science and expert in many of them."[19]

Born learned from Haber that lattice energies had never been calculated, apart from rough estimates made by Albrecht Kossel and by Haber himself. Haber now improved Born's methods of numerical calculation for lattice energies by inventing a graphical representation that is still used today under the name of the Born–Haber cycle. As Haber anticipated, this work caused a small sensation among chemical experts, and in the following years Born was frequently invited to speak at chemistry congresses and to take part in the discussions.

At Haber's institute itself James Franck, head of the physics department, carried out experiments that won him the Nobel Prize in 1925. His work provided experimental verification of Niels Bohr's atomic theory; it was carried out with the help of several students, including Hertha Sponer and Walter Grotrian, and occasional collaboration from Paul Knipping. Sponer remained Franck's research assistant for many years, even in Göttingen, and like Franck fled to America. The two married in 1944, after the death of Franck's first wife, Ingrid. Grotrian later worked at the Institute for Astrophysics in Berlin.

Also important for Franck was his collaboration with Gustav Hertz on the interactions between electrons and atoms. Like Franck, Hertz was from Hamburg; while Franck was Jewish, Hertz was half Jewish. Hertz later developed an important method for the separation of isotopes using diffusion. When the Nazis came to power, he refused to swear loyalty to them and went to work in industry in a laboratory that the Siemens firm set up for

*Max Born in 1932.*

him in Berlin. After World War II he went first to the Soviet Union. From there he traveled to East Germany to join the University of Leipzig, but after his retirement he returned to Berlin, where he died in 1975. He and Franck were awarded the Nobel Prize in 1925 for their discovery of the laws governing the impact of electrons and atoms.

Franck attended high school in Hamburg. He first studied chemistry in Heidelberg, where he met Born, and the two became lifelong friends. Franck then went to Berlin and, influenced by Emil Warburg, studied physics. He also completed his doctorate with Warburg. After research in Berlin on the forces between electrons and atoms, and an interlude in Frankfurt, he carried out research with Hertz on the physics of gas discharges. They continued this work in Haber's institute after World War I.

Franck first met Haber in 1911 in Berlin, where he also participated in the physics seminars that were then organized by Emil Warburg. As Franck remembered in his old age, Haber was the first of "the noble class of

*Geheimräte"* that took a young man seriously. During the war Franck was called into service from Haber's institute and was sent to join Pioneer Regiment 35-36 (see Chapter 7). As he reported, he became Haber's confidential assistant at the front; it was his job to inform Haber of the various battle actions and how they had gone.[20] In 1917 Haber suggested that Franck come to his institute after the war. Although Rubens, the director of the physics institute at the university, wanted Franck back, he accepted Haber's offer. Thus it was that in 1919 Franck took over as head of the physics department in Haber's institute.

Here Franck and Hertz continued experiments on the interaction between electrons and atoms begun in 1912 and 1913. The experiments were significant because they delivered experimental proof for the formulae in Planck's and Einstein's postulates that atoms are characterized by a quantized structure. Bohr's model of the atom, proposed in 1913, was based on this assumption. The experiments of Franck and Hertz showed that individual mercury atoms absorbed and emitted energy in certain quantized steps. These results clearly proved the existence of Planck's energy quantum and put the Planck-Einstein postulate and Bohr's model of the atom on a solid experimental footing. Furthermore, they supplied a new method for measuring Planck's constant.

Through Bohr's mediation Franck was offered the chair of experimental physics at the University of Göttingen's Second Physics Institute in 1920. Franck and Bohr began working in Göttingen at the same time, during the summer semester of 1921. The relationship between Franck and Haber remained cordial, and Franck often visited Haber in Berlin. There he always found "receptive understanding that, in working further along the ideas I had expressed, led far beyond them. I would see a keyhole somewhere, and Haber would open the door."[21] Franck and Haber worked directly together only once—on the oxidation of sulfite solutions as a chain reaction.

Another group that became especially active in the first few years after the war was the department of colloid chemistry under Herbert Freundlich. Freundlich had worked in this field before the war and had been occupied with the chemistry of interfaces since 1907. He had worked with the adsorption isotherm $a = c^{1/n}$, derived empirically by Wilhelm Ostwald and Karl Boedeker in 1905. Freundlich attempted to confirm it and to determine its theoretical significance. In connection with this research he examined the adsorption of various gases and organic substances by active charcoal and the phenomenon of capillary condensation.

*Herbert Freundlich before 1933.*

Haber took Freundlich into his wartime institute in 1916 on the basis of his much-acclaimed work. Thanks to Freundlich's expertise, the air filters in gas masks developed during the war were of unusually high quality. The collaboration between Haber and Freundlich was especially close. When the war ended and Haber was reorganizing his institute, he made Freundlich head of his department, and, soon afterward, his deputy in the institute. Freundlich often led the seminars. His further work in the field of colloid chemistry made him one of its most important pioneers, along with Wilhelm Ostwald, Hermann Staudinger, Lev Landau, and others. He also carried out pioneering work in the field of capillary chemistry, and his book about this subject still sparks great interest.[22]

Haber's work in the first years after the war included a few purely scientific papers, one of which was his Nobel Prize lecture on the preparation of ammonia from nitrogen and hydrogen, published in 1922 in *Die Naturwissenschaften*. In the same year Haber published a paper in which he returned to his investigations of the fundamental problems of the Bunsen flame. In 1911 he had published several papers with Gerhardt Just on his observations at the time. Of the two most important properties of the Bunsen flame—luminescence and ionization—the latter had already led him to the discovery of electron emission during chemical reactions. Now he took up the well-known but little-understood phenomenon of chemical luminescence.[23] To define the relationship between thermal energy and radiation energy, he drew upon the well-defined gas reaction of sodium with the halogens, which gives off a flame with pure chemical luminescence that radiates the sodium line at a temperature well below 500°C. The simple and unambiguous nature of this reaction allowed him to make a fundamental advance, namely the interpretation of chemical luminescence as the reverse of photochemical or sensitized photochemical reactions. Haber's pioneering work was the first to clarify the obscure area of chemical luminescence, and it created a solid basis for subsequent developments. Further research on chemical luminescence, much of it carried out in Haber's institute, confirmed the principle he had proposed.

Another publication of Haber's from this period dealt with his discussions with Max Born of Born's calculation of energy changes based on the theory of lattice energy, as discussed earlier.[24] In his paper Haber describes the points of view that led to their common deliberations. These show that Born's discussions with Haber greatly influenced his theory and that the points that were still unclear were the topic of various conversations.

In conclusion, one guest at the institute who worked there in 1922 should be mentioned. Margarethe von Wrangell came from Estonia, where she directed the experimental agricultural station in Tallinn (formerly Revel). During the war she had lectured in Berlin and other German cities on the mineral resources of Estonia, including its phosphorite reserves. She later received her habilitation at the Agricultural College at Hohenheim near Stuttgart. She developed a special system for using phosphoric acid as a fertilizer, which she described in her book *Gesetzmässigkeiten bei der Phosphorsäureernährung der Pflanze* (Principles of plant nutrition with phosphoric acid). In 1921 an article in the journal *Deutsche Landwirtschaftliche Presse* (German Agricultural Press) addressed von Wrangell's system of phosphoric acid fertilization; the same journal published Haber's discussion of von Wrangell's work. As her system had been sharply criticized from several sides, Haber's declaration that "through Miss von Wrangell's investigations . . . a clear advance has been made" was very important to her.[25] In the ensuing years Haber supported von Wrangell in many ways. She worked for about a year in his institute and finally received a chair in 1923 at Hohenheim Agricultural College. Her correspondence expresses her enthusiasm for Haber.

## Gold from the Sea

Inflation began to increase so dramatically in Germany at the end of 1922 that the financial condition of the state, and consequently of the public services, was headed for catastrophe. This situation was worsened by the occupation of the Ruhr region by French troops and the central government's support for passive resistance rather than action. Haber and his institute were, as prevously described, driven into extreme financial need. But he saw a possibility that could lead them out of financial calamity. He proposed to analyze the gold content of seawater and, if enough gold was found, to develop a technique for extracting it and thereby secure this resource mainly for the German state. Testing this possibility occupied Haber from 1923 to 1925 and made up the major part of his scientific endeavors during this time.

Johannes Jaenicke later reported: "In the spring of 1920 Haber surprised a small circle of trusted coworkers with the decision to start a thorough investigation of the presence of gold in seawater."[26] Haber described his reasons for starting this project in a lecture held on 29 May 1926 at a session of the German Chemical Society:

> From the 1890s right up to the present there has been a continuous series of proposals in the professional literature about extracting gold from seawater, and the newspapers repeatedly report on successful attempts made here and there all over the world using one of these processes. As far as I know, nothing reliable about the success of such efforts has ever been made public. But given the present state of our knowledge, the matter did not seem impossible when I took it up after the world war and looked into it. For even though we did not know exactly how much gold is contained in seawater, and occasionally an observer trying to prove the existence of gold in seawater obtained a negative result, still so much of the data were clustered around values of 5 to 10 milligrams per cubic meter that one could well believe that one could count on this value over wide regions of the sea.[27]

The "gold from the sea" group. At the front (from left to right), Schmittspahn (technician, seated), Hans Eisner, Fritz Haber, Walter Zisch, Kuckels (technician, seated); at the back (left to right) Fritz Epstein, Groth (secretary), W. Wolff (engineer), Hans Lebrecke, Friedrich Matthias, H. Ehlermann, Bahr (laboratory assistant), Johannes Jaenicke.

In 1903 the Swedish physical chemist Svante Arrhenius had calculated that, assuming a concentration of 6 milligrams of gold per metric ton of seawater, eight million tons of gold were available.[28] Haber had discussed the matter with Arrhenius, who continued to regard his assumption as realistic. Furthermore, Haber had studied various publications and had found they contained data that assumed at least a whole milligram of gold per metric ton of seawater. Haber discussed this idea for a project with his coworkers, and as Jaenicke later reported:

> Haber's thoughts and his own unique lecture style quickly dispersed initial doubts about the solubility of the problem among the group of young helpers whom he chose to work on this project, which was wrapped in the deepest secrecy right from the beginning. Their doubts quickly changed to enthusiasm, which was enhanced by all the difficulties that eventually arose, because all our efforts were for the liberation of the fatherland.[29]

This incident shows once again how Haber could transmit his own patriotism to others, how he could fire others with enthusiasm about something he himself felt was an important challenge. Why Haber kept this project so secret is not entirely clear. Presumably he wanted to keep his work hidden from the Allied inspectors who came and went in his institute as they pleased. Therefore he spoke about it only with a very few people outside the institute, and, within the institute, only with those who were actually involved in the project. Secrecy was also agreed upon in a later contract made with Degussa and the Metallbank in the autumn of 1922, as discussed in more detail below.[30] Only four or five years later, when it was clear that the project had not been successful, did Haber make it public.

The investigators whom Haber entrusted with the work were led by Johannes Jaenicke, who had worked in Haber's institute during the war and later became a scientific researcher at the Metallgesellschaft in Frankfurt. He greatly admired Fritz Haber, and (as noted in the preface) in the 1950s he was asked by the German Chemical Society and other associations to write his biography, though he never completed it. Thirteen other assistants, some of them with permanent positions in the institute and others working as doctoral students, took part in these investigations, including a number whom Haber viewed as young friends—Hans Eisner, Fritz Epstein, Friedrich Matthias, and Kurt Quasebarth. After 1933 several fled Germany to the United States or South America.

Work began in 1920 with an examination of standard solutions made up to imitate seawater, since drawing samples from the sea would have attracted the attention of the Allied commissions. The samples contained gold chloride at a concentration of 5 milligrams per cubic meter, which at the time was assumed to be the gold content of seawater. Various analytical methods were studied, of which the most satisfactory was the microcupellation of gold, obtained by its precipitation from solution with lead sulfide.

Cupellation is an ancient analytical procedure. It was known to the Babylonians and is mentioned in the Bible by the prophet Jeremiah (circa 600 B.C.): "The bellows are burnt, the lead is consumed of the fire, the founder melteth in vain; for the wicked are not plucked away. Reprobate silver shall men call them" (Jeremiah 6:29-30).

Working out this procedure—and especially constructing an apparatus that could be installed in a laboratory aboard a seagoing ship—now required financial support that the institute could no longer provide. Haber therefore approached the managements of Degussa and the Metallgesellschaft, as these companies were involved in the extraction of gold and other precious metals. Since Haber had worked with Degussa on pest control during the war, he already had good contacts among its managers. At the Metallgesellschaft he approached the chairman of the board of directors, Alfred Merton. Merton was a great supporter of the KWS and had also been elected to the senate of the society. That the Metallgesellschaft owned its own bank, the Metallbank, made it easier to finance the project, and a contract was drawn up.

The method adopted for extracting the gold was based on many different processes. The precious metal was first adsorbed under reducing conditions on colloidal sulfur, which spontaneously splits off from sodium polysulfide in seawater. The rapidly coagulating suspension was filtered over fine-grained sand whose surface was coated with sulfur from the same source. This procedure completely removed the gold from the water, allowing the concentrate to be easily processed.

This was the state of affairs in the summer of 1923. The laboratory-scale process then had to be tested on the high seas. With the support provided by Degussa and the Metallgesellschaft, a laboratory was set up on the passenger ship *Hansa*, owned by Hapag (Hamburg-Amerikanische Paket AG, the Hamburg-American Steampacket Company). A passage to New York and back was booked for Haber and his assistants, Eisner, Matthias, Hans Lehrecke, and Walter Zisch.[31]

After a short stay in Hamburg while the laboratory was set up on the ship, the *Hansa* left with 923 passengers, of whom 522 were emigrants. Writing Jaenicke in 1967, Hans Eisner described the efforts made to keep the undertaking secret:

> In order to avoid passport formalities, Haber and his assistants were signed on as crew members. Those who could not be hidden in this way appeared on the crew lists as extra paymasters. On landing in New York, the whole crew had to report on deck in rank and file. Haber, with the extra paymaster assistants, stood among a number of students, who made the journey as dishwashers, and employees of Hapag, who also had difficulties with their passports. He visibly enjoyed it when the extra paymaster Fritz Haber was called up to receive his landing card from the immigration officer. Later, when one of the reporters asked him why the *Hansa* had so many paymasters, he said, "Because of the many zeros." This was right in the middle of the inflation.[32]

Immediately on reaching the open sea, Haber and his assistants began taking test samples, using a special device rigged up on board. This work did not escape the passengers' notice, and the wildest rumors arose. Even the officers spread strange stories, probably partly at Haber's request, in order to distract the passengers from the real purpose of the work. After the ship landed in New York, a newspaper published an article with the headline "German Scientists See Way to Drive Ships by Using Mysterious Force." Various crew members were questioned. One passenger said that he had heard that if the experiments were successful, all machines operating at the time, even the most up-to-date ones, would become junk, and that propelling vehicles would cost only half as much. The hoax seems to have succeeded completely.

This journey gave the researchers their first experience in fitting out and using a floating laboratory. Haber himself did not participate in a further journey to North America but had the coded analytical data sent to him in Berlin. In the autumn of the same year he traveled with his assistants from Hamburg to Buenos Aires on the *S.S. Württemberg*, a journey made with additional support from the Emergency Association of German Science (see Chapter 12) and the German Navy. On board was an improved laboratory, set up to study the warmer water of the South Atlantic. Eisner also made this trip. In the letter cited earlier he describes the festivities on crossing the equator:

It was on our gold journey to South America. As we approached the equator and preparations began for the usual celebration and baptism of the novices, one of the officers asked me, "Can we also baptize the *Geheimrat?*" I said, "Naturally," because I knew Haber would enjoy it. The next morning the *Geheimrat* asked me, "Do I have to go through with this?" I didn't feel very honest as I said, "I don't believe you can avoid it."

Haber asked me to get three bottles of wine ready. At the right moment he dived elegantly into the pool and in a speech in rhyme offered Neptune the three bottles of wine, asking to be allowed to empty them and then fill them with seawater for testing. His dive impressed the crew and the passengers and was immortalized in a drawing on the evening menu. Haber's baptismal name was "Alchimistaton" [the supreme chemist].[33]

As a condition of the support for the journey provided by the Emergency Association of German Science, Haber was obliged to make an appearance in Buenos Aires so as to try to raise more money from the Germans in Argentina. He gave the German Club in Buenos Aires a highly patriotic lecture on the theme of German chemistry during the last ten years.[34]

In a letter to Jaenicke, Haber wrote mainly about the difficulties encountered on this journey. He began with the words, "Our journey was carried out because we were not certain whether the procedure would work properly on the high seas. This certainty is as lacking today as a month ago."[35] That uncertainty extended even to the medium used for filtration, as Haber described in detail. Thus while analyses were made directly on board during these sea journeys, to an increasing extent bottles were filled with seawater and then examined in the institute. Haber also described the steps taken to refine the analytical procedures further.

This particular revision first became necessary because the seawater samples taken on the journeys to North and South America showed quite different gold contents. The procedure for working the samples up was also inadequate and had to be fundamentally revised. But after some of the measured samples were found to contain considerably less gold than the five milligrams per cubic meter assumed, it first had to be determined whether the analysis itself was faulty. Therefore the decision was made to analyze all the samples in the laboratory rather than at sea.

Once all possible sources of error were painstakingly excluded, it became obvious that the previously determined values were far too high. Haber still did not give up. He obtained samples from various places assumed to have a relatively high gold content—for example, from San Francisco Bay, with the

Doppelschraubendampfer „Hansa"
Hamburg-Amerika-Linie
Brutto Register 16700 tons
Länge 202 m. Breite 20.5 m.
Maschinenkraft 15000 H.P.
Höchstgeschwindigkeit 17,5 Seemeilen

*The steamship* Hansa.

help of a Professor Kofoid. He also approached Martin Knudsen, the rector of the university in Copenhagen, who arranged for the Danish research ships *Dana* and *Godthaab* to collect samples of seawater and ice from the coastal waters of Iceland and Greenland. Finally he persuaded the Emergency Association to endorse a plan that allowed his last assistant on the gold project, Quasebarth, to cross the Atlantic on the research ship *Meteor* in order to obtain thoroughly authentic research material. About five thousand samples were collected and examined.

The results were shattering for Haber. The gold content in the samples from San Francisco Bay averaged 0.01 milligrams of gold per metric ton of seawater; the highest individual sample contained 0.055 milligrams of gold per metric ton. An average of 0.047 milligrams of gold was found in the Arctic Ocean, and the samples from the *Meteor's* cruise had a mean gold content of 0.008 milligrams per metric ton of seawater, with the highest individual value at 0.044 milligrams per metric ton.

The failure of the "gold from the sea" project was a great disappointment for Haber and his assistants. In 1927 Haber ended his description of the project with the words:

> There is nothing as varied as the conditions in the oceans. Perhaps one day, somewhere, a place will show up where gold may be found, where precious

*Crossing the equator on the* Württemberg.

metals regularly accumulate. Perhaps such a gold-bearing region will be in an accessible climate, and these conditions will once again arouse thoughts about processing seawater. I have given up looking for this dubious needle in a haystack.[36]

However, searching for this "needle" has continued even after Haber's work. In fact other procedures for winning gold from the sea have been suggested, and various concentrations of gold have been found.[37] The values obtained in the last decades fit well with those obtained by Haber and his assistants (a mean of 0.008 milligrams of gold per metric ton of seawater).

## The Work from 1926 to 1933

Early in 1925 Haber returned from his world trip, and over the following months he was extremely busy with the gold project. In 1926 he again turned to more general scientific themes. His health, however, had become quite poor, and his personal problems, which culminated in his divorce from his second wife, prevented him from devoting all his energy to the institute. In addition he took on many public responsibilities in 1926 and 1927.

Despite these distractions, in 1926 there began a period in the institute's history that may be described as the second scientific heyday of Haber's life. The range of themes under study in the institute was quite astounding, and some of this work opened up new research areas. The variety of problems and the different approaches taken to solve them characterize the generosity with which Haber permitted his various researchers independence in the direction and style of their work. One can see why Haber's institute produced a remarkable number of people who later occupied professorial chairs, including Karl Friedrich Bonhoeffer, Aladar von Buzagh, Ludwig Ebert, Ladislaus Farkas, Karl-Hermann Geib, Paul Goldfinger, Walter Grotrian, Paul Harteck, Hartmut Kallmann, Hans Kautsky, Hans Kopfermann, Fritz London, Michael Polanyi, Karl Söllner, Hertha Sponer, Alexander Szabo, Heinrich Thiele, O. H. Wansbrough-Jones, Joseph Weiss, Karl Weissenberg, and Hans Zoch. Under Fritz Haber's intelligent direction they all brought the institute to flower during this productive period.

Besides the colloid chemistry department run by Freundlich, a second department now developed under Polanyi. Its main field of study concerned the processes within flames and explosions, the radiation they emit, and the fundamental processes that could be explained by them—subjects that had occupied Haber for most of his scientific life.

Polanyi and numerous coworkers, among them Eugen Wigner and Henry Eyring, investigated "highly diluted" flames. These experiments—cleverly designed and elegantly carried out—considerably advanced the understanding of the individual steps in chemical reactions. Previously such reactions had been understood only in broad outline, with a focus on starting and end products. Polanyi, however, examined reactions that are much simpler than the processes one generally knows as flames and that therefore are much better suited for pioneering studies. Polanyi's work also yielded fundamental concepts on the elasticity of solids and on the mechanism of polymerization.

Another set of investigations was also related to flames and explosions insofar as they derived from the study of hydrogen atoms: Bonhoeffer's numerous and versatile researches of hydrogen atoms, Harteck's research on hydrogen and oxygen atoms, and—even if there is only a loose connection—the successful discovery by these two of para-hydrogen.

After James Franck left for Göttingen, Rudolf Ladenburg was appointed his successor. Besides a brief project on the use of electricity to purify gases, in which Haber showed great interest, Ladenburg concentrated on the research fields of his choice: the dispersion of electrically excited gases and vapors and the magnetic rotation of the plane of polarization. This work includes his and Kopfermann's proof that "negative" dispersion in a neon gas discharge tube is an indicator of stimulated light emission (a prerequisite for the later development of laser emission). After Ladenburg moved to Princeton in 1932, his post remained unfilled.

One of Haber's closest coworkers, as administrator of the institute, was Hartmut Kallmann. Many pre-1933 publications testify to his research on the border between physics and chemistry, carried out with the help of numerous young assistants. This work was wide ranging but dealt particularly with the ionization of gases and the splitting of gas molecules by slow electrons, which finally led to an effective process for accelerating positive ions for atom transmutation, and with the mass spectrometry of isotopes and the Compton effect.

Haber himself was fully occupied with the material and organizational concerns necessary for financing the entire institute and procuring new funding. In addition he held the heterogeneous activities of the institute together with a confident mastery. Even as he left individual researchers full freedom in their work, he was also able to keep full intellectual control over the whole enterprise.

*(Top to bottom) Paul Harteck, Karl Friedrich Bonhoeffer, Ladislaus Farkas, and Adalbert Farkas.*

At the end of the 1920s Haber busied himself with the group that had gathered around Bonhoeffer, which included Harteck, Geib, and Farkas. Most likely the results this group had obtained on the behavior of free atoms and free radicals led Haber to consider using new methods to delve into problems that had occupied him when he was young, that is, the study of flames, particularly the Bunsen flame and autoxidation. His first publication in this area, "Bandenspektroskopie und Flammenvorgänge," written with Bonhoeffer in 1928, is remarkable for its richness of ideas and fruitful suggestions.[38] Haber and Bonhoeffer were the first to investigate the band spectra and thermal effects of potential flame reaction processes. They discovered that the characteristic ultraviolet band system produced by flames of hydrogen and its compounds, and already known as the "water band system," is caused by the hydroxyl radical.

The results of the many investigations carried out in the decade after Haber entered this field generally supported his hypotheses and led to further development. His original formulas for the reaction mechanisms were used for a long time with only a few slight modifications, which points to his uncanny ability to recognize chemical problems and use new concepts in physics for their solution.

Another area that Haber examined was why unpredictable explosions occur in reaction vessels filled with hydrogen and oxygen. Clarification of the conditions governing such situations led to the discovery that radical chain reactions occur. He also studied the role played by the radicals present in flames, and his laboratory demonstrated that radicals can be created when atomic hydrogen or oxygen interacts with hydrocarbons (except methane) at room temperature.

Another research area, autoxidation, became prominent once again in Haber's scientific research. Carl Engler first brought this problem to Haber's attention, and Haber had investigated it in Karlsruhe. (For Haber's earlier work on oxidation by free oxygen—e.g., that in flames and explosions—see Chapter 4.) In the intervening period major changes, to which Haber had contributed greatly, had occurred in ideas on the reaction mechanism.

In 1928, along with Franck, Haber began his investigations of the oxidation of sodium sulfite by free oxygen in aqueous solution.[39] Haber and his experienced coworkers made a detailed analysis of both the thermal and the photochemical aspects of the reactions. These investigations led Haber and Franck to suggest an important modification of Franck's original interpretation of anionic absorption spectra as electron affinities.[40] They did not work out these new ideas in great detail. Rather, they were looking to achieve a better understanding of complex oxidation-reduction reactions, especially those of biochemical interest, through the basic principle of univalent reaction steps. Contemporary biochemists discussed these new considerations and suggestions passionately. This work demonstrates once again Haber's strong interest in organic and biochemical processes.

The discussion of these principles of radical and univalent reactions in connection with reactions that occur in a mixture of peroxidase and catalase led Haber to start an investigation that was to be his last scientific work: the kinetics of the decomposition of hydrogen peroxide catalyzed by iron salts.[41] The masterful analysis of this complex reaction led to a special result that was important for Haber, namely that a small change in conditions can cause a change in mechanism from a chain reaction to a radical reaction, or vice versa. This again shows how important his concept of univalent reaction steps and simple electron transitions was for explaining the mechanisms of reactions in solutions.

Haber's last five or six years of scientific work, carried out with his co-workers in his institute and with such friends as Franck and Willstätter, once again reveal his astounding mental ability. Superior effort, often to the last ounce of his physical strength, was a constant habit throughout his life. He could never totally relax, and he found idleness unbearable. His mind had to be constantly active. During his many travels, including those to scientific conventions or conferences on the promotion of science, whether he was on the train or in a hotel room, his thoughts were always on a scientific problem. Thus he was able, at an advanced age and in addition to all his other activities (which would have fully occupied anybody else), to carry out the interesting and pioneering scientific work discussed in this chapter. His coworkers and friends later carried his ideas to many parts of the scientific world, where, especially in the United States, they became the forebears of a new generation of researchers and teachers who today shape our picture of physical chemistry.

## Endnotes

[1]  Paul Harteck, "Physical Chemists in Berlin, 1919–1933," *Journal of Chemical Education* 37 (1960), 462–466 (quotes from pp. 462, 465).

[2]  Wilhelm Jost, "The First Forty-five Years of Physical Chemistry in Germany," *Annual Review of Physical Chemistry* 17 (1966), 1–14.

[3]  Otto Benecke, "Aus der Geschichte der KWG: Finanzkrise und Neubau 1921" (On

the history of the KWG: Financial crisis and reconstruction, 1921), in *Mitteilungen aus der Max-Planck-Gesellschaft*, December 1954 (issue 5), 239–248.

[4] Fritz Haber to Adolf von Harnack, 12 Jan. 1920, MPG, Dept. Va, Rep. 5, A1-337.

[5] Haber to Friedrich Schmidt-Ott, 15 Feb. 1920, MPG, Dept. Va, Rep. 5, 1699.

[6] Overview of the budget years 1914, 1919, and 1923, signed by Herbert Freundlich, MPG, Dept. I, Ia, 1179.

[7] Haber to the Prussian Ministry of Science, Art and Education, 7 Aug. 1922, MPG, Dept. Va, Rep. 5, 1772.

[8] Haber's reports in protocol of the senate of the Kaiser Wilhelm Gesellschaft from 7 Dec. 1935, MPG, General Administration, A1, Rep. 1a, 1271.

[9] P. C. Witt, "Wissenschaftfinanzierung zwischen Inflation und Deflation" (Financial support of science in times of inflation and deflation), in *Forschung im Spannungsfeld von Politik und Gesellschaft: Geschichte und Struktur der Kaiser Wilhelm/Max Planck Gesellschaft* (Research in the tension between politics and society: History and structure of the Kaiser Wilhelm/Max Planck Society), ed. Rudolf Vierhaus and Bernhard vom Brocke (Stuttgart: Deutsche Verlags-Anstalt, 1990), 636.

[10] Protocol of the meeting on 15 Feb. 1917 in the offices of Kriegschemikalien AG on pest control, Geheimes Staatsarchiv Preussischer Kulturbesitz, Berlin, Rep. 76 Vc, Sect. 2, Tit. 23, Lit. A, sheets 8–10.

[11] Karl Escherich, *Leben und Forschen* (Life and research) (Berlin/Hamburg: Verlag Paul Parey, 1944).

[12] Report on the activities of the Technical Committee for Pest Control (Tasch), 1918, undated, Geheimes Staatsarchiv Preussischer Kulturbesitz, Berlin-Dahlem, Rep. 76 Vc, Sect. 2, Tit. 23, sheet 119-129.

[13] Ferdinand Flury, "Die Tätigkeit des KWI für physikalische Chemie und Elektrochemie in Berlin-Dahlem im Dienst der Schädlingsbekämpfung" (The activities of the KWI for Physical Chemistry and Electrochemistry in Berlin-Dahlem in the area of pest control), *Verhandlungen der Deutsche Gesellschaft für Angewandte Entomologie, 2. Mitgliederversammlung* (Berlin: Paul Parey Verlag, 1924), 61–75.

[14] Letter with appendix from Haber to the Prussian Minister of Education Schmidt-Ott, 30 Oct. 1918, Geheimes Staatsarchiv Preussischer Kulturbesitz, Berlin-Dahlem, Rep. 76 Vc, Sect. 2, Tit. 23, folios 161–169.

[15] Draft of a regulation for pest control with highly poisonous substances, from Jan. 1919, Geheimes Staatsarchiv Preussischer Kulturbesitz, Berlin-Dahlem, Rep. 76 Vc, Sect. 2, Tit. 23, folio 183.

[16] W. Trappmann, *Schädlingsbekämpfung* (Pest control) (Leipzig: Verlag W. Hirzel, 1927), 346–349.

[17] Ferdinand Flury and Albrecht Hase, "Die Anwendung von Cyanderivaten zur Schädlingsbekämpfung" (Use of cyanoderivatives for pest control), *Münchener Medizinische Wochenschrift* 27 (1920), 77; Walter Heerdt, article in *Verhandlungen der Deutsche Gesellschaft für Angewandte Entomologie, 3. Mitgliederversammlung* (Berlin: Paul Parey Verlag, 1921), 36; C. Becher, *Schädlingsbekämpfungsmittel* (Substances for pest control) (Halle: VEB Knapp Verlag, 1953), 323f.

[18] Max Born and Alfred Landé, "Über die Berechnung der Kompressibilität regulärer Kristalle aus der Gittertheorie" (Calculating the compressibility of regular crystals according to the lattice theory), *Verhandlungen der Deutschen Physikalischen Gesellschaft* 20 (1918), 210; Born, "Über kubische Atommodelle" (About cubic atom models), ibid., 230.

[19] Max Born, *My Life: Recollections of a Nobel Laureate* (New York: Scribners, 1978), 188.

[20] Memorandum on an interview with James Franck, on 16–17 April 1958, MPG, Dept. Va, Rep. 5, 1449.

[21] Ibid.

[22] Herbert Freundlich, *Kapillarchemie* (Capillary chemistry) (Leipzig: Akademische Verlagsgeschichte, 1930–32).

[23] Fritz Haber and Walter Zisch, "Anregung von Gasspektren durch chemische Reaktion" (Excitation of gas spectra by chemical reaction), *Zeitschrift für Physik* 2 (1922), 302.

[24] Fritz Haber, "Betrachtungen zur Theorie der Wärmetönungen" (Considerations on the theory of heat tonality), *Verhandlungen der Deutschen Physikalischen Gesellschaft* 21 (1919), 751.

[25] W. Andronikow, *Margarethe von Wrangell: Das Leben einer Frau 1876–1932* (Margarethe von Wrangell: The life of a woman, 1876–1932) (Munich: Albert Lengen, Georg Müller Verlag, 1935).

[26] Johannes Jaenicke, "Habers Forschung über das Goldvorkommen in Meerwasser" (Haber's research on gold deposits in seawater), *Naturwissenschaften* 23 (1935), 57; see also "Notiz zur zweiten allgemeinen Sitzung des Vereins Deutsch. Chemiker" (Notice for the second general session of the German Chemical Society), *Z. Angew. Chem.* 39 (1926), 662.

[27] Fritz Haber, "Gold im Meerwasser" (Gold in seawater), *Z. Angew. Chem.* 40 (1927), 303.

[28] Svante Arrhenius, *Lehrbuch der kosmischen Physik I* (Leipzig, 1903).

[29] Jaenicke, "Habers Forschung" (cit. note 26).

[30] Ibid.; and contract between Fritz Haber, Degussa, and the Metallbank, 14 Nov. 1922, company archives of the Metallgesellschaft, Frankfurt am Main, and of Degussa, Frankfurt am Main (no archival number).

[31] The Hamburg-Amerikanische Paket Aktiengesellschaft (Hapag) to the Metallbank, 12 Dec. 1922; and Dr. Peters of the Metallbank to Hapag, 14 Dec. 1922; both in archives of the Metallgesellschaft, unnumbered.

[32] Hans Eisner to Johannes Jaenicke, 5 Sept. 1967, MPG, Dept. Va, Rep. 5, 102.

[33] Ibid.

[34] Fritz Haber, "Die deutsche Chemie in den letzten Jahren" (German chemistry in recent years), in Haber, *Aus meinem Leben und Beruf* (From my life and work) (Berlin: Verlag Julius Springer, 1927).

[35] Haber to Jaenicke, 12 Nov. 1923, MPG, Dept. Va, Rep. 5, 075.

[36] Haber, "Gold im Meerwasser" (cit. note 27), 314.

[37] F. H. Lancaster, "The Gold Content of Sea Water: The Unfulfillable Dream of Its Extraction," *Gold Bulletin* 6:4 (1973), 111.

[38] Karl Bonhoeffer and Fritz Haber, "Bandenspektroskopie und Flammenvorgänge" (Band spectroscopy and flame procedures), *Z. Phys. Chem.* 137 (1928), 263.

[39] Fritz Haber, "Über die Autoxydation" (On autoxidation), *Naturwissenschaften* 19 (1931), 450.

[40] James Franck and G. Scheibe, "Über Absortionspektren negativer Halogenionen in Lösung," *Z. Phys. Chem. Abt. A*, 139 (1928), 22–31.

[41] Fritz Haber and Joseph Weiss, "Über die Katalyse des Hydroperoxydes" (On the catalysis of hydroperoxide), *Naturwissenschaften* 20 (1932), 948; and Haber and Weiss, "The catalytic decomposition of hydrogen peroxide by iron salts," *Proceedings of the Royal Chemical Society (London)* A417 (1934), 332.

*Chapter 12*

# Haber's Promotion
# of the Sciences,
# 1920–1933

*Friedrich Schmidt-Ott.*

*Previous page: Fritz Haber in Japan with Minister of Education Okada (left) and Shimpei Goto (right), at a presentation of a gift of books.*

IN 1923 FRITZ HABER USED THE FOLLOWING WORDS TO DESCRIBE THE relationship between the state, society, and science:

> This social state [the Weimar Republic], which the revolution set up in the place of the previous one, this state, whose whole existence affirms the claims of the broad working class for a higher quality of life and that sees as just compensation for the unheard-of achievements of the people during the war that it should give equal opportunities for improvement to those with equal abilities and provide its support to all those in need, such a state is an extraordinarily costly one. Tormented from the outside for reparations and pressured by internal demands that it must fulfill if it is not to quit, it must make constant advances in its modes of operation and activities, and it can achieve that only through advances in the sciences.[1]

## Haber and the Emergency Association of German Science

With words couched in the language of the times, Haber described a situation that is still relevant to any modern state, and especially to Germany. As a result of this perception Haber, along with others, set up the Emergency Association of German Science (Notgemeinschaft der Deutschen Wissenschaft), today the German Research Association (Deutsche Forschungsgemeinschaft). At the festivities held on 31 October 1930 that marked the tenth anniversary of the Emergency Association, its president, Friedrich Schmidt-Ott, was asked who was in fact the "father" of the association—that is, who had first thought of launching it. Schmidt-Ott answered this question in his opening remarks:

> Who the actual father of the Emergency Association is will remain shrouded in darkness. I believe that we have all worked together. It was an idea that

259

guided us. Our friend Haber, with great energy and on his own unique initiative, took care of the matter. He claims that the Emergency Association was actually born on the steps of a house in Potsdamerstrasse where we were invited to a meeting of the Union of German Technology [Verbund Deutscher Technik] and where we both had to wait about half an hour on the stairs, as it was just at the time of the Kapp revolt [a short unsuccessful revolt by right-wing politicians and army officers against the democratic state on 13 March 1920]. In any case we were already discussing then that all sciences, including the technical sciences, had to be united in a single alliance.[2]

Haber and Schmidt-Ott became acquainted in the period before the war. Schmidt-Ott had been an assistant of Friedrich Althoff, who was then the Prussian minister of education, until 1908. Schmidt-Ott had taken over the department for the arts in 1903 and since then had been called Art-Schmidt to distinguish him from all the other Schmidts. (He did not add the name Ott—his wife's maiden name—to his surname until April 1920, on the occasion of their silver wedding.) He had a good relationship with the kaiser and was himself appointed minister of education in 1917. The collapse of the empire and the removal of the monarchy upset him greatly, as it also did Haber at first.

The financial need of the sciences was then extreme, but the national government and the German parliament had more pressing problems: unrest throughout the country, an influenza epidemic, and rampant inflation. The German economy was still severed from the rest of the world's, and unemployment was rising rapidly. In this context the plight of the sciences was also desperate. Contacts with foreign countries barely existed. The nation's individual states were not able to provide even partial financing for the universities and institutes. Keeping the school system going was difficult enough.

Thus that conversation on the stairs in March 1920 which led to the creation of the Emergency Association. It was to be an independent body, not connected to any political party, and as such it would be the most appropriate channel through which the state would support research. But it was imperative that the idea have broad support in order to have a decisive effect on the parties and convince parliament. So Haber immediately broached the idea to the Prussian Academy of Sciences, in a session held on 25 March 1920 before members of the University of Berlin, the Charlottenburg Institute of Technology, major technical and scientific associations, the Kaiser Wilhelm Institutes, and the Prussian State Library. They all came to the meeting at Haber's urging. As a member of the faculty Haber proposed to the rector of the University of Berlin that the university join the Emergency Association under Schmidt-Ott's direction and call upon all universities to do likewise. He added:

> It seems indispensable that such a venture, though independent in form, in execution must rely on close agreement with the responsible federal and state ministers.
>
> We therefore recommend that German science join in a free union in an Emergency Association under the leadership of a man whose personality guarantees the proper relationship with official authorities responsible for maintaining the sciences at the federal and state levels.[3]

The founding of the Emergency Association has been described in detail in two works, one by Kurt Zierold in 1968, which emphasized the credit due Haber, and the other by Thomas Nipperdey and Ludwig Schmugge on the occasion of the fiftieth anniversary in 1970 of the German Research Association.[4] Walther Jaenicke has also written an account of Haber's role in the founding of the Emergency Association.[5] Thus, no detailed description of events is necessary here.

In the first years of the Emergency Association, Haber, as second vice president, was often involved on its behalf. He also worked to promote public awareness of science. He maintained contact with the media of that time, mainly the press, knowing as he did how difficult it was to win the interest of the daily press in such a topic.

By 1927 the Emergency Association had reached its zenith. It enjoyed special respect, as it had already effectively promoted many areas of science. But from the end of 1928, and especially in 1929, the association passed through a crisis, partly because of Schmidt-Ott's authoritarian style. Major disagreements even began to arise between Schmidt-Ott and Haber, as the concluding lines of a letter that Haber wrote to Schmidt-Ott in June 1929 show:

> Antagonisms increase in secret whenever difficulties increase. The difficulties, however, are increasing in the Emergency Association with the continuing economic calamities in the parliament, which, in my opinion, will not end in the next few years. . . .
>
> In my innermost self I am convinced that there will be a 9 November 1918 [the date on which the emperor renounced his throne and the Social Democrats proclaimed a republic] within the Emergency Association, and therefore I once more heartily beg Your Excellency to alter matters and to preserve yourself for the Association and for science.[6]

Economic deterioration marked 1931 and 1932. The government was able to survive only by issuing emergency decrees. Unemployment rose above six million. If one considers that every unemployed person represented a family of three or four, about a third of the German population was affected by this scourge of the capitalist economic system. The Emergency Association also received less funding at this time, though the reduction was limited.

In the summer of 1932 Germany's national chancellor, Franz von Papen, abolished the Prussian government through a coup d'etat. Consequently the Emergency Association dispensed with appointing five new members in October, as required by its charter. The necessary changes in the charter were made at the general meeting on 11 October. The national minister of the interior appeared at this meeting and presented Schmidt-Ott and the members of the committee, including Fritz Haber, with the Goethe Medal, which President Paul von Hindenburg had created for the hundredth anniversary of Goethe's death. The committee was to be elected at this general meeting. The membership remained unchanged, which meant that Haber was also reelected.

And then on 30 January 1933 Adolf Hitler came to power. At first the Emergency Association was unaffected. In March there were elections for the committees of the various scientific fields, with about 50 percent participation. As always some Jewish names were among those elected. This was remarkable because after the burning of the parliament building on 27 February, the first wave of Nazi terror against the Jews had raged through Berlin and other cities. And a few days later the so-called Enabling Act was passed, which practically invalidated the Weimar Constitution. On 7 April the infamous Law on the Restoration of the Civil Service was announced. Non-Aryan officials, with the exception of former soldiers at the front, were to be dismissed from the civil services.

Because of this law Haber was forced to dismiss his closest coworkers. He felt that he could not remain in his post as director of his institute and resigned on 30 April 1933 (see Chapter 13); on 9 May he informed Schmidt-Ott that he was also resigning from the vice presidency of the Emergency Association. Schmidt-Ott's presidency came to an end soon afterward. The minister of the interior, Wilhelm Frick, who a month earlier had been full of praise for the president of the association, now made it clear that he should resign. Thus Schmidt-Ott decided to give up the presidency, and the other members of the committee also resigned.

When a memorial ceremony for Haber was being organized in Dahlem in January 1935, Schmidt-Ott wrote to Max von Laue: "You had most kindly suggested to me that at the Haber ceremony I should say some words about my relationship to the person being celebrated. I would rather not, as first of all my voice . . . would not suffice in the unfavorable conditions of the room." Schmidt-Ott then described his relationship to Haber at length, but he emphasized that he only wrote these pages as "personal words." He asked Laue to read in public only the last sentence: "Thus, during the building up of the Emergency Association, we were close friends, and even after his death I owe him the warmest thanks."[7]

And "warmest thanks" is what we still owe Haber today for his great contribution to founding and preserving the German Research Association. It is possible that without him similar support for German science might have arisen, but it is doubtful whether it would have been established so quickly after World War I or been so effective in its first thirteen years. Finally, we should not forget that the principles of the association that Haber and Schmidt-Ott established still characterize this organization for the promotion of German research.

## The Hoshi Foundation, a Journey to Japan, and the Japan Institute

Toward the end of the world trip that Haber and his wife Charlotte took in 1924 (see Chapter 9), Haber wrote from on board the *Batavia*, to Wilhelm Solf, the German ambassador in Japan: "The world has become a bit bigger and richer for me, and you have contributed a great deal in teaching me to see. The best things that one can bring home from a long journey are new friendships and an interest in new things."[8]

In the 1920s Solf had achieved extraordinary results with German-Japanese relations, which had become strained after World War I. His efforts after his appointment as ambassador are what caused Japanese-German contacts to develop quickly and (within a few months) normal relations to be resumed. In the next few years some notable events laid the foundation for a close and lasting exchange of ideas.

How did it come about that Haber's visit to Japan was for him the most important event on his world trip? Two critical factors must have contributed: the Hoshi Foundation and Albert Einstein's visit to Japan in September 1921.

*Wilhelm Solf.*

In 1920–21 the Japanese industrialist and businessman Hajime Hoshi gave an initial donation of 80,000 yen (about 160,000 gold marks) to Wilhelm Solf for a foundation to promote the sciences in Germany. Solf directed the donation to the Foreign Office in Berlin, where it was placed at the disposal of the Grants Distribution Committee of the Emergency Association of German Science in the spring of 1922. At the beginning of 1923 Hoshi came to Berlin and was received by representatives of the government and of the Emergency Association. Hoshi also visited Haber in his director's residence and invited him to visit Japan. Haber accepted Hoshi's invitation in part because he had also been invited to the centennial of the Franklin Institute in Philadelphia as a representative of the Prussian Academy of Sciences, the Kaiser Wilhelm Society, and the German Chemical Society. Thus Fritz and Charlotte Haber had occasion to circumnavigate the globe from the West to the Far East. On 2 September 1924 the Habers sailed from Hamburg on the Hapag ship *Reliance*.

The ceremonies at the Franklin Institute began in mid-September. Participants included representatives of many universities, scientific associations, and industrial organizations. Various journals reported on the meeting. In a speech at one of the dinners Haber briefly summarized the development of the United States:

> Today your nation appears to a visitor like one of the countries of an old culture. The first period of commerce lies far in the past; the second period of technical progress is also gone; and the third period, that of Science, has begun, in which the country is not dependent upon the Old World for either products or processes, but devises with its own creative genius the methods of work by whose aid it prepares its products.
>
> It is not now the congratulations of the wise teacher to the aspiring pupil that I extend. It is the respect of the older expert for the independence and splendid results accomplished by the younger colleague.

He concluded with a remark that was not made by "a German to an American but by a naturalist to naturalists" in which he characterized the condition of the economy as governed by lawyers, soldiers, financiers, and industrialists.

> Now they are disputing with one another about reconstruction, and, for the ordinary looker-on, it seems as if in place of the reigning princes, who for centuries governed the world, we now have the controlling banker. But this is only a superficial aspect. The banker and lawyer, the industrialist and merchant, in spite of their leading positions in life, are only administrative officials, and the sovereign is Natural Science. Its progress determines the measure of the prosperity of man; its cultivation is the seed from which the welfare of future generations grows.[9]

After the ceremonies in Philadelphia the Habers traveled across the United States. In October their ship sailed from San Francisco Bay, and after a short stay in Hawaii they reached Japan at the end of the month. There they were received in Yokohama Harbor by Hoshi and Solf.

At the reception banquet on 3 November, Haber thanked Hoshi for the invitation he had received in Berlin. He passed on the thanks of German chemical science for the generous help that Hoshi had given with his donation. Haber then gave Hoshi a gift and a letter from the German president, Friedrich Ebert, as well as a commemorative volume published by the

Committee on Japan of the Emergency Association for German Science, containing a photograph of the members of the committee. He then gave the Japanese minister of education a donation of books from German scientific associations, various publishers, and the chemical industry.

During his visits and conversations Haber began to realize what strength and energy lay hidden in the countries of the Far East. He concluded one article, written in Berlin after the end of his journey, with the words: "Just as it is sure that at present the world's center of gravity lies in the United States, so am I certain that the future of world development lies on the shores of the Pacific."[10]

Acting on this conviction, Haber tried to create, through the cooperation of scientific and cultural circles in Germany and Japan, an atmosphere that would eventually lead to technical and economic collaboration that would be especially advantageous to Germany. He was convinced that this could occur only if attitudes toward Japanese scientists and industrialists were to change, which was possible only if the cultural and intellectual traditions of Japan were understood. In this project Wilhelm Solf became Haber's special ally. Thanks to his excellent understanding of Asian culture and mentality and his extensive experience as a diplomat, the ideas developed during the talks in Japan could be realized and a German-Japanese cultural institute founded.

Fritz and Charlotte then undertook a ten-week trip around to the cultural sites and industrial cities of Japan, including the northern regions of the country. In Hakodate, on the island of Hokkaido, they visited the grave of Haber's uncle Ludwig, and there a memorial stone was unveiled in a solemn ceremony.

Finally, after they had once more been guests of the industrialist Michida and of Count Shimpei Goto, and after Haber had discussed further plans with Solf in Tokyo, the eventful days and weeks in Japan came to an end. The travelers journeyed through Korea, Manchuria, Shanghai, Indonesia, Ceylon, and Egypt to reach Europe in the middle of March 1925, landing in Genoa.

The negotiations that Haber had conducted on his travels, especially in Japan, were now expected to produce results after his return, and Haber would not have been true to himself had he not immediately taken up this new task. From March to May 1925 he met with various representatives of the Kaiser Wilhelm Society, the ministries, and the Emergency Association, working to realize his plan of founding a Japan Institute. Finally, on

2 May, he was able to lay his request for support before representatives of the Prussian Ministry of Education, the National Ministry of the Interior, the National Ministry of Finance, and the Kaiser Wilhelm Society.[11] The wish to link the founding of this institute in Germany with the founding of a corresponding institute in Japan caused delays. Haber's expectation that the founding would take place in June or July 1925, as he had written to Solf, was not fulfilled.[12] Solf came to Berlin in October 1926 and assured Haber that the institute in Tokyo was certain to be established on 1 April 1927.

The Japan Institute at last opened officially in Berlin on 4 December 1926. Its rooms were on the fourth floor of the Berliner Schloss, formerly the kaiser's residence, facing the large courtyard. The ceremonial opening took place in the banquet hall of the Kaiser Wilhelm Society. Berlin's scientific elite was there, including the members of the Japan Institute's board of trustees. Shimpei Goto, His Excellency Kumatao Honda (the former Japanese ambassador), and Wilhelm Solf were named honorary members.

Haber had finally reached his goal. As chairman of the board of trustees he gave the opening speech. Here he emphasized the significance of the institute's special character: "The founding of the twin institutes in Tokyo and here signifies a new stage in our relations with other nations. We have other institutes for foreign studies, but they are not complemented by parallel institutes in the foreign country. This difference results in their not being organized in the same way." Haber mentioned embassies and consulates and also chambers of commerce as the corresponding structures in the political field. He then added:

> There remains one other great sphere, which must be served in a similar fashion, that is, the field of cultural affairs. In our times this field has gained greatly in importance for the relations between people. Our connections with Japan, however, seem to me to be of special significance, justifying the first establishment of this new type of institute that will serve the mutual interests of Germany and Japan.[13]

The parallel institute was indeed founded in Tokyo in April 1927. Haber congratulated Solf on this "significant achievement." Solf left Japan about 1 January 1929 and stayed for some time in Lausanne. Haber wrote to him there:

> I cherish the double wish, as an individual and as chairman of the Japan Institute, that I may see you again soon. In the former capacity I wish to be assured of your well-being and to shake your hand. In the latter capacity

I should very much like to hear whether you would like to take over my position at the next meeting of the board of trustees and the associated general meeting at the beginning of May.[14]

Solf assured Haber that he would be happy to become Haber's successor at the Japan Institute, and he did take over on 15 April 1929, although Haber continued to maintain close contact with the institute.[15] He remained the representative of the Kaiser Wilhelm Society on its board of trustees up to the middle of 1932. His successor to this post was the zoologist Richard Goldschmidt, who had also visited Japan in the 1920s. He too was Jewish, and in 1933 he asked Solf to strike his name off the list of trustees, remarking, "I really do not think I need to give a special reason for this request."[16] Haber, however, remained a member of the board of trustees by his own wish. He wrote Max Planck, the president of the Kaiser Wilhelm Society, in explanation: "If I were to resign voluntarily, then I would give our Japanese friends the impression that I am repaying the many honors they gave me with ingratitude, in that I am giving up all interest in their country."[17]

On his departure from Germany in 1933 his membership on the board of trustees naturally lapsed. Solf remained chairman of the Japan Institute up to his death on 6 February 1936. His successors were two former admirals, Paul Behnke and Wilhelm Foerster, an indication of the new political direction that followed the Nazis' rise to power.

Once it became known in Japan that Haber wanted to emigrate from Germany, both Setsuro Tamaru, his old friend and coworker, and Hoshi invited him there. But Haber no longer had the strength for such a long journey and the strain connected with it. These signs of friendship indicate that Haber had not been forgotten in Japan. Indeed, his son Lutz and his daughter, Eva, were later invited there.

After World War II, attempts were made to preserve some activities of the Japan Institute, but the government of the Federal Republic of Germany was not willing to support its reestablishment. Finally, in 1987, a Japanese-German Center was founded in the former building of the Japanese embassy in Berlin.[18] This institute also sees as its main task the promotion of scientific exchange, in the humanities and social sciences as well as in the natural sciences and engineering.

From today's vantage point the Japan Institute might seem a quirk of history. The Jew Fritz Haber founded a cultural, scientific establishment that was later exploited by the anti-Semitic Nazis for their belligerent policies of alliance. His efforts on behalf of the Japan Institute served a very different purpose. He wanted to reconnect German science and culture, and their organizations, to the international world of culture and science, which had excluded Germany from many fields after World War I. The founding of the Japan Institute was one of Haber's methods for reaching this goal.

## Haber and International Scientific Cooperation

The world trip that Haber took in 1924 and his work to create the Japan Institute constituted one example of his endeavors to reconnect German science to science in other countries after World War I. His activities in various scientific organizations in Germany—at the beginning of the 1920s he was vice president of the Emergency Association of German Science and a member of the senate of the Kaiser Wilhelm Society, and from June 1922 to May 1924 president of the German Chemical Society—and his contacts with various politicians in Prussia and nationally, placed him where he could present his opinion to the seats of power, mediate, and finally push decisions through. Thus he played an essential role in the return of German scientific societies to the international arena.

International scientific relations between the warring powers had collapsed after World War I. The slanderous charges voiced in scientific circles during the war, first in Germany, but then in the allied countries, especially France, had created a climate that considerably hindered rebuilding any cooperation. After the war, scholars from the allied countries declared that they would bring the fight against German claims to supremacy into the intellectual sphere and carry it on even in peacetime.[19] The German scholars found the boycott humiliating. Their pride was wounded, so a backlash began; they declared a counterboycott.

Fritz Haber, once listed as a war criminal, certainly did not enjoy a good reputation among Germany's former enemies. It is thus surprising that he of all people became a great mediator, as much on the behalf of the allied boycotters as of those who supported the counterboycott. The task that Haber took upon himself was clearly a difficult one.

In 1923 Haber was invited by the national minister of the interior to work on Germany's scientific relations with other countries. After overcoming many difficulties, Haber, working through his Dutch colleagues Friedrich Went, president of the Section of the Natural Sciences of the Dutch Academy, and Hugo Kruyt, chairman of the Chemical Council of the Netherlands, tried to clarify for the French and the British the conditions stipulated by the boycotting German academies. Among these conditions were giving the international unions of individual disciplines more autonomy and once more allowing German as an official language (the International Research Council had excluded it in 1919). Went and Kruyt tried to arrange a meeting between German and French scholars on neutral ground at the end of March 1926, and they sent invitations to the German academies, which took their time in answering.

Shortly before a meeting of the International Research Council at which the Germans were to be formally invited to join, Kruyt happily reported to Haber on this forthcoming event.[20] But Haber was not satisfied with the style of the invitation. He objected that Germany had not been invited in a form worthy of its scientific standing and that the invitation did not differ from one that might be made "for example, to Siam"[21]—an allusion to the earlier decision to invite Siam (which supported the Allied countries) to join.

However, Haber did not give up his mediation. He now tried to carry out negotiations through the British, and the German Ministry of Foreign Affairs activated diplomatic channels. But nothing helped. The reactions of the academies and the universities to the invitation from the International Research Council remained unfriendly, and informal negotiations remained the only path left open to him.

Even after several new initiatives there was still no answer by the fourth general meeting of the International Research Council in July 1928 to the invitation sent to Germany two years earlier. Nor did Haber succeed in having a German representative named to attend a consultation that took place in Paris in September 1929. The cartel of the German academies had decided that the matter of membership in the International Research Council could rest. Haber went along with this point of view with resignation. The time for joining was not yet ripe, he explained in a conference at the Ministry of Foreign Affairs, at least not for the "right wing" of the German professoriat.

Haber then began concentrating more strongly on Germany's membership in international scientific societies, especially the International Union of Pure and Applied Chemistry (IUPAC). The professional societies of the neutral countries supported German membership, but there was still resistance, especially from France. Haber wanted to overcome that resistance once and for all, and at the end of 1927 a special opportunity presented itself: the celebration in Paris of the centennial of the birth of Marcelin Berthelot.

In his report on these celebrations, to which he was invited, Haber stated his opinion that in France in his field not only left-wing scholars but also, with only a few isolated and therefore unimportant exceptions, right-wing professors wanted real cooperation with Germany. "I have no doubt that . . . a firm ground for this [German-French] understanding has been created."[22]

In the next two years Haber strove above all to obtain entry to IUPAC in a form that his German colleagues could also fully accept. His election in 1928 as president of the Union of German Chemical Societies shows clearly that these colleagues recognized his ability to carry out that assignment. Entry into IUPAC was to be achieved at the end of 1931, but Haber tried to effect as close a cooperation with the organization as possible even before this. Various meetings at congresses, in Scheveningen in the Netherlands and Liège in Belgium among other locations, served this purpose.

Haber's strategy succeeded. In July 1931 the Research Council was converted into the International Council of Scientific Unions (ICSU). The autonomy of the individual professional unions was considerably strengthened, in line with German suggestions, and other points they made were also taken into account during the revision of the council's charter. At a meeting of the Union of German Chemical Societies on 13 October 1931 Haber, as chairman, was able to announce this outcome—and that on behalf of the union he had declared its final entry into IUPAC.[23]

Shortly afterward Haber was elected vice president of IUPAC. There seems to have been a move in 1932 to select him as its president. He commented on this intention in a letter to the members of the board of the Union of German Chemical Societies.

> I see this as an international honor intended for our country, and I would not like to see this honor go to another country because of any refusal on our part. Considering Germany's position in chemistry, it is only fitting that we take the leadership. However, I do not believe that I can accept the nomination. I suffer from heart cramps [angina pectoris], which frequently force me to exercise special restraint and which sets limits on my ability to act as a representative, just as it does on my scientific activity. To predict the development of this disease over the years to come is quite impossible.[24]

He wanted to suggest in his place the name of Willstätter, who was slated to follow him as chairman of the German union if he resigned. Because of the rise to power of the Nazis, however, Willstätter, who was also a Jew, never replaced Haber in either role.

A few years after the National Socialists rose to power in Germany, the scientific organizations were subordinated to the so-called *Führer* principle. Nor could the societies of chemical science and industry evade these measures. A good description of these events is given in a Festschrift for the centennial of the German Chemical Society.[25]

After Germany's defeat in World War II the scientific organizations also collapsed. Owing to the occupation, new organizations could only be created slowly and with difficulty, in both the German Federal Republic and the German Democratic Republic. After various attempts to achieve common representation at the international organizations, the Federal and Democratic Republics finally became separate members of IUPAC via their umbrella organizations—the Central Committee of German Chemistry in the Federal Republic and the Academy of Sciences in the Democratic Republic.

The scientific organizations created by the German Democratic Republic were disbanded after Germany was reunited in October 1990. The two chemical societies merged as did the other professional societies. Today there is once again a single German representation at IUPAC.

## Endnotes

[1] "Wissenschaft und Wirtschaft nach dem Kriege" (Science and the economy after the war), lecture by Fritz Haber, held at an event sponsored by the Reichspresident, 20 Mar. 1923, *Naturwissenschaften* 11 (1923), 753. The same lecture was held at the parliamentary evening at the Parliament on 23 Jan. 1921, reprint in *Internationale Monatsschrift für Wissenschaft, Kunst und Technik* 15:2 (1921), 253, on the occasion of the celebration of the 10th jubilee of the KWG (Berlin: J. Springer, 1921).

[2] *Aus der Arbeit der Notgemeinschaft der Deutschen Wissenschaft* (From the work of the Emergency Association of German Science), Schriftenreihe Deutsche Forschung (German Research Series), vol. 16 (Berlin: Karl Sigismund Verlag, 1931).

[3] Kurt Zierold, *Forschungsförderung in drei Epochen* (Promotion of research in three epochs) (Wiesbaden: Franz Steiner Verlag, 1968); and Thomas H. Nipperdey and Ludwig Schmugge, *50 Jahre Forschungsförderung in Deutschland: Ein Abriss der Geschichte der Deutschen Forschungsgemeinschaft 1920–1970* (Fifty years of promotion of research: A summary of the history of the German Research Association 1920–1970) (Bonn–Bad Godesberg: Deutsche Forschungsgemeinschaft, 1970).

[4] Ibid.

[5] Walther Jaenicke (for Johannes Jaenicke), "Fritz Habers spätere Jahre und die Notgemeinschaft der Deutschen Wissenschaft" (Fritz Haber's later years and the Emergency Association of German Science), *Fridericiana: Zeitschrift der Universität Karlsruhe*, special issue, "Zum Gedenken an Fritz Haber" (Fritz Haber, in memoriam), 35 (1964), 56–65.

[6] Fritz Haber to Friedrich Schmidt-Ott, 25 June 1929; cited in Nipperdey and Schmugge, *50 Jahre* (cit. note 3), 61.

[7] Friedrich Schmidt to Max von Laue, 7 Dec. 1952, MPG, Dept. Va, Rep. 5, 1172-2.

[8] Fritz Haber to Wilhelm Solf, 6 Jan. 1925, Bundesarchiv Koblenz, Solf Nachlass, folio 10.

[9] "Franklin Institute Centenary," *Chemical and Metallurgical Engineering* 31 (1924), 492ff.

[10] Fritz Haber. "Der erwachende Osten" (The wakening East), *Industrie und Handelszeitung* 121 (26 May 1925).

[11] Identical letters from Haber to the national Ministries of the Interior, of Finance, and of Foreign Affairs, and to the Prussian Ministry of Science, Art, and People's Education, 2 May 1925, MPG, KWG 1, Rep. 1A, 984.

[12] Haber to Solf, 28 May 1925, Bundesarchiv Koblenz, Solf Nachlass, folio 4.

[13] Fritz Haber, speech at the opening of the Japan Institute, MPG, Dept. Va, Rep 5, 2034.

[14] Haber to Solf in Lausanne, 26 Jan. 1929, Bundesarchiv Koblenz, Solf Nachlass, folios 177, 178.

[15] Solf in Lausanne to Haber, 5 Feb. 1929, Bundesarchiv Koblenz, Solf Nachlass, folios 179–183.

[16] Richard Goldschmidt to Wilhelm Solf, 20 April 1937, MPG, Dept. Va, Rep. 5, 2041.

[17] Fritz Haber to Max Planck, July 1933, MPG, KWG 1, Rep. 1A, 988.

[18] Japanese-German Center, "Festschrift on the Occasion of the Dedication of the Former Building of the Japanese Embassy as the Japanese-German Center" (Berlin, 8 Nov. 1987).

[19] Brigitte Schröder-Gudehus, *Deutsche Wissenschaft und internationale Zusammenarbeit 1914–1928: Ein Beitrag zum Studium kultureller Beziehungen in politischen Krisenzeiten* (German science and international cooperation 1914–1928: A contribution to the study of cultural relations in times of political crisis) (Geneva: Dumaret & Golay, 1966).

[20] Hugo Kruyt to Fritz Haber, 19 June 1926, Kulturelle Abteilung, Archiv der Auswärtige Amt, Berlin (Cultural Dept., Ministry of Foreign Affairs), VIb, KuW, 607/1-11824.

[21] F. Haber to the Ministry of Foreign Affairs, 29 June 1926, Kulturelle Abteilung, Archiv der Auswärtige Amt, Berlin (Cultural Dept., Ministry of Foreign Affairs), VIb, KuW, 607/1-11389.

[22] Fritz Haber to Adolf von Harnack, 31 Oct. 1927, MPG, Dept. Va, Rep. 5, 1926.

[23] Minutes of the meeting of the Verband Deutscher Chemischer Vereine (Union of German Chemical Societies), 13 Oct. 1933, MPG, Dept. Va, Rep. 5, 2233.

[24] Fritz Haber to the board of the Union of German Chemical Societies, 5 Sept. 1932, MPG, Dept. Va, Rep. 5.

[25] Walter Ruske, *100 Jahre Deutsche Chemische Gesellschaft* (100 years of the German Chemical Society) (Weinheim: Verlag Chemie, 1967).

*Chapter 13*

# Emigration
# and
# Death

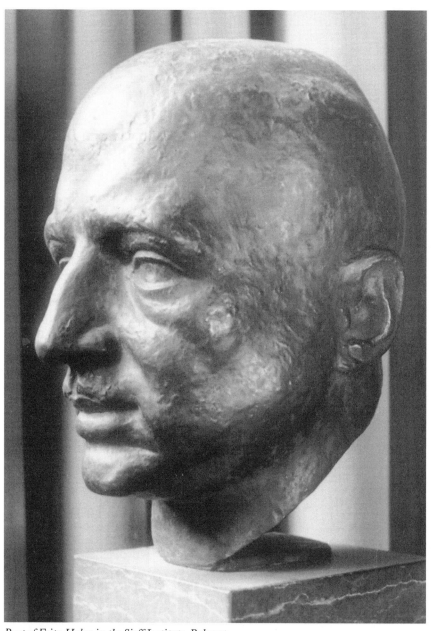

*Bust of Fritz Haber in the Sieff Institute, Rehovot.*


*Previous page: Employees of Haber's institute at their farewell party (see also p. 284).*

$W$HEN PRESIDENT HINDENBURG APPOINTED ADOLF HITLER national chancellor, Haber was not in Germany. He had gone to the French Riviera for rest in December 1932, and he spent over two months in Cap Ferrat, the small peninsula near Nice. He had planned this recuperative journey long before. As he wrote his young friend and medical adviser, Rudolf Stern, in October: "I requested a holiday of two months during the winter in order to spend it in a frost-free climate." And he reported on the state of his health: "Of all your recent advice none has proved more useful than that of pressure on the neck artery. . . . In any case, the bottom line is that the light attacks, which can be cut off just by this, as you emphasized, no longer require the use of nitroglycerin and that I have a new reason for being grateful to you."[1]

As Stern reported, the elections in November 1932, which seemed to offer a glimmer of hope on the political horizon, influenced Haber's health for the better. Haber observed political developments with intense uneasiness and was sensitive to every political change. That explains then why he did not feel rested after staying at Cap Ferrat, a matter that caused Stern great concern. Haber became increasingly worried about the future, though whether these worries also concerned his professional future is unclear. He certainly knew about the strongly anti-Semitic attitudes of the National Socialists, but in early 1933 he had not fully recognized the consequences for Jews of Hitler's takeover.

During these days he wrote to his friend Richard Willstätter: "I am fighting with diminishing strength against my four enemies—sleeplessness, the financial demands of my divorced wife, my increasing disquiet over the future, and the feeling of having made serious mistakes in my life."[2] Was this last remark a hint about his relationship to Judaism? Willstätter was a practicing Jew, and Haber had often discussed Jewish questions with Albert Einstein, who had already left Berlin. Haber now saw that his previous views were starting to crumble. He must have realized that his efforts to suppress his Jewishness in the face of his desire to be a good, patriotic German, rather than helping his situation in Germany in 1933, made it more difficult.

He regarded the continued direction of his institute as his most important task, with no consideration of his other burdens. The scientific work had to continue despite all the political upsets.

## Haber's Conflict and His Decision

Spring holidays usually began in March, but as usual not all the scientists took their holidays. At the end of the month, after the Nazis had achieved full control, a storm broke over the Kaiser Wilhelm Society and its institutes. Haber had seen it coming, for it had been brewing in his institute. Some of the workers who were National Socialists had begun to accuse other institute employees of communist activities, and Haber tried to protect the accused.

But even the well-informed Haber did not fully understand how immediate the danger was. On 7 April 1933 the Law on the Restoration of the Civil Service came into effect. The Kaiser Wilhelm Society and Haber's institute were special targets of the Nazi hunt for Jewish scientists. Thus the *Zeitschrift für die Gesamte Naturwissenschaft*, the science newspaper of the national student body, wrote, repeating the Nazi slogans of the year: "The founding of the Kaiser Wilhelm Institutes in Dahlem was the prelude to an influx of Jews into the physical sciences. The directorship of the Kaiser Wilhelm Institute for Physical and Electrochemistry was given to the Jew F. Haber, the nephew of the big-time Jewish profiteer Koppel. The work was reserved almost exclusively for Jews."[3] (Haber, of course, was not related to Koppel.)

By mid-April the personnel expert at the Prussian Ministry of Education, which oversaw Haber's institute, had made clear that it would not be acceptable for the institute to reopen after the holidays in its previous form. Haber then had two meetings, on 20 and 22 April, with Schmidt-Ott, who as vice president of the Kaiser Wilhelm Society was standing in for Max Planck, who was on leave.

In the previous weeks Haber had been casting about for a way to handle this crisis, but he could not reach a decision. At his last meeting with Schmidt-

Ott, Haber gave him the letters of resignation of his department heads, Freundlich and Polanyi, required by the new law. Haber called this "the most important step in the required reorganization" because "they were quite independent in the choice of their assignments and, as a natural and necessary consequence, also in the choice of their coworkers, and an almost automatic consequence of their departure is that it eliminates numerous further separate questions concerning the desired reorganization." And he added that this naturally would apply to his own department on his departure. He also said, probably ironically, that the reorganization "would be most effectively eased by the acceptance of these resignations and the agreement to my own decision." The only request he made was for the possibility "of an ordered retrenchment over the next five months." And he declared in a resentful tone, "Without this change I cannot take any part in the required reorganization."[4] The goal of his demand was to gain a transition period for his Jewish coworkers that would allow them to secure a means of livelihood in their professions in other countries.

Haber's attempts to delay the dismissal of his Jewish coworkers had only minimal success. Haber, like all his colleagues, received the questionnaires for their coworkers relating to enforcement of the 7 April law at the same time. The employees themselves had to fill these out, and their answers were painstakingly checked. Just like the department heads, Freundlich and Polanyi, who had "voluntarily" handed in their resignations, all the other Jewish members of the institute had to give up their positions. That applied to Haber's old friend Fritz Epstein, who had relieved him of administrative work, as well as to the research assistants Ladislaus Farkas, Leopold Frommer, Hartmut Kallmann, Karl Söllner, Ernst Simon, and Joseph Weiss, all of whom left Germany in the course of the year. His longtime coworker Paul Goldfinger stayed in Germany until 1937. The technician Martin Schmalz, the secretary Irene Sackur, and Haber's private secretary, Rita Cracauer, also had to leave the institute in 1933. The directive for immediate dismissal applied to three department heads, six research assistants, and three other coworkers, whereas one, Goldfinger, fell into the category of those who could receive temporary protection from dismissal, because he had been a state official in 1914 and a soldier at the front during World War I.

Haber worked especially hard to help his private secretary, Rita Cracauer, and to get her an adequate transition period. Cracauer, whose coworkers called her not only the "memory" but also the "soul of the institute," stayed on to the end of the year, after which she went first to England and then later to Israel. She maintained close contact with the Haber family, especially with Hermann, and other members of the institute who had fled to England and America continued to correspond with her for many years.

Haber also attempted to retain Irene Sackur, the secretary working in Freundlich's department, on the grounds that her father, Otto Sackur, had been killed in the institute while working on research for new explosives during World War I. Haber had been similarly involved in trying to prolong the stay of his other workers, especially Kallmann and Farkas.

Meanwhile Schmidt-Ott and other Kaiser Wilhelm Society officials had been trying to pacify Haber and at least to delay his resignation—to no avail. The pressures from the Prussian Ministry of Education had convinced Haber that he could not continue to head the institute under these circumstances. He submitted his resignation, dated 30 April 1933, to Bernhard Rust, the national and Prussian minister of education. It contained the following text, cited here in an abbreviated form:

> I herewith request that on 1 October 1933 I be relieved of my official full-time Prussian position as director of a Kaiser Wilhelm Institute as well as of my secondary Prussian post as full professor at the local university, and that I be allowed to retire. According to the directives of the National Civil Service Law of 7 April 1933, whose application to the institutes of the Kaiser Wilhelm Society is stipulated, I have the right to remain in office, although I am descended from Jewish grandparents and parents. But I do not wish to make use of this dispensation any longer than is required for the ordered closing of the scientific and administrative duties that I am obliged to carry out in my position. . . .
>
> My decision to request retirement derives from the contrast between the research tradition in which I have lived up to now and the changed views which you, Minister, and your ministry advocate as representatives of the current large national movement. My tradition requires that in a scientific post, when choosing coworkers, I consider only the professional and personal characteristics of applicants, without considering their racial make-up. From a man in the sixty-fifth year of his life you will expect no change in the thinking that has directed him for the past thirty-nine years of his university life, and you will understand that the pride with which he served his German homeland all his life now stipulates this request for retirement.[5]

Haber also sent his resignation to Max Planck, president of the Kaiser Wilhelm Society, who was shocked at this development. Planck made a last attempt to reverse the course of events by requesting a meeting with Adolf Hitler, who did not accept Planck's arguments.[6]

*Max Planck.*

Haber was relieved after making his final decision. He had suspected how difficult the next months would become and how adversely his health would be affected. As he wrote Rudolf Stern: "The feeling of being a useless bit of life on this earth is really wretched." And in June he wrote, "I don't want to complain about my emotional suffering and to express the bitterness that fills me and that often enough breaks out of me when it would be better to keep it to myself. I have lived too long."[7]

## Last Months in Dahlem

Despite his bitterness Haber wanted to stay until he and Max Planck, president of the Kaiser Wilhelm Society, had completed the tasks he had set himself: transferring the institute to a worthy successor and establishing a livelihood for the coworkers he had been forced to dismiss. His overriding sense of duty drove him to do this.

Three physicists and physical chemists whom Haber respected highly seemed to him the most suitable successors for the directorship of the institute. He chose as his preferred candidate the Nobel laureate James Franck, who had once worked in Haber's institute and was now a professor of experimental physics in Göttingen. As the second candidate he considered the physical chemist Karl Friedrich Bonhoeffer, who had worked closely with him on various research questions in the late 1920s and early 1930s and was now working at the Physical Chemistry Institute in Frankfurt. Finally he considered the theoretical physicist and Nobel laureate Max von Laue, who had been associate director at the Kaiser Wilhelm Institute for Physics since 1914. Two of these possible successors actually directed the institute after World War II, Bonhoeffer in 1949, while the institute was still housed in Göttingen, and Max von Laue from 1950 to 1960 in Dahlem.

But Haber and Planck's hopes were not to be fulfilled in the 1930s. James Franck, who was also dismissed as a Jew, left Germany in the autumn of 1933, first spending a year in Copenhagen with Niels Bohr and then traveling to the United States. There he worked first at the Johns Hopkins University in Baltimore. In 1936 he went to the University of Chicago, where, in 1938, he received a chair in chemistry. He participated in the Manhattan Project because, like many other physicists in America, he feared that Germany would be the first to produce the atomic bomb. Later, after the total defeat of Germany in 1945, Franck and other physicists, especially Leo Szillard, composed a memorandum to the U.S. Secretary of War in which they tried to draw attention to the dangers of a nuclear arms race.[8] Bombs fell on Hiroshima and Nagasaki despite their protests.

As Franck was no longer available, Haber then began to carry out an intensive correspondence and many discussions with Bonhoeffer about the succession. But the National Socialists, supported by the military, showed increasing resistance to Haber and Planck's plans. Meanwhile Bonhoeffer was negotiating with the University of Leipzig over an appointment as director of the Institute for Physical Chemistry there. During his meetings in Berlin, Bonhoeffer apparently received the impression that Haber and Planck's efforts had little chance of success, so he looked for a position elsewhere.

Haber's proposed reorganization of the institute and transfer of the directorship to Max von Laue had also become untenable. The idea thus arose of naming a provisional director. Time was pressing because Haber wanted to travel to a conference in Spain and to visit his son Hermann in Paris on the way. Haber and Planck agreed to ask Otto Hahn to take on the role of provisional director. Hahn was officially scheduled to take over this job on 1 October, after Haber had left. But Haber and Hahn had already had various meetings in July about concluding matters in the institute. On this topic Hahn reports: "The winding up was naturally extremely painful for Prof. Haber, and I often had conversations with him about it. I remember that we spoke for a long time about Kallmann's staying and what we could do with the other non-Aryan members of the institute."[9]

Haber left Dahlem for his journey to Spain, while Planck went on holiday. Planck wrote Haber what can be seen as a farewell letter. It began with the following lines: "Before my departure I want to add a personal word of farewell to you. With what feeling you will leave the place of your long, fruitful, and glorious work, I do not even wish to imagine. Just the bare attempt makes my heart spasm." At the end of the letter Planck asks Haber to "keep his friendly attitude toward him even from afar."[10]

In the end the National Socialist government accepted none of Planck's ideas for the directorship of the institute, and Hahn had to retire. Gerhard Jansen from Göttingen was appointed temporarily, but he stayed only until 1935, when he was replaced by Adolf Thiessen, who directed the institute until 1945.[11]

Thus first Haber and then the Kaiser Wilhelm Society lost the fight over Haber's successor and the management of the institute. In addition, Haber's admonition to carry out military technological research in the field of gas

*Photograph taken in 1933 at the farewell party of employees of Haber's institute, held in the institute's garden. Haber is seated in the second row, third from right.*

warfare in the institute in Dahlem was brushed aside for the time being. Admittedly, up to the end of World War II, the institute was heavily involved with such projects. Most of the scientific research and development in this field, however, was carried out in industry, while the further development, testing, and application were carried out mainly at the experimental station in Breloh on the Lüneburger Heide, the place that Haber had suggested in a letter to General Hermann Geyer in May 1933.[12]

As for Haber's decision to stay until he had found his Jewish colleagues some prospect of a post abroad, one consequence was that as the official director of the institute, he had to carry out their dismissal himself, and some of these colleagues were good friends. With this task he had taken on a burden he could hardly bear. Some friends and relatives could not understand why he had not simply left Germany after submitting his resignation. But Haber could not. It was clear to him that if he did not act, others would, and he would have been much less able to help.

The flood of letters Haber wrote to colleagues in other countries testifies to his concern for and efforts on behalf of his employees. He also took the trouble to secure the future of his friends and relatives. As has already been noted, numerous coworkers in his institute were affected by the National Socialist laws. Some left the institute before 1933. Rudolf Ladenburg had already gone to the United States in 1932, while Friedrich Matthias and Hans Eisner no longer worked at the institute. (The latter left for private industry first in Spain and then in Montevideo.)

Haber did not have to extend himself for his two department heads, Freundlich and Polanyi. They had such excellent scientific reputations that they had no problem finding positions abroad. Both went to England, Freundlich to University College, London, and Polanyi to Victoria University in Manchester. Freundlich later taught at the University of Minnesota in Minneapolis.

Haber was especially active on Kallmann's behalf. It was important to him that Kallmann continue his work on the behavior of ions under high energy and electric current. Kallmann stayed in Germany and was able to work, using his contacts with IG Farben and the electrical manufacturer AEG. He was married to a woman who was not Jewish, and that saved him from the concentration camps.[13]

Ladislaus Farkas had an unusual fate. He had a brother, Adalbert, who had worked previously at the Haber institute. Both had worked with Bonhoeffer at that time, and since then they had all remained friends. Some of the letters written by the two brothers to Bonhoeffer have been preserved and provide a lively picture of their life in the 1930s.[14] The brothers went to England, where they probably (although not certainly) met with Haber while he was in Cambridge between October 1933 and January of the next year. Adalbert Farkas first stayed in Cambridge, and then went to Philadelphia in 1941. Ladislaus Farkas worked for a year in Bristol, but then traveled to Palestine to take up the directorship of the physical chemistry institute that was being set up by the Hebrew University of Jerusalem.[15] In September 1933, when Weizmann asked Haber, through his son Hermann, to recommend a professor of physical chemistry, Haber had named Ladislaus.[16] Weizmann apparently had not forgotten. Ladislaus traveled frequently to Europe, visited Bonhoeffer in Leipzig, and bought various pieces of equipment for his institute. He became a great supporter of Jewish studies at the Hebrew University until 1948, when he was killed in the battle for Jerusalem.

Irene Sackur, too, was unable to keep her post at the institute, although many people, such as Planck, Hahn, and even Friedrich Glum of the Kaiser Wilhelm Society, stood up for her. She went to Palestine and worked for many years at an agricultural institute near the Weizmann Institute. She married there and later lived in Rehovot near Tel Aviv.

When Haber left Berlin, he had not quite achieved his aim of finding jobs abroad for all the Jewish workers dismissed from his institute. But for those without jobs he had made many connections that proved helpful in the future. Now he could think about himself, even though he realized that in his poor state of health (which he still did not want to accept) he was scarcely capable of carrying out further great scientific projects.

## Emigration and Haber's Sojourn in Cambridge

Haber left Dahlem at the beginning of August 1933. His future was extremely uncertain: officially, he remained director of the institute until 1 October, but he had had so many humiliating and painful experiences since May that after his trip to Spain he first wanted to rest for several weeks.

What possibilities were available to Haber, and in what country should he settle? Should he go to France to be near his son? Some old acquaintances tried to find him a permanent new home. Aihito Sata, who taught in Osaka and who had been a friend since the time of the founding of the German-Japanese Society, corresponded with both Wilhelm Solf and Haber about the possibility of moving Jewish-German scientists to Japan. Haber's old friend Setsuro Tamaru and Hajime Hoshi, who had been such a generous donor, also invited Haber to come to Japan. Haber corresponded with Hans von Euler, a professor of chemistry, in Stockholm, about possibilities in Sweden. And a friend of Haber's in Spain, the banker Julio Kocherthaler, discussed possibilities for scientific work there. The question also arose quite early as to whether a temporary or a longer stay in England would allow him to pursue his work. Support for Haber's moving to England came from old antagonists from World War I, whom he had met after the war: Brigadier Harold Hartley; Sir William Pope, now a professor at Cambridge University; and F. G. Donnan, now a professor at Imperial College, London.

It is amazing that of all people it was Hartley, Pope, and Haber's former French antagonist in World War I, Henri Maraour, who became active on behalf of Haber and his coworkers. Whereas others, including scientists, still harbored strong resentment of Haber and those who had developed chemical weapons in World War I, former adversaries in gas warfare research showed a great deal of understanding for the position in which Haber and his coworkers found themselves.

Haber left Berlin on 5 August 1933 and traveled first to Paris to visit his son and his son's family. He stayed there briefly and then journeyed on to Santander on the Calabrian coast in Spain, where a meeting of IUPAC was to be held at the university and where Haber had long planned to give a lecture.

In Paris he met Richard Willstätter, who was also on the way to Santander, although they made the journey separately. In his autobiography Willstätter describes his shock at the state of Haber's health. Haber nevertheless traveled on to Santander and gave his lecture.

Carrying out a planned commitment at all costs and against all common sense and medical advice was typical of Haber, even at the end of his life. But his strength was now exhausted. Under the circumstances returning to Berlin was impossible. So he traveled via Paris to Switzerland, where he tried to recuperate at Visp in the upper Rhône valley. Hardly had he recovered a little strength, however, than he could not resist visiting Chaim Weizmann in Zermatt, at an altitude of 1,500 meters. In August, he, with Willstätter, had met Weizmann in Paris before going on to Santander. Now he wanted to discuss traveling to Palestine that same year. (Their meeting in Zermatt is described later in this chapter.)

Haber's excursion to Zermatt had disastrous consequences. Before he could reach Visp again, he suffered a serious collapse in Brig, Switzerland. Haber thought he had had a stroke, but Rudolf Stern thought it was more likely a heart attack.[17] Once Haber had recovered somewhat, he drove to the Swiss sanatorium in Mammern at the lower end of Lake Constance, where he remained under competent medical supervision during September and October. He had to abandon his plans for visiting Budapest, going to Orselina in Switzerland, and starting the journey to Palestine via Genoa and Alexandria.

Meanwhile Hartley and Pope had been active. They reported on their progress to Haber, mainly by passing the information on to his son Hermann, as they did not always know where Haber was. By the end of July, Hartley had been able to secure a laboratory for Haber's further work.[18] The question of an assistant had not been settled, but Joseph Weiss was supposed to come later from Berlin, and he in fact did arrive to help Haber with his work. Haber informed Pope that he would gladly accept an offer of a chance to work in Cambridge. So Pope wrote back that he had asked the vice chancellor of Cambridge University to invite Haber officially.[19] The next day the vice chancellor sent Haber a friendly and respectful invitation.[20]

When Pope returned to Cambridge after a long vacation, everything was prepared for Haber. The vice chancellor also sent written invitations to Else Freyhahn, Rita Cracauer, and Joseph Weiss, which they were to present at passport control on entering England. Pope had already advised Haber to do the same. Pope had also submitted an application to the Academic Assistance Council for Weiss's support.[21] All details for Haber's stay at Cambridge had been attended to.

At the end of October, Haber left Mammern and traveled to Paris to meet his son. He stayed there only a few days and went on to London, where he met Weizmann on 4 November. From there he traveled to Cambridge and took up quarters with his sister at the University Arms Hotel. At Pope's institute, with Joseph Weiss, he began his last investigation, on the catalytic decomposition of hydrogen peroxide.

In the following period in Cambridge, which lasted only a little over two months, Haber was gripped by various moods and emotions. He was certainly happy that he could at least continue with a small part of his work. Many of his former coworkers visited him. He met with Freundlich, Polanyi came from Manchester to Cambridge, and Ladislaus Farkas worked in Cambridge for some of the time. Kallmann later described a meeting there:

On 15 December I traveled to London in order to settle various matters, and naturally I visited Haber in Cambridge. There I experienced some unforgettable hours. In the afternoon we gathered for a scientific colloquium in his hotel room in Cambridge; all his laboratory assistants from Dahlem were there, and I was there as a guest, along with a friend I had brought from London. Then began a scientific discussion more wonderful than you could possibly imagine. All cares, all difficulties, all pressures were forgotten in that moment. And so the Dahlem circle arose anew under Haber's influence in Cambridge, unfortunately only for a short time.[22]

This time was a comfort for Haber. He also met with other old friends and acquaintances. Paul Harteck came to Cambridge in 1933 to work with Ernest Rutherford. Max Born was also in Cambridge at this time, and he and his wife often met with Haber and his sister. He wrote in his memoirs that Haber had seemed "ill, depressed, lonely, a shadow of his former self" in Cambridge.[23] But Haber was not as lonely in Cambridge as Born had assumed. What so distressed Haber was his still-uncertain future. Again and again he tried to reach a satisfactory solution to his financial problems with the German authorities, especially regarding the so-called emigration tax. He had received no answer by the time of his death.

In this period a second inquiry came from the vice chancellor of the university, asking whether Haber wished to stay longer in Cambridge. He invited Haber to continue his research until the end of the academic year, in which he would turn seventy.[24] Haber wrote his friend Richard Willstätter on the subject:

> Now I sit here in my wanderings, awaiting the things to come. The university here has taken a step that is certainly unusual in that they have offered me an appointment without saying to what. I am officially addressed as "Dear Professor" and the document itself is known as a "call." Naturally it is a purely honorary appointment to participate in directing scientific work in the chemistry department in close coordination with the professor of chemistry [Sir William Pope]. . . . I have suffered further from my problems, of which fatigue and insomnia are the worst. Now I suffer from the uncertainty about the German business. . . . In the most favorable case my sister and I want to travel at the end of the year to Palestine for two months, which I badly need. That I do not see you is an especially hard misfortune for me. I have not followed up on connections to other countries apart from England. My scientific achievement, at least for now, is pitiful.[25]

Yet Haber must have found some relaxation in this "pitiful" scientific work. But now, as his son Hermann had predicted, Haber's health, which had improved during October and November, again began to deteriorate. In December, Haber reported to Rudolf Stern that he had had in his hotel room "exactly the same sort of attack [as in Brig] but slightly weaker." He commented, "But I didn't make a fuss about it this time, and I managed just the same."[26] However, he did not have the prescription given him by the doctor in Mammern, nor did he have morphine to ease the pain.

Else Freyhahn later told Stern that Haber spent his last ounce of strength on his research, which he wanted to finish. He more or less ignored the pains that increased as the raw English winter set in. She begged her brother to travel to the south, to Madeira, Portugal, or to Tunisia, and both Stern and Hermann supported her efforts. But Haber stayed in Cambridge until the end of January.

Toward the end of December, Haber saw that his strength was rapidly diminishing. He reported to Willstätter that he had "reduced the sleeping tablets stepwise until [he] no longer took them and now spent some nights awake, but the following days were not worse for this." And he described his condition:

> I manage the agony of these times very badly, and even though I feel your friendship more than the stronger words and cooler feelings that lie behind the other letters, I still remain prey to the continual unrest caused by the negotiations about moving over here. It is a defect of age that one has no patience. . . . Fundamentally, I believe about no one but you that knowledge [*Wissenschaft*] comes with age. For me this knowledge is a requirement, and I now write in English so that I can still publish a few things. But I would rather dispense with this habit and, like the English, get my happiness from trying to reduce my golf handicap to a maximum of plus four.[27]

At the end of December and beginning of January, Haber's plans for a journey south began to take shape. Stern advised Haber against a long journey, such as to Palestine, and also regarded Madeira as unsuitable for a winter recuperation because no reliable heart specialist worked there. He invited Haber to travel with him to Tunisia, where he had to go on business.[28] Haber apparently was unenthusiastic about these recommendations and seems to have given Stern a fairly brusque answer, although he later apologized. Haber had nothing against a stay in Orselina, which had also been discussed.[29] In any case Haber wrote to his friend Willstätter that the doctors had advised him against a journey to Palestine, and he asked Willstätter to travel there in his place.

Haber left Cambridge after only two months. He wrote a farewell letter to the vice chancellor of the university in the hope that he could return there. He thanked him in the following moving words for the kindness shown him in Cambridge:

> In these weeks I have learned that in this country, where the memories of ages past do not fade, the chivalry from King Arthur's time still lives among its scientists. . . . I have the strong hope that I will be able to return in a few weeks. I feel the uncertainty of the future like a physical weight on my old shoulders, and I am sure that the odds are imponderable whether my physical strength will suffice to bear the coming earthquakes.[30]

## Haber, Weizmann, and the Palestine Project

In early 1933 a closer relationship developed between two men who up till then had taken diametrically opposed positions on the way in which Jews in the Diaspora should conduct themselves. Haber supported the assimilation and integration of Jews into the society of the country in which they lived. Weizmann opposed integration in principle and was an ardent Zionist who saw Palestine as the true home of the Jews. The differing attitudes of the two men stemmed partly from their different origins but also from the fact that Weizmann had very early become an active member of the Zionist movement, whereas Haber had hardly been aware of the movement during his youth.

Chaim Weizmann was born on 17 November 1874 in the small town of Motol in the Kobrinin district of the Grodno area, in what was then western Russia (now Belarus). His father was one of those eastern European Jews who had recognized that the only chance of escaping from his poverty was through further education. And he was one of the few eastern Jews who advocated a Jewish nation. He sent his son to a modern secondary school in Pinsk and later moved his entire family to this larger city. There Chaim Weizmann became interested in the Hebrew language and in chemistry, which he wanted to study after graduation from high school. As it was extremely difficult for a Jew to study at a Russian university, he went to Germany and began to study chemistry at the Darmstadt Institute of Technology. After two semesters he went to Berlin to study at the Charlottenburg

Institute of Technology. Here he met many other Jewish students who, in a sort of pre-Zionist movement, preached the love of Zion. After Theodor Herzl's book *Der Judenstaat* (The Jewish nation) was published, Weizmann immediately became one of his followers. In 1898 he went to the University of Fribourg in Switzerland, where he obtained his doctorate a year later. In 1901 he became a research assistant to Augustyn Bistrzycki, one of Carl Gräbe's former students at the University of Geneva. He stayed there until 1906 and then went to Manchester, where he became an Anglophile. He retained these feelings for the rest of his life, a characteristic partly responsible for his successes as well as his failures.

In Manchester, Weizmann divided his time between science and work for the Zionist movement. When World War I broke out, he offered his services as a scientist to the British government. In 1912 he had discovered a new process, based on fermentation, for making large amounts of acetone, which was needed for manufacturing cordite. Weizmann now worked with the British on scaling up the process.

In the autumn of 1914 Weizmann became acquainted with the editor of the liberal newspaper the *Manchester Guardian*, Charles Prestwich Scott. Through Scott, he made connections with such leading liberal politicians as Lloyd George, Herbert Samuel, and Arthur J. Balfour. These connections were to become important when Weizmann lobbied the British government for an official consent to the Zionist goal—making Palestine available as a homeland for Jews. And he actually succeeded. On 2 November 1917 Balfour, then the British foreign minister, announced that "Her Majesty's government regards with favour the establishment of a national home for the Jewish people in Palestine."[31] The Balfour Declaration became the starting point for all the efforts of the Zionists and of Weizmann to bring about the settlement of Jews in Palestine under the British mandate after World War II.

In 1931 Weizmann set aside his research and preoccupied himself with establishing Jewish scientific institutions in Palestine. He had laid the foundation stone for the Hebrew University of Jerusalem in 1918, shortly after the British had conquered the city, and he was repeatedly active on the university's behalf. From 1932 on he was busy building up a scientific institute (later named the Daniel Sieff Research Institute) in Rehovot, near Tel Aviv. When Hitler rose to power in Germany, Weizmann wanted to bring to Palestine as many Jewish scientists as possible, including prominent individuals. He tried especially hard to win Richard Willstätter and Fritz Haber.

*Chaim Weizmann (left) with Yitzhak Wilkanski, at the opening of the Daniel Sieff Research Institute on 3 April 1934.*

In 1932 Weizmann visited Haber in Dahlem and was extraordinarily impressed by his institute. At a meal in Haber's official residence Haber showed great interest in Weizmann's work in Palestine. In the course of a conversation on technological and scientific matters Haber said several times, "Well, Dr. Weizmann, you might try to introduce that into Palestine."[32]

The two men kept up further contact by letter. In 1933 Hermann Haber informed Weizmann about the events in Dahlem and his father's resignation. Weizmann apparently then suggested that Fritz Haber come to Palestine. A few weeks later Haber visited Weizmann on his vacation in Zermatt, and Weizmann described an incident from the visit:

> During the dinner, at which my wife and my son Michael were also present, Haber suddenly burst into an eloquent tirade. The reason was the following: The eighteenth Zionist Congress was then being held in Prague. I had refused to attend, not wishing to be involved in any political struggle. During the dinner repeated calls came from Prague, and frantic requests that I leave Zermatt at once and betake myself to the Congress. I persisted in my refusal, and though I said nothing to Haber about these frequent interruptions, except to mention that they came from Prague, he guessed their purport from something he had read in the papers, and he said to me with the utmost earnestness:
>
> "Dr. Weizmann, I was one of the mightiest men in Germany. I was more than a great army commander, more than a captain of industry. I was the founder of industries; my work was essential for the economic and military expansion of Germany. All doors were open for me. But the position I occupied then, glamorous as it may have seemed, is as nothing compared with yours. You are not creating out of plenty—you are creating out of nothing, in a land which lacks everything; you are trying to restore a derelict people to a sense of dignity. And you are, I think, succeeding. At the end of my life I find myself a bankrupt. When I am gone and forgotten, your work will stand, a shining monument, in the long history of our people. Do not ignore the call now; go to Prague, even at the risk that you will suffer grievous disappointment there." . . .
>
> I did not go to Prague, much to Haber's disappointment. But I made use of the opportunity to press upon him our invitation to come out to Palestine and work with us. I said, "The climate will be good for you. You will find a modern laboratory, able assistants. You will work in peace and honor. It will be a return home for you—your journey's end."
>
> He accepted with enthusiasm, and asked only that he be allowed to spend another month or two in a sanatorium. On this we agreed—and in due course he set out for Palestine, was taken suddenly ill in Basel, and died there.[33]

In spite of the serious heart attack that Haber suffered in Brig, he wrote to Weizmann, still enthusiastic about their meeting: "Dear, very dear Mr. Weizmann, I feel the need in my heart to thank you and your wife for the hospitality shown me in Zermatt." He told them about his heart attack and said that it had had no bad consequences, "but I remain the undiminished master of my limbs, my speech, and my mental abilities."[34]

At the beginning of October, Haber's plans for traveling to Palestine became more concrete. Weizmann was able to inform Haber that work was developing favorably in Rehovot, and he wrote:

> I am pleased to inform you that the outer shell of the building has been completed and the people are now beginning with the interior fittings. I am sure that the laboratory will be ready for work in January, so that we will have a lot to do when we all begin to arrive there during December. I have charged colleagues in Palestine with looking for accommodations for you and for us, and I would like to know roughly what sort of accommodations you will need. Who will be traveling with you? Of course, the type of housing will be somewhat simple at first, yes, possibly spartan, but we will soon have comfortable quarters for you. Will you bring some of your library with you? And will your sister and your secretary accompany you? Please excuse me for bothering you with questions about such details, but it is better to clarify them in advance so that we can make the necessary arrangements.[35]

Haber wrote back immediately to say that difficulties had arisen in Berlin that had to be settled before he could undertake such a long journey as the one to Palestine. But he informed Weizmann that after a stay in Budapest he and his sister would make their way there.[36]

In October there was every indication that Haber would soon realize this plan. His son was also in favor of the move, and Rudolf Stern was keen for Haber to travel for the winter to Palestine, which he thought would be good for Haber both climatically and psychologically. Hermann and Fritz wanted to discuss the exact dates with Weizmann during a scheduled meeting in Paris.[37] Thus at the end of October, Weizmann was still convinced that Haber would travel to Palestine in November and would arrive there about 1 December.

Meanwhile Haber arrived in Paris. Hermann had notified Weizmann earlier that Haber wanted to go to London to see him there. Hermann hoped that he could still convince his father to leave soon for Palestine. Fritz, however, was worried about his financial affairs in Germany and convinced that they would not be cleared up for four to six weeks.

On 4 November, Haber went to London and stayed for three days with his sister at the Hotel Russell. There he talked with Weizmann at length about his difficulties in Germany and the journey to Palestine, now fixed for the end of December. Weizmann telegraphed a colleague in Rehovot, asking him to reserve two bedrooms and a living room with bath from late December for two months.[38]

Haber again contacted Weizmann shortly after his arrival in Cambridge.[39] He appeared somewhat at sea about conditions in England, but he immediately mentioned some scientific work that he had discussed with Weizmann in London. Haber and Weizmann wrote each other almost daily. Weizmann thought that Haber would soon acclimatize to Cambridge, and he hoped that he would find the atmosphere pleasant and friendly. He also invited Haber, along with Freundlich, Simon Marks, and any others Haber could suggest, to meet at his house to enjoy long and quiet conversations. Marks was an owner of the Marks and Spencer chain of clothing stores and a sponsor of Weizmann's activities.

On 27 November, Haber went to London and attended a luncheon given by Marks. Weizmann discussed Haber's further plans, as the dates they had agreed on had been postponed. He also asked Haber to discuss with Max Born whether he too might come to Palestine to join the Hebrew University of Jerusalem.

On 15 December, Weizmann wrote a memorandum on the standing of the Daniel Sieff Research Institute and its program in agricultural and applied chemistry. He mentioned that "Professor Fritz Haber would spend some of the winter months in the institute in Rehovot; Professor Richard Willstätter, with whom I am working on various scientific problems, advises us regularly, not only on questions of personnel but also on the institute's program. He has kindly agreed to come to Palestine for the opening of the institute in March."[40]

All was ready for Haber's arrival in Palestine, but on 6 January he wrote Weizmann a letter that in effect signaled the end of those travel plans. Haber began:

> I have been working on this letter for a long time.... Should I put everything on paper, with the result that I bore an overworked friend with explanations that never alter any of the facts in life and any of the feelings that signify the actual tenor of a life? The briefest way to say it is that everything of consequence has been postponed and through this delay has assumed an altered and distressing form.[41]

Haber then described how his affairs in Germany had still not been settled. He added that some people in Germany were in such a bizarre state of mind that they were speculating on what would happen if war were to break out and Haber were then either to be interned or to work for the English.

In the meantime the condition of my heart is changing as winter progresses and anxiety continually increases. And the idea that seemed self-evident to me, that I could set out on and complete the journey to Palestine for recuperation, has been changed by my state of health into the very opposite. I have asked . . . a consultant doctor here about the possibility of traveling to Madeira this month. He warned against this journey as too great an undertaking and thereby has implicitly forbidden the journey to Haifa. Added to the fear that the German authorities will make difficulties for me when I am far away is the new and sharper fear that the journey would not give me a rest but would instead make me worse.[42]

Haber then added some general remarks that served to sum up the plans for having him collaborate in the work at the Sieff Institute in Rehovot:

Truly, I do not envy you your great task. Each day I feel more strongly that only those things are worth doing that we risk doing from a broad perspective. But we need strength for that, and trust that our health will endure, and it seems to me that the conditions needed for your success depend more and more on overcoming an inner deficiency among the Jews of my homeland that Hitler's Germany has not uprooted up to now. They feel closer to citizenship in Germany than to Zionism and lack the purity and simplicity of their own spiritual direction. Since Hitler's policy has evoked a positive response from the economy, the days of the Jewish prophets fade into the forgotten past, and all the usual overemphasis on a physically bearable existence has moved into the foreground of their interests again. No one who sits at his desk preaching about the Maccabees escapes being ridiculous, and no one who expects peaceful citizens to turn into Maccabees escapes the lunatic asylum. I have known the wartime battlefields on which French and English Jews shot German Jews, just as French and English socialists shot German Social Democrats, and that has left behind a stain that it is painful to bear.

I write all this not as the opinion of a man who feels responsible, but from the age that the year 1933 has bestowed upon me and in the wish to be as useful to you as my strength still allows and with all my wishes for your success and for the well-being of your family, which has given a true feeling of friendship to my tired soul.[43]

Ten days later Haber announced that he intended to travel to London on 24 January and from there to Paris. He wished to visit Weizmann and his wife. "What we will do after we have reached Paris, God alone knows."[44] Haber's departure from Cambridge was further delayed, so that he and his sister did not arrive in London until 26 January. There he was received by Weizmann. Both then met Joseph Blumenfeld, Weizmann's brother-in-law and Hermann Haber's employer. Writing Hermann and Rudolf Stern, Weizmann describes how Haber, just forty-eight hours before his death, was still overflowing with spirit and turned the conversation into a real experience.[45] It was a shock for him to hear on 2 February that Haber had died shortly after this meeting.

The Daniel Sieff Research Institute was inaugurated on 3 April 1934. Richard Willstätter was among the guest speakers. Other German-Jewish scientists whom Weizmann had invited to work in Palestine were not present. And so it was that Haber's friend opened the institute and paid tribute to Weizmann's achievements.

Long before this, Weizmann had had a vision. He had imagined that in Rehovot a research establishment would arise equal in size and content to research institutes in Europe and North America, that it would have modern facilities and be laid out in a green park with decorative flower beds. This vision has become a reality. The grounds of the Weizmann Institute in Rehovot are resplendent with green lawns, flower beds, and modern research facilities. Lying almost hidden behind the administration building is the old Sieff Institute. And in a nearby library building stands a bust of Haber, which commemorates the gift of Haber's library to the Sieff Institute. And in the Ullmann Institute, in a green inner courtyard, there is a memorial stone with this inscription:

> This institute stands as a living monument to
>
> | | |
> |---|---|
> | Fritz Haber | 1868–1934 |
> | Richard Willstätter | 1872–1942 |
> | Carl Neuberg | 1877–1956 |
> | Otto Meyerhof | 1884–1959 |
> | Max Bergmann | 1886–1944 |
> | Rudolf Schoenheimer | 1898–1941 |

If one walks down the long path through the institute grounds, one reaches a memorial with inscriptions that commemorate Weizmann. Finally one reaches the house in which he spent the last years of his life. He also lived there after he had been elected president of the young state of Israel, to whose founding in 1948 he had made a decisive contribution. He died in 1952, and his gravestone lies below his house, under green trees and framed by colorful floral hedges.

*The gravestone of Fritz and Clara Haber (née Immerwahr) in the Hörnli Cemetery, Basel (photograph taken in 1958).*

## Death in Basel

The journey that took Fritz Haber and his sister from England to Switzerland at the end of January 1934 must have been an enormous strain for him. Rudolf Stern and Hermann were already waiting for him at his hotel in Basel. When Haber entered, they were shocked to see how terrible he looked. Stern reports about the hours that followed:

> He was not capable of speaking for even a few minutes without having a severe heart attack. He agreed to go to bed and asked me to examine him thoroughly. As I have always done, I reassured him with calming words and promised him that the weeks in Orselina [where Haber wanted to go] would do him good. He always reacted to this psychological treatment with amazing gaiety. Nothing could keep him in bed any longer. He got up and came

downstairs and—almost without pausing—discussed future plans for his son and himself. Each of us had a chance to talk to him alone, and he showed great interest in everything we told him. I insisted that we all retire early, and we said good night with plans for the next morning.

But hardly had we separated than he called me to his room. He had a sudden heart flutter related to a pulmonary edema. I asked Professor [Rudolf] Staehelin, the leading heart specialist in Basel, to come for a consultation, and he immediately appeared at the hotel. Together, we tried everything until his heart no longer responded to our medical efforts. He never returned to consciousness and died within a few hours.[46]

A short ceremony attended by close relatives took place on 1 February at the crematorium of the Hörnli Cemetery at Basel. Richard Willstätter came from Munich and delivered the funeral oration.

Haber had made his last will in the winter of 1933. In this so-called "Cambridge will," which was recognized as valid, he had decided on the following:

> My body is to be cremated, and the ashes are to be buried in the cemetery in Dahlem, just like those of my first wife, whose ashes lie in the same place. If the anti-Jewish movement in Germany makes it impossible or disagreeable for my son or his survivors to carry out this request, or should he or his survivors later want to alter it after having carried it out, then he should take my first wife's ashes and mine to the place where he would like to see them buried. The grave should be marked with the inscription of my name, Fritz Haber, my date of birth, 9 December 1868, and the day of my death. Perhaps there can be added, "He served his country in war and peace as long as was granted him."[47]

Hermann Haber later remarked about this inscription, "As you see, the inscription on the gravestone is ambiguous. The 'as long as was granted him' usually means 'as long as he lived.' In my father's case, however, it could mean 'until the events in 1933 made further service to his country impossible.' I never found out how he meant it."[48]

Later, on 29 September 1934, the urn was buried in a section of the Hörnli Cemetery for which there was no fee. On Hermann Haber's request Clara Haber's urn was buried in the same grave on 27 January 1937. Their names, along with their birth and death dates, are inscribed on the gravestone.

# Endnotes

[1] Fritz Haber to Rudolf Stern, quoted in Rudolf Stern, *Personal Recollections*, Leo Baeck Institute Year Book 8 (New York, 1969), 99.

[2] Fritz Haber to Richard Willstätter, 24 Feb.1933, MPG, Dept. Va, Rep. 5, 1202.

[3] L. Glaser, "Juden in der Physik," *Zeitschrift der Gesellschaft für Naturwissenschaften* 5 (1939), 272.

[4] Fritz Haber to Friedrich Schmitt-Ott, 27 April 1933, former Staatliche Zentralarchiv der Deutsche Demokratische Republik, Merseburg, Dept. I, Rep. A, 541.

[5] Quoted in Richard Willstätter, *Aus meinem Leben* (From my life) (Weinheim: Verlag Chemie, 1958), 273.

[6] Max Planck, "Mein Besuch bei Adolf Hitler" (My visit to Hitler), *Physikalische Blätter* 3 (1947), 143; and Helmuth Albrecht, "Max Planck: 'Mein Besuch bei Adolf Hitler— Anmerkung zum Wert einer historischen Quelle,'" in *Naturwissenschaft und Technik in der Geschichte: 25 Jahre Lehrstuhl für Geschichte der Naturwissenschaft und Technik am Historischen Institut der Universität Stuttgart* (Science and technology in history: 25 years of the Chair for History of Science and Technology at the Historical Institute at the University of Stuttgart) (Stuttgart: Verlag für Geschichte der Naturwissenschaften und Technik, 1993), 41.

[7] Fritz Haber to Rudolf Stern, in Stern, *Personal Recollections* (cit. note 1), 99–100.

[8] David Nachmansohn, *German Jewish Pioneers in Science 1900–1933* (New York: Springer, 1979), 75.

[9] Interview of Otto Hahn by Johannes Jaenicke, MPG, Dept. Va, Rep. 5, 1453.

[10] Max Planck to Fritz Haber, 1 Aug. 1933, MPG, Dept. Va, Rep. 5, 1153.

[11] For more on subsequent events see D. J. Stoltzenberg, contribution to "Beitrag zur Geschichte des KWI für Physikalische Chemie und Elektrochemie" (The history of the Kaiser Wilhelm Institute for Physical Chemistry and Electrochemistry), *Berichte zur Wissenschaftsgeschichte*, 14 (1991), 15–23.

[12] Fritz Haber to General Geyer, 15 May 1933, MPG, Dept. Va, Rep. 5.

[13] Burghard Weiss, "Höchste Spannung: Fritz Haber, Hartmut Kallmann und das "Tandem-Prinzip": Ein frühes Kapitel der Beschleuniger-Geshichte" (Maximum stress: Fritz Haber, Hartmut Kallmann and the tandem principle: An early chapter in the history of the catalyst), *Kultur und Technik* 1 (1997), 42–49.

[14] Ladislaus Farkas to K. F. Bonhoeffer, 6 April 1933; Adalbert Farkas to Bonhoeffer, 11 April 1933; and L. Farkas to Bonhoeffer, 26 April 1933; all MPG, Dept. III, Rep. 23, 19.5.

[15] L. Farkas to Bonhoeffer, 4 Aug. 1933, ibid.

[16] Chaim Weizmann to Hermann Haber, 12 Sept. 1933, Weizmann Archive (WA), Rehovot, Correspondence Haber-Weizmann.

[17] Stern, *Personal Recollections* (cit. note 1), 100.

[18] William Pope to Fritz Haber, 29 July 1933, MPG, Dept. Va, Rep. 5, 1156.

[19] Pope to Haber, 7 Aug. 1933, ibid.

[20] Vice-chancellor of the University of Cambridge to F. Haber, 8 Aug. 1933, MPG, Dept. Va, Rep. 5, 1178.

[21] Pope to Haber, 25 Sept. 1933, MPG, Dept. Va, Rep. 5, 1156.

[22] Hartmut Kallmann, "Fritz Haber, in memoriam" (speech at a memorial ceremony for the 12th anniversary of Fritz Haber's death on 2 Feb. 1946), MPG, Dept. Va, Rep. 5, 1285.

[23] Max Born, *My Life: Recollections of a Nobel Laureate* (New York: Scribners, 1978), 261.

[24] Vice-chancellor of the University of Cambridge to Fritz Haber, 20 Nov. 1933, MPG, Dept. Va, Rep. 5, 1158.

[25] Fritz Haber to Richard Willstätter, 21 Nov. 1933, MPG, Dept. Va, Rep. 5, 910.

[26] Haber to Stern, undated, MPG, Dept. Va, Rep. 5, 905.

[27] Haber to Willstätter, 20 Nov. 1933, MPG, Dept. Va, Rep. 5, 1202.

[28] Stern to Haber, 17 Dec. 1933, MPG, Dept. Va, Rep. 5, 1176.

[29] Haber to Stern, from early January 1934, MPG, Dept. Va, Rep. 5, 1176.

[30] Haber to the vice-chancellor of the University of Cambridge, undated, MPG, Dept. Va, Rep. 5, 1178.

[31] Chaim Weizmann, *Trial and Error* (New York: Harper, 1949), 208 (see also pp. 203–207).

[32] Ibid., 352.

[33] Ibid., 353–354.

[34] Fritz Haber to Chaim Weizmann, 6 Oct. 1933, WA.

[35] Weizmann to Haber, 2 Oct. 1933, WA.

[36] Haber to Weizmann, 5 Oct. 1933, WA.

[37] Margarethe Haber to Weizmann, 6 Oct. 1933, WA.

[38] Telegram from Weizmann to Dr. Magasanik, 9 Nov. 1933, WA.

[39] Haber in Cambridge to Weizmann in London, 9 Nov. 1933, WA.

[40] Weizmann, memorandum, 15 Dec. 1933, WA.

[41] Haber to Weizmann, 6 Jan. 1934, WA.

[42] Ibid.

[43] Ibid.

[44] Haber to Weizmann, 15 Jan. 1934, WA.

[45] Chaim Weizmann to "his friends" (Hermann Haber, Rudolf Stern), 4 Feb. 1934, WA.

[46] Stern, *Personal Recollections* (cit. note 1), 102.

[47] Testamentary instructions for the burial of F. Haber, extract from a letter from L. F. Haber, 4 May 1959, MPG, Dept. Va, Rep. 5, 664.

[48] Hermann Haber to J. A. Coates, 11 April 1933, MPG, Dept. Va, Rep. 5, 664.

*Chapter 14*

Epilogue

*Memorial tablet at the Fritz Haber Institute, inscribed with words from the memorial address given by Max von Laue.*

F RITZ HABER'S DEATH TOUCHED MANY RELATIVES AND FRIENDS AS WELL
as those in scientific circles. Hermann Haber received many letters of con-
dolence from various groups: from the friends of Fritz Haber's youth, such
as August Marx and Fritz Milch; from Haber's friends and acquaintances
from his Karlsruhe period, including van Aken, Ernst Riesenfeld, Georg
Bredig, Ernst Berl, Alwin Mittasch, and Walther Nernst; from friends of
the Berlin period, among them Heinrich Wieland, James Franck, Aihito
Sata, Setsuro Tamaru, Friedrich Schmidt-Ott, Albert Einstein, Richard
Willstätter, Karl Friedrich Bonhoeffer, and Otto Meyerhof; and from people
Haber knew from the period of his emigration, particularly Sir William
Pope and Chaim Weizmann. These letters give a further, if incomplete, pic-
ture of the many people with whom Haber had contact, both in his personal
life and within the framework of his scientific life.

At the beginning of 1934 it was still possible to report on the death of a
German-Jewish scientist in the German press. Press, radio, and film were
not yet firmly under the control of Josef Goebbels, the National Socialist
minister of propaganda, so that merits of Jews could be mentioned and even
honored. Even so, there were considerable problems in the scientific journals. When Max von Laue wrote Haber's obituary in *Naturwissenschaften*,
Johannes Stark protested against some of his expressions, especially that
"Laue had set up a comparison with Themistocles in such a tendentious
fashion, as if Haber had been banished by the National Socialist government."[1] Laue had written: "Themistocles went down in history, not as the
person banished from the court of the Persian king, but as the victor of
Salamis. Haber will go down in history as the ingenious inventor of the
process for combining nitrogen with hydrogen."[2] Laue responded to Stark's

letter, stating that even Stark himself did not mention Fritz Haber in a list of those who had "voluntarily" resigned.

Various obituaries appeared in other journals. Carl Neuberg published an article in a Berlin newspaper, the *Central Vereins Zeitung*. Richard Willstätter wrote a short, sober obituary on behalf of the Bavarian Academy of Sciences, concluding with the words, "Fritz Haber's unique quality comprised his ability to collect and concentrate his strength in aiming for lofty goals: his penetration to the depths and right to the bottom of problems, his grasp of correlations and effects, his originality of ideas and broad view, his directness and clarity." This obituary appeared in 1935 in the academy's yearbook, and Willstätter reprinted it in his autobiography.[3]

Wilhelm Schlenk dedicated a surprisingly personal obituary to Haber in the *Berichte der Deutschen Chemischen Gesellschaft* (Journal of the German Chemical Society), as can be seen from its conclusion: " 'The times pass and we pass with them.' This was one of the most beautiful expressions that Fritz Haber used shortly before our last farewell. Certainly he has gone from this world. But he has not completely left us; for 'A master who his best did give, / lives and acts beyond the grave!' [Ein Meister der sein Bestes gab, / Der lebet, wirket übers Grab!]"[4]

Max Bodenstein made a memorial speech about Fritz Haber at the Prussian Academy of Sciences, which concludes:

> Haber's death is not what dissolved the work group of [his] institute. Haber was a Jew, and the overwhelming majority of his coworkers were also Jews. [Bodenstein was wrong here.] Conflict with the National Socialist state was therefore a given. Haber believed there was no other way to solve this than by submitting his resignation—on 2 May 1933. Thus he himself experienced the dissolution of his institute. His death, which his badly shaken health had already threatened often, came a year too late to save him from this pain. We feel and can identify with the tragedy of this fate.[5]

These words were chosen so as not to anger the National Socialists. As it was with Einstein, so also with Haber: to mention Jews who had been members of the academy for such a long time required extreme care in the Nazi state.

The pressure by the National Socialist regime against any commemoration for Haber reached its peak a year after his death. During 1934 an increasing number of people called for a memorial celebration to mark its first anniversary. Max Planck finally took over organizing such a ceremony. The program was set up, and invitations were sent during the second week of January 1935. The ceremony was to take place in Harnack House, the guest and assembly house of the Kaiser Wilhelm Society, and introductory words by Max Planck and two memorial speeches, one by Otto Hahn and the other by Karl Friedrich Bonhoeffer, were to be framed by two pieces of music. On 17 January a notice appeared in the Berlin financial newspaper, *Börsen Zeitung,* announcing the ceremony.

Max Planck had invited Hermann Haber (then living in Paris) and other members of the family. Hermann declined, after some hesitation and correspondence with Richard Willstätter, in a polite, respectful letter addressed to Planck.[6]

Hermann's decision proved wise. For scarcely had invitations arrived and the planned memorial ceremony become known in wider circles, than the campaign by the National Socialists began. The national and Prussian minister of education, Bernhard Rust, seeing this memorial as a provocation to the National Socialist State, forbade all officials and employees working under him to attend the ceremony and sent out a decree to that effect to rectors of all universities, institutes of technology, and other research and educational institutions.[7] The rector of the Charlottenburg Institute of Technology, Hans von Armin, immediately posted this decree "for information and consideration." It was also posted at the University of Berlin and at other institutions.

Planck, however, was not so readily intimidated. He wrote to the minister that he did not see that this commemoration was provocative. He added that he would greatly regret such a view as it could easily "be interpreted as a sign of weakness, in contrast to the general trust in the stability of our public affairs that has been expressed in the last few days."[8] And he reminded the minister that a prohibition would cause a quite undesirable sensation abroad. Planck was careful enough to end these remarks with a declaration of faith in the Führer and his government.

Minister Rust answered Planck with a "Heil Hitler!" and informed him that he could not retract his prohibition because Haber had opposed the National Socialist State.[9] He had to take into consideration, however, that the matter had already attracted the attention of the press both at home and abroad, that foreign participants were expected, and that the Kaiser Wilhelm Society had private members. He therefore suggested to Planck that the ceremony take place, but as a purely internal and private event of the Kaiser Wilhelm Society. Also forbidden to attend were members of other such organizations as the Office of Technology, the National Association of Science and Technology in the area under Fritz Todt (the official in charge of technology and technological organizations), the teaching staff of the Charlottenburg Institute of Technology, and the members of the German Chemical Society.

Otto Hahn later reported on subsequent developments and on the ceremony itself:

> Even the dispensation allowing participation was retracted again. Professor Bonhoeffer was forbidden to hold the memorial speech that had been planned, and I was called a few days before 29 January by the rector of the University of Berlin, who was at the same time a director of one of the Kaiser Wilhelm Institutes in Dahlem, to be told that, as rector, he was unfortunately obliged to forbid me from giving the memorial speech as planned. But I was able to tell Professor Eugen Fischer that I had resigned from the philosophical faculty in 1934, that is, I was no longer part of the university. (I had been only an honorary professor.) Professor Fischer answered—with obvious relief—that in this case he could not give me any further orders.
>
> An application from [Adolf] Windaus, a professor at Göttingen, with the request to receive a dispensation for attending the ceremony, was rejected. Windaus was telephoned in Göttingen on 29 January at the time the ceremony was taking place in Dahlem: They wanted to be sure he had not gone to Berlin!
>
> Thus the following grotesque situation occurred on the morning of 29 January. Privy Councillor Planck picked me up at my institute before the ceremony. The decree that all members of the Kaiser Wilhelm Institutes were forbidden from going to Harnack House was hanging on the notice board.
>
> Planck was, however, excited and pleased that the ceremony was going to take place in spite of everything, unless perhaps on our short way from Thielallee to Ihnestrasse a group sent by the Party would try to prevent us by force from entering Harnack House. But nothing happened. One had to add one's name to a list at the entrance.
>
> The lovely, large reception room at Harnack House was full. Relatives of Haber's sat in the front rows: There were naturally not many. [It is unclear whom Hahn meant here. They could have been only very distant relatives who still were in Berlin. Johannes Jaenicke wrote to Hahn, before his report, that none of Haber's relatives were present. He could not recall having met a member of the family in Harnack House.[10]] Apart from this Privy Councillor [Carl] Bosch, Director Hans Kühne, and other leading members of the IG Farben A.G. were present. They had been told by Bosch to come. Others who appeared were His Excellency Schmidt-Ott, Professor Willstätter from

*Otto Hahn in January 1933.*

Munich, Dr. A. Petersen and Dr. Jaenicke from the Metallgesellschaft in Frankfurt, and Elisabeth Schiemann, associate professor of botany from the University of Berlin.

Only a few others from our Kaiser Wilhelm Institute had defied the prohibition—Lise Meitner, Fritz Strassmann, and Max Delbrück.

Most of the participants were women, wives of Berlin professors, the wives of members of the Kaiser Wilhelm Society, the wives of personal friends of Haber's. They came as representatives of the men who had been prevented by a brutal prohibition from bidding final farewell to an important person and scientist.

The ceremony was dignified and impressive. Privy Councillor Planck gave the introductory address, pointing out that had Haber not made his magnificent nitrogen discovery, Germany would have collapsed, economically and militarily, in the first three months of World War I [a slight exaggeration of the conditions at the beginning of the war]. In his speech General Joseph Koeth [who had worked together with Haber in the Military Raw Materials department during the war] also emphasized Haber's great significance during the World War. Without Haber's discoveries and organizational talents they would not have succeeded in maintaining their resistance to the enemy's blockade over the many years.

The two main speeches by me and Bonhoeffer dealt with Haber's personal side and the significance of his famous institute as well as his scientific work. As Professor Bonhoeffer was not able to be present—he had been forbidden to come—I read Bonhoeffer's manuscript in his name. Members of the Berlin Philharmonic Orchestra framed the dignified and completely successful ceremony.

The final directive from the ministry: Nothing is to be reported about the ceremony, and the speeches are not to be published.[11]

Today no comment on these events is necessary.

Victims of persecution had to receive support from outside the borders of the dictatorship. It was in England, for example, that J. E. Coates gave a Haber Memorial Lecture to the Chemical Society on 29 April 1937. This well-researched report, mainly about Haber's scientific work, is the first detailed work on his life. Coates was one of Haber's most productive assistants in Karlsruhe and admired him greatly, as did so many of his colleagues and students. The concluding sentence of Coates's memorial lecture expresses that admiration: "All those who knew him will remember with lasting affection the man who enriched their lives. He will live on as a great chemist and will be honored for his services to humanity. He deeply wished to be remembered as someone who served his country in war and peace."[12]

Haber's merits were honored in many ways after World War II and the end of the National Socialist dictatorship. On the twelfth anniversary of his death a memorial ceremony took place on the grounds of his former institute, and his close coworker Hartmut Kallmann gave the eulogy. A new dedicatory plaque was also unveiled on the so-called Haber linden tree. Kallmann hoped that "one day this institute will once again count among the most important research institutes in the world" and thought that "this would be the best thanks and the greatest memorial for the international scientist, for the great personality, for our Fritz Haber."[13]

Kallmann's wish has been fulfilled. The institute is now honored with the name "Fritz Haber Institute of the Max Planck Society." Under the directorships of Karl Friedrich Bonhoeffer (1948–1985), Max von Laue (1951–

1958), Rudolf Brill (1958–1969), and Heinz Gerischer (1969–1985), and later under the teams of department heads who directed it together, the institute has again achieved a high rank in the scientific world, as its numerous outstanding researches in the field of physical chemistry testify.[14]

## Endnotes

[1] Johannes Stark to the Board of the German Physics Society, 1 Mar. 1934, MPG, Dept. Va, Rep. 5, 1752.

[2] Max von Laue, "Fritz Haber gestorben," *Naturwissenschaften* 22 (1934), 97.

[3] Carl Neuberg in *Central Verlags Zeitung*, 8 Feb. 1934; and Richard Willstätter, *Aus meinem Leben* (From my life) (Weinheim: Verlag Chemie, 1958), 255.

[4] Wilhelm Schlenk, "Fritz Haber—Nachruf" (Obituary), *Ber. Deutsch. Chem. Ges.*, 67 (1934), A20.

[5] Max Bodenstein, "Gedächtnisrede auf Fritz Haber" (Memorial address), *Sitzungsberichte der Preussichen Akademie der Wissenschaften, Physikalisch-Mathematische Klasse*, 28 June 1934, p. 3.

[6] Hermann Haber to Max Planck, beginning of Jan. 1935, MPG, Dept. Va, Rep. 5, 1375.

[7] Bernhard Rust, minister of science, education, and popular instruction, to the rectors of the universities, institutes of technology, etc., 15 Jan. 1935, MPG, Dept. Va, Rep. 5, 1850.

[8] Max Planck to the national minister of science, etc., 17 Jan. 1935, MPG, Dept. Va, Rep. 5, 1850.

[9] Rust, national minister of science, etc., to Planck, 24 Jan. 1935, MPG, Dept. Va, Rep. 5, 1850.

[10] Johannes Jaenicke to Otto Hahn, 12 Dec. 1959, MPG, Dept. Va, Rep. 5, A11.

[11] Otto Hahn, "Zur Erinnerung an die Haber-Gedächtnisfeier vor 25 Jahre" (The Haber commemoration 25 years later), *Mitteilungsblatt der Max-Planck-Gesellschaft* 1 (1960), 3.

[12] J. E. Coates, "The Haber Memorial Lecture," *Journal of the Chemical Society (London)* 30 (1939), 1642.

[13] Hartmut Kallmann, "Dem Andenken von Fritz Haber: Rede anlässlich der Gedächtnisfeier am 12. Todestag von Fritz Haber am 2.2.1946" (In memory of Fritz Haber: Speech held at the memorial ceremony for the 12th anniversary of his death on 2 Feb. 1946), MPG, Dept. Va, Rep. 5, 1285.

[14] "The Fritz-Haber-Institut, Berlin," *Berichte und Mitteilungen der Max-Planck-Gesellschaft* 1986 (7).

# Index

Harteck, Paul, 225, 249, 250, *251*, 252, 289
Hartley, Harold, 135, 162, 287, 288
Hase, Albrecht, 168, 227, 234
Hasse, Otto, 165, 166
Hausrath (Karlsruhe friend), 47
heat theorem, 57–58, 84–85, 116
Hebrew University, 286, 292, 296
Heerdt, Walter, 234
Heereswaffenamt. *See* Army Ordnance
  Department
Helferich, Burkhardt, 137
Helmholtz, Hermann von, 17, 18, 57, 109
Hertz, Gustav, 137, 225, 227, *228*, 236–237, 238
Herzl, Theodor, 292
Herzog, Reginald O., 48, 65, 139, 227
Hevesy, Georg von, *228*
Heymons, Richard, 232
Hindenburg, Paul von, 145, 262, 277
Hirschkind, Wilhelm, *60*
Hitler, Adolf, 181, 199, 208, 262, 280, 292. *See also* anti-Semitism; National Socialists
Hittorf, Johann Wilhelm, 42
Hodsman, H. J., *60*, 64
Hoechst Dyeworks (Farbwerke Hoechst), 32, 48, 83, 93–95, 144, 166
Hofer, H., 78
Hofmann, August Wilhelm von, 17, 18, 22
Hofmann, Karl A., 168
Holdermann, Karl, 67, 81, 89
Holz, Adolf, 55
Honda, Kumatao, 267
Hoshi, Hajime, 264, 265, 268, 287
Hoshi Foundation, 263–269
Howell (researcher on nitrogen fixation), 78
Hutton, R. S., 50–51
hydrogen, 98–99, 100, 250, 252
hydrogen cyanide, *224*, 232–233, 234
hydrogen peroxide, 65, 253, 288

IG Farben (Interessengemeinschaft der Deutschen Teerfarbenfabriken), 99, 101, 141, 166, 167, 180, 231
Ihne, Ernst von, 115

Immerwahr, Clara. *See* Haber, Clara Immerwahr
Immerwahr, Georg, 46
Immerwahr, Phillip, 44–45
Imperial Chemical Institute (Chemische Reichsanstalt), 94, 109
Imperial Chemical Institute Association (Verein Chemische Reichsanstalt), 109
Imperial Office of the Interior, 110
Imperial Physical and Technological Institute (Physikalisch-Technische Reichsanstalt), 109
Ingold, Christopher, 66
Institute for Applied Zoology (Munich), 232
Institute for Chemical Technology: at Karlsruhe Institute of Technology, 38, 59, 64
Institute for Chemistry: at University of Berlin, 17–18, 109, 110, 217–220; at University of Jena, 32
Institute for Military Science, 226
Institute for Physical Chemistry: at Karlsruhe Institute of Technology, 48, 59, 61; at University of Leipzig, 27, 109
Institute for Physics: at University of Berlin, 109
institutes of technology, 52; Stuttgart Institute of Technology, 89. *See also under* Charlottenburg Institute; Karlsruhe Institute; Swiss Federal Institute
Interallied Control Commission, 162, 163, 226
interferometer, 61, 116, 117
International Chemical Congress, 37–38
International Council of Scientific Unions (ICSU), 271
International Research Council, 270–271
international scientific cooperation, 269–272
International Union of Pure and Applied Chemistry (IUPAC), 270–272, 287
ionic crystals, 236
Ipatieff, Vladimir N., 165–166
iron: as catalyst, 90, 99, 100, 131; electrochemistry of, 55–56
Isgarischev (researcher in Karlsruhe), 64